The Military–Peace Complex

Series Editors: Victoria M. Basham and Sarah Bulmer

The *Advances in Critical Military Studies* series welcomes original thinking on the ways in which military power works within different societies and geopolitical arenas

Militaries are central to the production and dissemination of force globally but the enduring legacies of military intervention are increasingly apparent at the societal and personal bodily levels as well, demonstrating that violence and war-making function on multiple scales. At the same time, the notion that violence is as an appropriate response to wider social and political problems transcends militaries: from private security, to seemingly 'non-military' settings such as fitness training and schooling, the legitimisation and normalisation of authoritarianism and military power occurs in various sites. This series seeks original, high-quality manuscripts and edited volumes that engage with such questions of how militaries, militarism and militarisation assemble and disassemble worlds touched and shaped by violence in these multiple ways. It will showcase innovative and interdisciplinary work that engages critically with the operation and effects of military power and provokes original questions for researchers and students alike.

The Military–Peace Complex

Gender and Materiality in Afghanistan

HANNAH PARTIS-JENNINGS

EDINBURGH
University Press

Edinburgh University Press is one of the leading university presses in the UK. We publish academic books and journals in our selected subject areas across the humanities and social sciences, combining cutting-edge scholarship with high editorial and production values to produce academic works of lasting importance. For more information visit our website: edinburghuniversitypress.com

Edinburgh University Press Ltd
The Tun – Holyrood Road,
12(2f) Jackson's Entry,
Edinburgh EH8 8PJ

First published in hardback by Edinburgh University Press 2021

Typeset in 10.5/13 ITC Giovanni Std by
Servis Filmsetting Ltd, Stockport, Cheshire

A CIP record for this book is available from the British Library

ISBN 978 1 4744 5332 5 (hardback)
ISBN 978 1 4744 5333 2 (paperback)
ISBN 978 1 4744 5334 9 (webready PDF)
ISBN 978 1 4744 5335 6 (epub)

CONTENTS

FIGURES

ACKNOWLEDGEMENTS

I dedicate this book to Marie, to whom I owe the greatest thanks. Without you, Marie, the research would not have been done, and you know how grateful I am to you for being an inspiration and a source of support and friendship. I also wish to thank Shamsia, Zaheed, Mustafa, Alex and the many others who showed me enormous kindness and made it possible for me to see so many wonderful and important spaces and talk to such brilliant people in Afghanistan. Shamsia, you are someone I came to admire deeply in a short space of time; your wit, intelligence and energy left a lasting impression. I must also thank Nargis Nehan, Hosai and EQUALITY for Peace and Democracy for allowing me to work with them briefly, use their offices at times and enjoy delicious staff lunches. Thank you also to the many people who spoke with me, from taxi drivers and friends to official respondents, offering such valuable insights as well as their time.

The research for this book started as part of my doctoral study at the University of St Andrews and for that I owe great thanks to Patrick Hayden, for supporting my scholarship application, Jaremey McMullin, who was my second supervisor, and most of all to Caron Gentry, my supervisor, mentor and friend. Thank you, Caron, for the intellectual support, the inspirational conversations and for rooting for me, always. Because of you, I have a PhD. At St Andrews, I learned so much, surrounded by such fantastic people – Nick Rennger, Karin Fierke, Jasmine Gani, Gurchathen Sanghera, Faye Donnelly, Jeffery Murer and others who shaped the intellectual environment so beautifully, as well as my friends: Andreas, Chris, Clara, Natasha, Helga, Jenna, Hannah, Elena, Luise, Alexis, Sophie, Aliya, Selbi, Fran, Antonio, Kieran, Lizzie, Mez, Becks, Arik, Rab, Fiona, Sonya, Jack, Naomi, Elle, François, Katarina,

Daria, Johana, Kate, Robbie, Dan, Caroline and many more who made my life there so memorable and joyful. Andreas, together we made it through, with a friendship that will last a lifetime. Chris, thank you for so many meaningful conversations – you are a natural scholar. Clara, you have always inspired me and made me laugh – I am so grateful to have found you and your particular warmth and genius. Natasha, your grace and moral strength taught me a lot. Jenna, thank you for making me feel valuable and for all the hilarious moments. Helga, you are one of the most giving people I have ever met – thank you for all that you are. Becks, you made me a part of your St Andrews family – thank you for bringing people together. Mez, living with you was a joy. Hannah – for the nuance.

Thank you to the Russell Trust at the University of St Andrews, who awarded me over £700 to fund my trip to Afghanistan.

Thank you also to my friends in Dublin for their encouragement, to those I met on my MA in Peace Studies which first sparked my interest in questions of global politics, intervention and peace, and to those who taught us so well on that programme – Iain Atack, Gillian Wylie, Etain Tannam, Jude Lal and others. Thank you to those I met along the way through academia, and who make it better on the hard days, especially to Katharine, Henry and James. Of course, the book would not have been finished without the support of my current institution, Loughborough University, and for that, as well as everything else, thank you especially to Caroline Kennedy-Pipe.

I also want to thank Marsha Henry, Paul Higate and Gurchathen Sanghera for their work on the research that became *Insecure Spaces*. It showed me a different way of thinking.

A huge and vital thank you to Victoria Basham and Sarah Bulmer for editing the series of which this book is a part, for being such wonderful feminists and such fantastic scholars in so many ways. And to the editors at Edinburgh University Press, Sarah Foyle and Jen Daly, who helped, facilitated and communicated with me through this project.

Finally, to the three people I love most dearly: my partner Ciaran, and my parents Kevin and Anne. Ciaran, thank you for being such a generous, humorous, eccentric, intelligent, linguistically astute and loving human and for helping me through this process. I am so lucky. Mum and Dad, I owe you everything. You are both gifted, sparkling, erudite, gentle people who make the world a better place. Thank you for the endless support. The gratitude and love I feel are beyond words.

ABBREVIATIONS

COIN	Counterinsurgency
FET	Female Engagement Team
FOB	Forward Operating Base
IO	International Organisation
ISAF	International Security Assistance Force
NATO	North Atlantic Treaty Organisation
NGO	Non-Governmental Organisation
PMSC	Private Military Security Company
PRT	Provincial Reconstruction Teams
UN	United Nations
UNAMA	United Nations Assistance Mission in Afghanistan
UNDP	United Nations Development Programme
UNICEF	United Nations Children's Fund
USAID	United States Agency for International Development

Introduction

One day in Bamyan a small group of us (there were two from Kabul, one from America and me, from Ireland) went sightseeing with a Bamyan resident. We visited the so-called City of Screams and the Red City, both the remains of cities once attacked by Ghengis Khan, and the empty spaces cut into the rock that had once been the famous Bamyan Buddhas (Figure I.1). At one point we were warned to be careful and keep to a white painted track in case of landmines, though most had been cleared. Climbing up into the spaces where the Buddhas once had stood, we could see footprints on the walls where – apparently – the Taliban who had blown up the statues had deliberately left marks as a sign of disrespect. Yet, looking out from where the Buddhas had once been, the stunning view created a sense of awe, peacefulness and deep respect for the beauty, strength and magnificence of the whole space. This experience could not be easily mapped onto the simplicity of war, peace or human history; it was a layered mix of elements, unquestionably shaped by violence but not reducible to it.

It was a great privilege to visit such a stunning site in the company of friends and to recognise its significance in terms of signalling a conflu-ence of momentous events written into the landscape. Going sightsee-ing in Afghanistan, including paddle boating in little swan boats in a lake in Band-e-Amir (Figure I.2) was one of the many experiences that unsettled any expectations or presumptions I carried about the country before my short visit in 2014 and made me think differently about what I was actually researching. If I am honest, I don't know exactly what my expectations were before I went, but I know that moments like this produced a sense of reflection and had a complex, visceral impact, with lasting sensory memories. Equally, like the embassy staff in the quotation that opened this chapter, I remember feeling the fear of a foreigner the first time I heard gunfire at night near where I was staying and the friend I was staying with reassuring me that it was probably just celebrations from a neighbouring wedding venue. I remember the sound of a bomb exploding in Kabul, and the WhatsApp messages I sent to check in with my host, the search on Twitter to find out what it was and who was harmed or dead, visiting a quiet and subdued Chicken Street Market a day or two later that had been affectively impacted by the recent attack. I remember arriving at a party mostly attended by internationals with my friend, her Afghan partner and his friends, finding it unexpectedly like a house party in the UK though with security guards and a strange atmosphere of underlying tension. I remember the surreal feeling of our little group of Westerners and Afghans driving through empty Kabul streets on the way home from that party, listening to The Killers' song (are we) 'Human'? I think about those I spoke to remotely in 2017, some of whom were still in Kabul, some of whom, both international and Afghan, sounded deeply exhausted and strained by their work and environment, the restrictions placed on them and their sense of insecurity. Or some of those formerly in the military, who indicated the burden their military service in Afghanistan had placed on their mental health. I remember moments during my trip to Afghanistan in 2014 when my whiteness stood out and I felt it draping me and my experience like a cloak, visually connecting me to a history of violence as well as to the embod-ied 'international'. I remember the deep awe I felt for some of the participants in the research I was conducting: a widely respected civil society leader who ran a women's shelter despite the dangers involved; a renowned activist who had pictures of herself with Michelle Obama on the wall; a young non-governmental organisation (NGO) worker from the US who chose a relatively low-paid job rather than focusing exclusively on the big-budget consultancy work accessible to her and who lived alone with her rescue dog in Kabul. I remember the female security guard at the airport on my way home to Ireland enquiring where I had bought the ring I was wearing and the moment of comfort that came from discussing the Chicken Street Market shops with her as she patted me down, in an otherwise tense and security-heavy context. I remember a lot of easy friendship, even in such a short space of time.

These fragments of experience are only indirectly linked to the discussions in this book. Yet through these experiences and thinking about them, alongside reflecting on my interviews and research materials, I recognised that in exploring post-2001 Afghanistan and the international involvement there, I also wanted to draw in some of that unsettling that had shifted my own parameters and engage with the everydayness and disjuncture of that project, the ways that ideologies and banalities intersected and echoed each other: the material, spatial and unnoticed, the gendered and embodied. So, part of what motivates me to write this book is that it is an attempt to capture some sensation of layering, violence, unease, multiplicity and the experiential, while also examining the international project in Afghanistan in new ways.

Figure I.1 Where a Bamiyan Buddha used to be. Author photograph.

Figure I.2 The paddle boats. Author photograph.

The focus of this book is an exploration of some of the assemblages and pathways that bind peace and war work together. In Afghanistan, the nexus of cooperation and operational boundary negotiations between military and non-military actors, referred to as 'civil-military relations' (Goodhand 2013: 287; see also Suhrke 2011: 10–11), as well as the increased militarisation of the humanitarian aid industry (Duffield 2010, 2012; Shannon 2009; Suhrke 2011), means that the two components – civilian and military – of the intervention and liberal statebuilding project and their activities are not always easy to disaggregate.

Here, I posit the military–peace framework as a paradigm that captures slippage and overlap between the 'civil' and the 'military' sides, but I also push the boundaries of this analysis and consider this slippage in new ways – namely the more everyday, embodied, gendered, racialised and material fragments that feed this nexus. My central argument is that military and peace work in the liberal mode cannot be logically separated, but rather are co-constituted and operate in a dynamic relationship to each other with fluid and shifting boundaries. My argument is not at all that they are the same thing, nor that they should be understood as having the same objectives and meaning. Yet I argue that an embodied analysis of military and peace actors, paying attention to the material, gendered and racialised dynamics of militarism, aid work, humanitarianism, military experience and peacebuilding work, is necessary to understand what I call the contemporary military–peace complex and its politics. I suggest that we gain a great deal analytically from considering these non-typical modes of slippage – the material, embodied and performative. I suggest that the military–peace complex, taken as a whole, has certain key features including gendered and racialised logics that manifest from the everyday to the institutional and have historical foundations and patterns as well as material and spatial signifiers that bind the collective actors of the paradigm together and separate them out from the majority of the Afghan population in particular ways.

In developing the conceptual framework of the military–peace complex I am answering a series of calls within international relations scholarship, including calls to theorise the international project in Afghanistan in holistic ways (Friis 2012); to centre feminist scholarship and insights within critical peacebuilding literature (McLeod and Reilly 2019); to push our thinking beyond intentionality in studying intervention (Rutazibwa 2019); to pay attention to humanitarian workers and their gendered frameworks as part of a wider engagement with the gendered structures of global politics (Read 2018); to explore different elements of militarism (Basham and Bulmer 2017); to recognise the vitality of the material (Mac Ginty 2017), the significance of the spatial (Kothari 2006c; Smirl 2008), the routine and the everyday within the intervention and statebuilding praxis (Autesserre 2014; Shepherd 2014) and the complex configurations of security, Othering and 'race thinking' that track between the everyday and the geopolitical in indirect ways (Basham and Vaughan-Williams 2013; Sabaratnam 2017).

Primarily, I am interested in how military work and peace work interact within the broad overarching remit of the liberal peace, specifically in Afghanistan. While excellent work has been done on the liberal peace in all its manifestations (see Dodge 2013; Joshi et al. 2014; Hudson 2012; Mac Ginty 2010a; Nadarajah 2013; Richmond 2009b; Sabaratnam 2013), there is still more to say on the entanglements it produces. Specifically, then, an exploration of the military–peace complex is an exploration of entanglement and, as Karin Barad (2007: ix) states, 'to be entangled is not simply to be intertwined with another, as in the joining of separate entities, but to lack an independent, self-contained existence'.

The military–peace complex is intimately connected to the liberal peace paradigm and many of the entanglements I analyse are bound up with its logics. Through the hierarchical framing and prioritising of certain economics (neoliberal), epistemologies and skills (report writing, training, grant bids, evaluations) the liberal peace approach was rendered commonsensical in post-conflict and conflict-affected spaces around the world (Mac Ginty 2012: 288) though arguably its dominance has now passed to a certain extent (Chandler 2012; Nadarajah and Rampton 2015; Richmond 2009a). Linked to ideas around governance, technocratic values and security sector reform, a Westphalian conception of the state is central to the liberal peace paradigm (Mac Ginty 2012: 290; Richmond 2009a: 564) and the ideological drive within it to perpetuate a global systemic status quo (Pugh 2004; Cox 1981). Heidi Hudson suggests that the liberal peace paradigm 'rests on two pillars: that effective liberal states are a bulwark against international instability; and that failing or conflict-prone states represent a threat to international security' (Hudson 2012: 445).

The idea of the military–peace complex parallels other scholarly frameworks and insights, such as (conceptually) Alison Howell's (2018) 'martial politics' which disrupts any idea of a civilian order pre-existing military connections, subverting the concept of militarisation, which presupposes the possibility of process, by emphasising the always already pre-existing entanglement between military and civilian domains within the liberal order. This is in addition to (practically) the framework of the development–security nexus, which highlights the increased securitisation of development activities (Stepputat 2012; Stern and Öjendal 2010) and elucidates institutional frameworks which identify 'security as a precondition for development' (Haastrup 2017: 202). Yet, through a reliance on feminist theories and methodologies as well as insights from new materialism – very broadly understood – and a small but significant literature on space and conflict, this book offers an important contribution by drawing together critical military and peace studies to emphasise the everyday performances that constitute the under-studied aspects of military–peace engagements.

Justification for Focus, Participants and Methodology

Afghanistan is an especially interesting and complex example of the military–peace complex in action, particularly due to its hybridised and shifting nature and the extent of its significance on the global stage, and within the domestic political arenas of intervening states. Roland Paris has suggested that the 'case of Afghanistan' has, for some, 'demonstrated the futility of "nation building", a vague term that often denotes the use of military intervention to achieve nonsecurity goals' (2013: 538). Jonathan Goodhand and Mark Sedra argue that

> [t]he Afghan intervention vacillated over time along a spectrum of consent and coercion, manifesting itself in a constant tension between transformational aspirations linked to statebuilding, democratization, and human rights on the one hand, and pragmatic, illiberal practices aimed at building a coercive apparatus of control on the other (2013: 240).

Paris argues that there needs to be a clear distinction made in scholarly discussion between peacebuilding after internal conflict, and peacebuilding linked to conflicts and counterinsurgency (COIN) campaigns in which international actors constitute one of the warring parties (2010: 338). Thus, it needs to be acknowledged from the outset that the Afghan example is an instance of the latter category and therefore potentially more likely to be subject to the militaristic dynamics that come with war than other peacebuilding projects (Paris 2010). As Roger Mac Ginty points out, this adds an overtly violent and force-based dimension to the ideologies and practices of the liberal peace paradigm: '[s]tatebuilding and formation projects in Afghanistan . . . can be described as technocracy at gun point' (2012: 301). In this book it is precisely these modes of symbiosis, interplay and collapse between ideas of security and peace, 'nation-building' and war, and peace work at gunpoint that I am interested in, and Afghanistan constitutes an exemplary case (see Suhrke 2011).

Afghanistan is often depicted as 'a vivid illustration of the idea of *permanent liminality* – a prolonged condition of being stuck in the *in-between* zone of war and peace'; it is thus always a '*potential war zone*' in which certain things take on heightened urgency, sensitivity and power (Mälksoo 2012: 492, original emphasis). Arguably, these narratives that circulate around Afghanistan, especially when linked to ideas of failed statehood, chaos and danger, feed into a wider neo-imperial discourse about spaces in need of civilising and tap into an always already racialised framework (Hanifi 2018; Khalid 2011; Nayak 2006; Said 1979). These narratives are part of the 'construal of Afghanistan as a zone of exception and of permanent crisis' (Manchanda 2017: 387). I am interested in some of the narratives and histories that fuel a wider understanding of Afghanistan as a site, and the problematic trends of some of these narratives and accepted histories that manifest in everyday ways within the international project. Equally, gender and gendered ideas are bound to Afghanistan's political trajectory. In the contemporary context, since 2001, gender has played a large part in the narrative and practice of peacebuilding and intervention in Afghanistan, and is a gendering/focus on gender that is crafted onto and runs alongside deep and ongoing insecurity and violence, as well as being superimposed upon a repetitive history of – often racialised – political battles over women's rights (Abirafeh 2009; Zulfacar 2006). It is for all of these reasons – its in-betweenness, the gender dynamics and the especially military character of peace work – that I focus on Afghanistan in this book.

The book is based on multiple sources, including a set of interviews, some limited research time in Afghanistan in 2014 and an ongoing research engagement with the context. My materials are varied. Methodically speaking, I take a kind of 'bricolage' approach (Aradau and Huysmans 2013: 607), drawing together fragments such as observations, leaked documents,[1] media articles and interview data in response to a particular research focus. I gathered my interview respondents through snowballing, meaning that I used initial contacts in the civilian and military domains to generate further contacts and often sought interview respondents through direct introductions (see Murer 2009: 119). I also reached out to people to whom I had no connection by emailing them or posting on a closed online forum for relevant people, explaining who I was and what I was interested in. I relied to some extent on a 'grounded approach', in that I had a theoretical overview, expectations and plan for my research topics prior to my research and interviews, but those original theoretical perspectives and expectations were 'subject to revision as insights emerged from interviews' (Basham 2009: 730). I accept that my research is a creative process, and in this way I am influenced by 'non-representational' research methods where styles 'strive to animate rather than simply mimic, to rupture rather than merely account, to evoke rather than just report' (Vannini 2015: 318), though I do not situate this book within those literatures directly. I am most strongly influenced by critical feminist methodological commitments (Tickner 2005; Zalewski 1995) whereby academic rigour and honesty is achieved through the acknowledgement of limitations, through reflexive practice and empathy (Shepherd 2014: 106), and through being sensitive to positionality and the power dynamics within research (Mehta 2014: 185).

Formally, I spoke with forty-one people as part of this research, almost equally divided between Afghan nationals (twenty-one respondents) and foreign (to Afghanistan) nationals. Ten participants were part of a focus group, two interviews had more than one participant and the rest were one-to-one. Some took place in Afghanistan in 2014, others happened while I was based in the UK and Ireland between 2014 and 2017. I also took part in participant observation for a month in Afghanistan (Kabul and Bamiyan), taking photos and keeping notes, which I have continued to reflect upon. All participants, with the exception of the ten university students who were part of a focus group in Bamiyan, are considered to be linked to, or working parallel to, the international project in Afghanistan to a greater or lesser extent (through work type, funding, project alignment and so on). My participants included civilians[2] working (broadly speaking) within the peace/statebuilding sector (Afghan and foreign to Afghanistan, with all the latter being nationals of Western countries), and military or former military personnel who served in Afghanistan as part of foreign military operations in the country. There are obvious limitations to this research in terms of scale and scope, and I use the other kinds of materials mentioned, in addition to scholarly work, to broaden my engagement. All my participants share a high level of education and qualification and an ability to offer enormous insight due to their experiences and expertise. I consider them to be expert interviews. International participants were usually experienced and familiar with different elements of the Afghan context. The Afghan participants I interviewed (all bar two of whom were women) were often in positions of authority, in some cases well-known in their professional context, and all aside from the university students worked within the civil society/NGO sector. All interview extracts are reproduced verbatim, and often reflect a conversational pattern of speech including grammatical imperfections and colloquialisms.

While I seek to avoid reifying false and unhelpful distinctions between the local and the international, I also recognise that this distinction did form a core theme that emerged in my research and I discuss it throughout the book. There are extensive angles and perceptions that I did not capture – for instance, the particular experiences of Black women in the US military, the experiences of female Afghan police officers, and many more. Moreover, though I draw upon quotes to support my arguments I recognise that these might not be representative of groups of people, that there is a huge diversity of perspective on the issues I discuss and that multiple counterarguments are possible. I seek only to put forward some arguments about the military–peace complex as I understand it, almost as the start of a conversation, and hopefully to open up some further questions to pursue. Since the discussions in this book are sensitive in some ways, I anonymise all interviews, giving respondents false names and general affiliations, and in some cases not providing respondent information at all.

Like Lisa Smirl (2015: l. 173), I want to note that '[a]lmost every aid worker [and, I suggest, individuals in the military too] comes to "the field" with the intention to improve other people's lives'. This book is not designed as a condemnation of individuals, whole organisations or sectors, nor to detract from the willingness of many to risk their lives for what they understand to be an important purpose. My critique of the military–peace complex as a paradigm is not meant to demonstrate condemnation or to argue for a parsimonious understanding of intentions in this context (see Rutazibwa 2019). Though some expressed views I do not share, in general, I liked and respected all my interview respondents, and found them as individuals to be politically complex, intellectually impressive and self-reflexive. Indeed, my respondents themselves were largely deeply critical of the international project and its consequences in Afghanistan, even though they were part of it or linked to it, and this highlights the inherent contradictions and disjuncture within that project.

My own positionality in the context of Afghanistan was primarily defined by being a youngish white female frequently associated with the 'international community' in some way. I was staying with an international, spending a lot of time with her and her Afghan partner and his friends in coffee shops, working on and off at an Afghan NGO (as an unpaid research assistant) but also socialising with other internationals at times. I did not have any formal security protection or processes in Kabul beyond getting lifts to the office in a regular car. This was largely because my host did not have any, and lived differently from many internationals, and because I was an independent researcher, not attached to any international organisation or entity. I travelled by taking taxis, getting lifts with others, occasionally on foot, such as around the market shops and to nearby houses, and once using a domestic airline. I never travelled in an armoured car. In Bamiyan my friend and I shared a room in an NGO building, which did have a guard at the gate. On a few occasions, I visited restaurants that served alcohol and catered to international clients and which had some heavy security measures in place. On balance, my positionality was mixed – I had access to different spaces and was clearly engaged with the privileged international lifeworld while not exclusively experiencing significant security practices or other aspects of international life. As a PhD student I had little money by UK standards, but was privileged economically in the Afghan context. Another aspect of privilege was through my access to Afghan civil society actors as interview respondents who, while not political elites in the traditional sense, were nonetheless important experts who to some extent moved in elite circles.

Positionality in this context refers to 'the perspective, orientation and situatedness of the researcher *vis-à-vis* the researchees' (Henry et al. 2009: 468). Implicit in this notion is the idea of power and differentials between types of status and identity. Positionality is also multiple, fluid and sometimes conflicting. Thus 'researchers' multiple positionalities do not always result in positions of power *over* researchers' (Henry et al. 2009: 469). A particular kind of positionality is therefore not a fixed or given phenomenon in any kind of research, particularly research involving lifeworlds in which identities and context are shifting, such as peacebuilding and conflict-affected environments. In line with a feminist research ethics, a critical feminist approach should seek to 'make bare the trajectory' of the research in some way, and explore, even internally, 'some of the consequences of their methodologies and presence in the field' (Henry et al. 2009: 469). Thus, I keep my own positionality in mind as I conduct my analysis.

On a related note, it is worth recognising here that Meera Sabaratnam has rightly questioned the focus of the critical liberal peace (and related) literature on international actors and international organisations. She argues that this focus denies a voice to those actors who are local to the context and elevates internationals to a position of superior importance in a research context (Sabaratnam 2013). My positionality as someone with access to internationals helped to shape my engagement and interests, and Sabaratnam's critique is salient to the focus of this book, though Afghan voices are central in this work as well. I take Sabaratnam's (2013) critique seriously despite my focus, and try to consider and weigh up its implications as a backdrop to my analysis.

Another criticism linked to researcher positionality within the literature on peacebuilding is offered by Oliver Richmond et al. (2015), who call into question the construction of the 'field' in academic research and policy practice. They argue that the field can be understood as a discursive creation marked and defined by distancing, essentialising and Othering: 'upholding and perpetuating the workings of modern power, globalization, global governance, and the [neo]liberal peace' (Richmond et al. 2015: 2).

As such, I seek to be cognisant of the idea that 'fieldwork as an academic practice requires the performance of spatial relations through the production of boundaries, binaries, hierarchies, and cultural imaginings' (Richmond et al. 2015: 7) and, indeed, this interest in the 'field' as a spatial concept forms a part of my analysis in Chapter 3.

In terms of timeframe, my research focus on Afghanistan generally spans from the intervention in 2001 to the troop drawdown in 2014 but, in more specific terms, my main focus is on the period between 2009 and 2014 when counterinsurgency was overtly the dominant military approach (at least in theory) and when there was a particularly securitised approach to the civilian peacebuilding project (see Duffield 2012; McBride and Wibben 2012; Suhrke 2011).[3]

Tools of Analysis

In order to explore and to craft a depiction of the military–peace complex, I call upon a specific analytical toolkit that allows me to seek out non-traditional areas of focus in war studies and less commonly recognised spaces and subjects of politics. This book is located within critical military studies and critical peace studies and is heavily and centrally influenced by feminist scholarship. It also draws on new materialism and the study of space in global politics. I discuss some of the core frameworks I will draw upon below, while others, such as insights from new materialist literature, I will discuss in the relevant chapters.

Gendering Conflict
Gender is a ubiquitous, central and underlying concept to the military–peace complex and can be framed as a 'foundational construct that affects and is affected by all other relations of power' (Shepherd 2014: 104). This is a political understanding of gender, in which gender performativity is always already a political experience and a politically powerful force. A feminist lens attentive to gender as a system and as something that shapes individual, collective and institutional practices often influences my analysis in the book, even when gender is not explicitly discussed (see Ackerly et al. 2019; Cohn 2011; Crenshaw 1989; Enloe 2007, 2010; Gentry 2014; Mehta 2015; Mohanty 2003; Shepherd 2009; Zalewski 1995).[4]

In the chapters that follow I am interested in how individual gendered performances feed into military–peace complex practice on an everyday, embodied level and the book thus sits within a wider tradition of scholarship where 'experience and bodies have always been front and centre' (Sylvester 2012: 483). I am interested in how everyday actions that may not seem obviously gendered can be better understood with the use of gendered analysis (see Basham 2013: 1–15; Mehta 2015). I am also interested in the way that gendered ideas fuel overarching paradigms, such as the liberal peace[5] or the counterinsurgency doctrine in Afghanistan (Billaud 2012; Khalili 2011; McBride and Wibben 2012). In all cases I am sensitive to the fluidity of gender, and the way that it can produce and mask contradiction. In order to better facilitate the discussions in this book, it is worth briefly outlining feminist engagement with war and militarism, and key categories, like militarised masculinities, that facilitate my analysis. Feminist work has illustrated the connections between gender and military praxis on multiple levels, highlighting the manner in which gender ideologies filter through militaristic language and cultural discourse (Cohn 1987, 2013), structural impetus (Sjoberg 2013; Wilcox 2013), and individual identity constructions and representations (Duncanson 2013, 2008). Scholarship has demonstrated the complexity of gender at each of these levels, the way it is adopted and revised selectively (Higate 2012c) and the manner in which it intersects with racial and national identity markers within militaries and military acts (Basham 2013; Higate and Henry 2009; Khalili 2011; Mann 2014). Feminist work has also problematised the links between ideology or representation and practices of militarism or violence at each of these levels – cultural, structural and individual – offering detailed accounts of how human agency interacts with gendered structural or ideational patterns, expectations or constraints (Bulmer 2013; Higate 2012c; Gentry and Sjoberg 2007; Manchanda 2014).

The links between feminist scholarship and problematising militarism and war are extensive. Betty Reardon (1996) first articulated the notion of a 'war system' in which a variety of global and national institutions are complicit in perpetuating patriarchal war practices. Cynthia Enloe (2000) has shown the relationship between military culture, military violence and gendered, militarised politics (see also de Mel 2007; Parashar 2013). Carol Cohn emphasises how war and military operations are 'permeated with symbolic associations with gender' (2013: l. 343). Cynthia Cockburn, Peace Medie and others have shown the complex ways that a feminist focus problematises the boundaries between 'war' and 'post-war' temporalities (see Cockburn 2014; Medie 2015). For Kimberly Hutchings, the formal structures of masculinity, consisting of the logics of contrast and contradiction, are what allow us to make sense of war (2008: 390) and thus structures of masculinity transcend individual bodies. Equally, in the context of conflict analysis Karin Fierke argues that the 'feminine is part of a structure of meaning that exits independent of women' (2010: 404) so that the feminine acts as a system of meaning beyond individual persons.

Within feminist scholarship and central to recognising the operation of war, 'hegemonic masculinity' is a normative identity category, more ideational than actual in terms of the number of men who achieve it in any real sense. From the moment it was first articulated 'it embodied the currently most honoured way of being a man, it required all other men to position themselves in relation to it, and it ideologically legitimated the global subordination of women to men' (Connell and Messerschmidt 2005: 832). Thus, hegemonic masculinity, while it may be unattainable, exerts a subordinating power over both men and women to a greater or lesser extent, depending on how it intersects with other relations of dominance and hierarchy (see Duriesmith and Ismail 2019). 'Militarised masculinity' is a gendered identity category specific to a militarised framework, though not necessarily exclusive to soldiers. It is best understood as the set of values and attributes designated hegemonic within a militarised context (Eichler 2014). Mirroring structures of 'hegemonic masculinity' (Connell 2005), the concept points to a kind of masculine identity that is privileged above all else in a military context, and functions as an all-pervasive standard with deep cultural and institutional roots. Maya Eichler states that: '[c]haracteristics associated with militarised masculinity have historically included toughness, violence, aggression, courage, control and domination' (2014: 82). It has been noted by Susanna Trnka (1995), for example, that military folk rhymes valorise aggressive masculine sexual dominance. Nicole Detraz states that 'toughness' and 'lack of emotion' are rewarded in soldiering (2012: l. 549). Importantly, militarised masculinity is not understood as something inherent to men – 'men are not innately disposed to war' – but rather there is a great deal of normative and ideational work required to construct and maintain the connection between masculinity and militarism, male identity and the capacity for violence (Prugl 2001: 335). For example, Victoria Basham has shown that part of this normative work can lie in the expulsion and rejection of modes of explicit homosexuality in a military context, in order to legitimise and make safe homosocial and homoerotic bonding within a hegemonic masculine framework (Basham 2013: 103–11).

Militarised masculinity is understood within a hierarchical context and is defined by its dominant relation to lesser masculinities and its subordination of femininities (Eichler 2014: 89). Feminist scholarship often understands it to be a constructed category that is built through all military praxis but most especially military training (Eichler 2014: 83). Thus, Sandra Whitworth argues that after experiencing basic training and coming out the other side:

> [t]he new soldier is both physically and emotionally tough – betraying little emotion, with the possible exceptions of anger and aggression. The soldier learns to 'deny all that is "feminine" and soft in himself,' and any who depart

from the ideal are neither men nor soldiers. (Goldstein 2001: 266; Whitworth 2004: 161)

Scholars such as Claire Duncanson (2013), Laleh Khalili (2011), Paul Higate (2003), Sarah Bulmer (2013), David Jackson (Bulmer and Jackson 2016), Eichler (Bulmer and Eichler 2017), and David Duriesmith and Noor Huda Ismail (2019) have pointed to the fluidity within the category of militarised masculinities, and the manner in which the traits valued within soldiering shift and change depending on context. Duncanson (2013) makes the important point that the concept of military masculinity can be prescriptive and can position men as inherently violent or indicate a path dependency in relation to military experience. Within my interviews and wider research, I have encountered multiple and complex relationships with ideas of masculinity and wish to reflect this non-linearity and diversity within my discussions while still highlighting the ongoing centrality of masculinity as a performative and structuring force.

At the macro level, feminist scholars suggest that military interventions are shaped by gendered logics linked to notions of hegemonic masculinity, and the system of values it prescribes. Laura Sjoberg (2013) and Lauren Wilcox (2013) write about the international state system as a gendered system, and thus all actions within and between states necessarily follow a gendered logic. Wilcox suggests that 'sovereignty and the sovereign state are conceived in masculine terms, as revealed by the representations of the state as a masculine body' (Wilcox 2013: 69). Anne Orford (1999) and Maria O'Reilly (2012) identify the importance of masculinity as a framework and guiding logic for those who intervene militarily. These and other feminist scholars point to the way in which gender and race operate in tandem to shape the ontological reality and narrative identifiers in which (primarily Western) military powers see themselves and their role in the international arena, and perpetuate racialised Self/Other binaries (Hudson 2014, 2012; Khalili 2011; O'Reilly 2012; Orford 1999). Sherene Razack, for example, has argued that a gendered culture of neo-imperialism underlies humanitarian interventions justified in the name of peace and protection (Razack 2004). Moreover, scholars point out that given the relational nature of gender as a construct, this kind of reliance on hegemonic masculine frameworks necessitates the feminising of an inferior Other (Orford 1999).

Female soldiers, as articulated by feminist scholarship, are often marked by modes of unease in part because of notions of protection that justify war-making, such as the need to protect women and children (Pin-Fat and Stern 2005; Khalid 2011; Young 2003b). Feminists have pointed to the manner in which military culture and practice tends to subsume individual women within a system of masculine-oriented hierarchies of gender identities (see MacKenzie 2012). Orna Sasson-Levy (2003) and Jennifer Silva (2008: 945) point to the tendency of female soldiers to perform 'male' traits as a means of gaining acceptance from their colleagues, thereby internalising and reinforcing a patriar-chal consciousness despite ostensibly transgressing traditional gender boundaries (see Parashar 2012, 2009). Wider logics of signification in relation to female soldiers also operate to neutralise their femininity or demonise it in specific ways. For example, women (including soldiers) who commit acts of violence are re-signified as maternal, deviant or sexually promiscuous so that 'their choices are trivialised by mother, monster, whore narratives, which describe them as non-culpable' (Gentry and Sjoberg 2015: 24). For Véronique Pin-Fat and Maria Stern, the female/feminised body in the masculine sphere of the military will always be expelled, re-signified, generative of deep unease since 'the markings of masculinity make possible the workings of the military only if they are maintained as seemingly distinct and, indeed, dichotomous' (Pin-Fat and Stern 2005: 33). Thus, as Basham articulates, 'the ways in which women's bodies are disciplined within the military not only constitute women as having certain (in)capabilities, but also reinforce the customariness of men's bodies in violence both in the everyday and geopolitically' (Basham 2013: 54).

Again, beyond the level of individuals, scholars have pointed to the particular role that notions of femininity have had within the concept of militarism as a whole, and relatedly how the dichotomy between masculinities and femininities threads through into notions of state-hood, security and war (Wilcox 2013: 69–71). This brings us back to the concept of militarised masculinities and the denigration of the feminine that is required to maintain this identity category and the hierarchies it perpetuates (Cohn 1999: 461). Arguably that which is understood as feminine is purged in a war-fighting context, partially through linking it with shame (when standards of masculinity are not achieved), the necessity to prove masculinity and the humiliation of those that cannot maintain the 'courage, power and authority exclusively associated with masculinity' in the logic of warfare and militarism (Sasson-Levy 2003: 451).

The manner in which femininity is expelled, subordinated or den-igrated in practices of war and security, in notions of rationality and practices of statecraft, reinforces the validation of certain hegemonic masculine tropes above all else, as discussed above (Basham 2013: 87–8; Cohn 1999; Pin-Fat and Stern 2005). Joshua Goldstein has argued that 'men's domination of women primarily plays a symbolic role in warfare: it serves as a metaphor for domination of the enemy' (Goldstein 2001; Prugl 2001: 336). As Saskia Stachowitsch argues,

> [f]eminist research has shown that the coevolution of the Western nation-state, modern military institutions, and hierarchical gender orders led to a privileging of militarised masculinity in the political sphere and institution-alised gendered dichotomies of 'just warriors' and 'beautiful souls' within the state. (Elshtain 1991; Stachowitsch 2015: 24)

Equally, that which is coded feminine – bodies, practices, ideas – is regularly folded into militarism at the level of strategy and military goals. Scholars such as Julia Welland, for example, suggest that counterinsurgency warfare is a gendered practice, rhetorically framed as 'softer' than other kinds of war-fighting, and thus attached to notions of the 'feminised' (Dyvik 2013; Welland 2015: 3). In a different vein, Duncanson discusses the category of peacekeeper masculinities as a departure from military masculinities, a way of doing soldiering that values work previously coded 'feminised' (Duncanson 2013: 134) thus demonstrating the fluidity of gendered perceptions within military operations, and their capacity to evolve. I will explore some of these arguments in detail in the chapters that follow and will continue to build on feminist insights and perspectives throughout the book.

Racialised Logics

Though I have touched on the intersections between race and gender above, it is important to highlight the centrality of considering racialised logics in order to understand the military–peace complex. Feminist work has highlighted that gender, while vital to political meaning, is not sufficient as a category of analysis (Davis 2016; hooks 2000) and that intersectionality (the complex configurations of experience and identities that produce modes of repression) as coined by Kimberlé Crenshaw (see, for example, 1991) and postcolonial insights (Mohanty 1984, 2003; Spivak 1988) are crucial to understand politics, power and marginalisation. In this book I draw on Edward Said's (1979) concept of Orientalism and its focus on practices of knowledge production, representation and Othering in producing ideas of the 'East' in the eyes of the 'West'. The very frame of reference that underlies intervention in Afghanistan – that Afghanistan was a 'failed' state where terrorism could thrive – manifests racialised logics. As Alison Howell and Melanie Richter-Monpetit (2019: 8) write about narratives of state failure, '[w] hile they may avoid overt reference to race, they operate within a lineage of racial discourse that emerged to justify colonialism and continuing trusteeship'. Racialised logics within the military–peace complex in Afghanistan were sometimes explicit, such as the concept of the unciv-ilised Muslim man prone to violence, which facilitates the possibility of 'saving brown women from brown men' (Cloud 2004; Dyvik 2013: 420; Said 1979; Spivak 1988: 297). The aesthetic and symbolism of the veil and the construction of the Afghan woman in different politi-cal contexts (including as refugees) have been well noted as racialised tropes (Abu-Lughod 2002; Abirafeh 2009; Ahmed-Ghosh 2003; Ahmed 1992; Bezhan 2014; Burki 2011; Khalid 2011; Jiwani and Dakroury 2009; Shepherd 2006; Zulfacar 2006). They could also be more implicit, echoes of colonial practices that trend affectively or in micro-political ways towards division and inequality stuck to racialised bodies (see Ahmed 2015). Race here emerges in part as a way of understanding self-definition that is historical and bound up with the historiography of citizenship, as articulated by Gloria Wekker (2016: 2):

> a racial grammar, a deep structure of inequality in thought and affect based on race, was installed in nineteenth-century European imperial populations and . . . it is from this deep reservoir, the cultural archive, that, among other things, a sense of self has been formed and fabricated.

The concept of whiteness is vastly important in terms of generating affective, embodied and aesthetic echoes of colonial logics and praxis, yet whiteness does not map directly onto the 'international' sphere or international bodies in Afghanistan. Soldiers and civilian liberal peace practitioners could easily be associated with different races – Black American or British for instance, Malaysian, Indian and so on. Because of this, the idea of the international, or of 'liberal' citizenship, is perhaps more useful for the purposes of this book. In the sense that whiteness is a reference point here it is not fixed as such but rather 'lived as a back-ground to experience' (Ahmed 2007: 150) and is bound to a sense of privilege when looking at the 'international' project as a whole (Ahmed 2007). Whiteness is also bound historically to the imperial project, to the political economy of empire, the stealing of resources and the enslave-ment and abuse of peoples, and as such it manifests in Afghanistan, as in the wider humanitarian/military intervention/war system, as linked to these histories. Moreover, neoliberal policies embedded within the liberal peace framework perpetuate particular racialised and gendered inequalities. As Basham articulates, '[t]he privileging of whiteness, of masculinity, of heterosexuality, of free market values, are not regrettable oversights; they are what allow liberal democracies to function as they do' (2013: 7), and this, I suggest, extends to foreign policy. I draw on the idea of whiteness as a system of privilege and set of lived experiences here in thinking about embodied divides generated through routine and institutional praxis, but often focus on the category of the international or 'liberal' citizenship to better capture the nature of the international project.

There is also the idea of the contemporary 'civilising mission', or an implicit dichotomy between liberal and illiberal, which manifests racialised logics. As Paul Higate and Marsha Henry point out, 'liberal democratic models have a tendency to be accepted non-consciously as morally and ethically "right" for those regions and states that require "civilizing"' (Higate and Henry 2009: 10). This can be messy or indirect. For instance, keeping in mind that hybridity in the liberal peace context can be understood as the mixing together of so-called local and international practices, ideas and so on, scholars such as Uma Kothari and Catherine Nash connect liberal hybridity to colonial governance. They both suggest that the colonial project was fluid and adaptable, rather than rigid and uncompromising: 'the complex ambivalence within the seemingly ridged ideologies of colonial discourse was compounded by its transmission into distinct local spaces' (Kothari 2006c: 237). Nash argues that colonial ideologies were not adopted easily but were 'threatened, challenged, negotiated, made and remade in the encounters between those brought together through colonialism' (2004: 112). Similarly, racialised logics within the military–peace complex are not necessarily clear-cut; they manifest in messy ways that sit underneath the paradigm and underlie its manifestations. Fundamentally important is the globalised intertextuality of Islamophobia and racism targeted specifically at Muslims that formed a bedrock of war on terror ideology and has constituted modes of politics ever since (though they also manifested before 2001) (see Eroukhmanoff 2015, 2019; Gentry 2015; Wekker 2016). Though explicit Islamophobia is not something I often encountered expressed directly in relation to Afghanistan, this backdrop undoubtedly shaped perceptions about and modes of self-definition in relation to the country in particular ways, and indeed shaped the nature of military intervention in the country to begin with (as well as the reaction to it inside Afghanistan).

In this book, I facilitate the reification of a divide between 'international' and 'local' through my discursive and analytical choices, and it is important to note that while these concepts help with my analysis, they are not fixed, stable or in any kind of logical opposition. Indeed so-called 'local' elites may have much more in common with internationals than they do with 'local' rural poor populations and so on (Paffenholz 2015). My use of these terms in this book should be read with that in mind. I use these frameworks as social categories drawing on insights from Emile Durkheim's (2012: 440–5) work and from scholars such as Jaremey McMullen (2013) to suggest that the categories of the international and the local functioned as socially meaningful signifiers. They serve in a way that McMullen (2013: 389) has described, drawing on Durkheim: 'categories do not communicate social facts but are themselves socially constructed (that is, categories not only express "social things" but are also "social things" themselves)'. As social categories, the 'international' and the 'local' signal dominant expectations and performances (carrying racialised and gendered baggage), without needing to encompass all the actual individuals to which they refer. In fact, these categories are best understood as to some extent cut loose from actual people individually (in the sense of encompassing all that they are and do) while maintaining a reputational and signification power derived from a confluence of expectations, interactions and performative practices.

Everyday, Experience, Performances
Also crucial to an exploration of the military–peace complex is a recognition that 'everyday life is a mix of taken-for-granted realities, habit, and routine, as well as impulse, novelty, and vivaciousness' (Vannini 2015: 320). The symbolic and ideational components of a given conflict-affected context are visible in practices that might otherwise be seen as banal, or peripheral to the important and deliberate acts of key actors. These practices are the everyday, the routine, the semi-conscious; they are 'intentional, but not always reflexive in a cognitive way' (Vannini 2015: 322). Since 'a number of (apparently) hidden or mundane practices and processes operate alongside macro-political processes to shape the precise form and configuration' of peace and statebuilding (McLeod 2015: 52), an exploration of the spaces in and logics through which they operate must be alert to the everyday, routine and habitual as well as the overarching, institutional and ideological.

In this vein Enloe suggests that war and militarism 'tends to insinuate itself into ordinary daily routines where it is rarely heralded or deemed noteworthy' (2000: 3). A focus on the everyday, which traditionally has been neglected in the study of war and war-affected contexts (Basham 2013: 8), demonstrates the banality of violence and exposes it as, at times, an unexceptional process and series of small decisions, without losing site of its wider geopolitical meaning and ideological roots. In this book I seek to 'underline the not-necessarily reflexive sensory dimensions of experience by paying attention to the perceptual dimensions of our actions and the habituated and routine nature of everyday existence' (Vannini 2015: 323), while also arguing that the military–peace complex is explicitly bound to geopolitical shifts and the wider, pervasive logics of neoliberalism.

In recent international relations scholarship focusing on peace, conflict, militarism and violence the notion of the everyday, the banal and the under-noticed has gained traction and significance (see, for example, Basham 2013; Duffield 2010; Holland and Solomon 2014; Mehta 2015). Paying attention to the smaller and less obviously political, power-centric or statist dimensions of peace and conflict allows a deeper access to an understanding of how power, politics and violence actually function, thread through lives and manifest in praxis on a human and social level (see Basham 2013; Enloe 2010).

In the chapters that follow I pay attention to geopolitical goals, processes, mandates and meaning but often look to how these unfold at the everyday level, and track between the everyday and the geopolitical. The concept of the everyday is prevalent in critical feminist scholarship (see, for example, Åhäll 2019; Mehta 2015; Vaittinen et al. 2015). The drive of second-wave and subsequent feminisms as both academic and political projects is marked by the push to expose and reframe the distinction between the private and the public, where that which was designated personal, social or private was coded apolitical and feminine while the public, political sphere was masculinised (see Basham and Vaughan-Williams 2013: 514). Carole Pateman has written that '[t]he dichotomy between the private and the public is central to almost two centuries of feminist writing and political struggle; it is, ultimately what the feminist movement is all about' (Pateman 1989: 181). Marked most particularly by the work of Enloe (see, for example, 2000; 2004; 2007; 2010), feminist military and war studies has sought to collapse the scholarly preference for a focus on states and powerful actors in public moments and turn analytical attention upon the everyday, marginalised, feminised and unnoticed, exploring how these aspects are crucial for the workings and maintenance of violence and conflict (Basham 2013; Frerks et al. 2014; Higate and Henry 2009).

A focus on the social and political significance of the everyday and routine can also be traced (at least as far and further back) to the Annales school of historical study (Moses and Knutsen 2007: 186). Fernand Braudel, a key Annales school historian, argued that 'mankind is more than waist-deep in daily routine. Countless inherited acts, accumulated pell-mell and repeated time after time to this very day become habits that help us live, imprison us, and made decisions for us throughout our lives' (Braudel 1977: 7).

Part of the significance of the unnoticed and the routine as political phenomena is their capacity to structure the conditions of possibility within collectives or particular social groupings. Again, this kind of understanding has deep roots in social and political scholarship. Durkheim's term for the 'set of generally accepted norms or rules embraced by all of society's members' was 'solidarity' (Moses and Knutsen 2007: 210). For Michel Foucault the term 'archaeology of knowledge' captured the sense of collective predispositions that guide choices and designate social meaning (Foucault 1972). Both these notions of social group pre-knowledge are affected by and manifested within the everyday. It is at this level that 'we are shaped by our environments and cultural interactions' (Murer 2010: 129). The small processes that make up daily life are thus marked with political meaning derived from their social content and collectively understood, if undernoticed, significance.

An important element of the everyday is the interaction between individual agency, routine and institutional or macro-level frameworks and how these relate to violence. The repetition and solidification of everyday behaviours into normative behavioural guidelines feeds into the crafting of particular structures, which in turn influences the choices individuals make on the everyday level. Iris Marion Young, drawing on Peter Blau, Jean-Paul Sartre and Anthony Giddens, frames structure as the collective product of a multiplicity of individual actions sedimenting into fixed parameters for action and thought over time (Young 2003a: 6). For Young, structure is spatial and self-referential, existing as pre-knowledge that guides actors' choices and, equally, being reified and solidified by those choices (Young 2003a: 6). She suggests: '[a]s I understand the concept, structure denotes a confluence of institutional rules and interactive routines, mobilization of resources and physical structures' (Young 2003a: 4). Violent structures are created when the processes described by Young contribute to the unequal treatment, suffering, injury and perhaps death of some portion of humanity, often while others benefit from structural conditions (Galtung 1969). Laura Shepherd draws upon Foucault as well as feminist conceptualisations of agency and power, to suggest that 'violence is not reducible to (physical) constraint or repression but rather encompasses regulative idea(l)s and performs ordering functions in our collective cognitive frameworks' (Shepherd 2012: 8). Related insights are also evident in other feminist writings on the relationship between violence, structure and individual agency, such as Caron Gentry and Laura Sjoberg's use of Nancy Hirschmann's 'relational autonomy framework' which conceptualises the power of structural restraint, while not shutting out the need to understand how people choose to behave (including violently) within structurally designated boundaries (Gentry and Sjoberg 2007: 189; Hirschmann 1989; Shepherd 2009: 211).

Moreover, paying attention to the everyday brings experience to the fore. Experience is the 'lived truth' of a particular temporal moment for a particular actor but is equally 'subjectively narrated' (McLeod 2015: 53). The body is of course central to any experiential framework since 'how the body "feels" the world impinges upon how the world is experienced and described' (McLeod 2015: 53). In paying attention to the bodies and embodied performances of actors within the military–peace complex, I also pay some attention to my own by occasionally incorporating my notes and experiences, since certain kinds of research 'begins from the researcher's body as the key instrument for knowing, sensing, feeling, and relating to others and self' (Vannini 2015: 321). Following Sara Ahmed (2015, 2010), I see a close relationship between bodies and emotions, and recognise the call in feminist work for 'reorienting research towards the affective and relational dimensions of peace activities' (Shepherd 2014: 112). Ahmed, concerned with a phenomenological post-structuralist feminist reading of emotions, points to the notion of affect as 'sticky': '[a]ffect is what sticks, or what sustains or preserves the connection between ideas, values, and objects' (2010: 5). She outlines affect as a way to recognise 'the messiness of the experiential, the unfolding of bodies into worlds, and the drama of contingency, how we are touched by what we are near' (2010: 30).

Affect is often understood as *'pre-personal'* (Gregory 2019, emphasis added) and is thus slightly different from particular emotions, and not individual as such but environmental (Shouse 2005). It is the conditions in which emotions can come to be articulated fully, a sensory perception of the parameters that are set for feelings to be felt. I perceive affect as 'amorphous potential that remains outside of discourse, which is difficult to articulate but none-the-less has effects within discourse' (Holland and Solomon 2014: 264). Affect is difficult to work with methodologically. Reading affect into discourse is challenging and uncertain.

However, following Ty Solomon (2012) and Bleiker and Hutchison (2008), I believe that it is possible to do so and that placing people at the centre of the study of conflict and peacebuilding requires an engagement with the affective environment in which certain types of violence percolate and self-sustain (see Partis-Jennings 2017).

In exploring felt experiences, I also pay attention to spatial dynamics and environmental affects, recognising that '[a]ffect is distributed between, and can happen outside, bodies which are not exclusively human, and might incorporate technologies, things, non-human living matter, discourses or even, say, a swathe of noise or a swarm of creatures' (Lorimer 2008: 552). Thus landscapes, things and our built environment are vital to global politics because they contribute to 'our sense of being in the world, although much of our engagement with it is unreflective' (Shepherd 2012: 11).

Moreover, my engagement with the everyday and embodied experience in this book is framed through a focus on performances – the enactment of specific sets of behaviours that have social and political consequences – within the military–peace complex. In part I draw on Karen Barad, who understands performativity as a material notion, arguing that '[a] performative understanding of discursive practices challenges the representationalist belief in the power of words to represent pre-existing things' (2003: 802). She suggests that language cannot fully grasp how performances operate in praxis and that 'performativity is precisely a contestation of the excessive power granted to language to determine what is real' (Barad 2003: 802). A focus on performance has the capacity to draw out what Paul Kirby and Marsha Henry call 'disjunctures, slippages and paradoxes' (Kirby and Henry 2012: 447). An exploration of how performance operates in military and peacebuilding work highlights the reification of certain hierarchical codes of identity and behaviour. Yet it equally elucidates the 'possibility of challenging and parodying these naturalized codes' (Fenster 2014: 195). Performance illuminates 'how individual behaviour derives from collective, even unconscious, influences and is manifest as observable behaviour, both overt and quotidian, individual and collective' (Davies 2008: 1) while at the same time 'making experience legible to others' (Davies 2008: 5).

Important to my conception of the military–peace complex is the idea that conflict-affected space is sometimes treated like a clean slate, in which actors can create a new reality from scratch (Smirl 2009), yet in actuality peacebuilding sites are burdened with extensive pre-knowledge and preconceptions, pre-existing power structures and normative repertoires that are entrenched from many angles (Higate and Henry 2009).

The external statebuilders (military and civilian) themselves come from a range of national and institutional backgrounds, each with its own set of expectations, mandates and rules, while the subjects of liberal peace interventions – national populations – are of course equally operating within pre-existing frames of reference and relations of power (see Higate and Henry 2009). Severine Autesserre uses the concept of 'practical sense' as articulated by Pierre Bourdieu, to access the manner in which the performative practices of peacebuilders (and those that engage with them) are produced by 'background dispositions' which 'every social being carries and uses constantly, if unconsciously' day to day (Autesserre 2014: l. 1039). Particular modes of praxis 'simultaneously embody, act out, and possibly reify background knowledge and discourse in and on the material world' (Bourdieu 1972, 1979; Autesserre 2014).

Overall, then, military–peace complex performances in a space such as Afghanistan are both novel and hybrid, in that new roles and relations are in the process of being formed under the particular conditions of liberal peace intervention, and equally they are performances marked by baggage from prior contexts, relationalities and preconditioning. These performances are made up of different aspects; discourses are performative, in that discursive systems gain social meaning through practice (Frerks et al. 2014: 6), while bodies and symbols are also central to performance, since performativity is by nature an embodied notion and often requires certain symbolic props to be rendered intelligible (Higate and Henry 2009: 18). These are performances linked to gender, nationality, security and forms of social recognition, and thus always include a certain set of understandings about the perceived target audience and the expectations of the sexed body (see Butler 1999).

The Structure of the Book

The rest of the book is structured primarily according to core themes, namely the performative intersections between actors, key logics of entanglement, and the material and gendered dynamics of the military–peace complex. However, before moving to the analytical body of the work, the first chapter of this book discusses the context of Afghanistan and is organised so as to draw out some of the key narratives that circulate around the country and its history as well as trying to provide the reader with a minimal background understanding. In particular I highlight the impact of war, and the production of a dichotomy between ideas of tradition and modernity that feed into certain conceptions of Afghanistan as an always already 'failed state'. While this chapter does not contribute as directly as others to the major overarching arguments of the book, it is necessary to lay out a backdrop against which to understand the analysis that follows. It also helps to understand the layers which shape the military–peace complex in Afghanistan, the manner in which its ideologies and logics cycle through recent histories as well as being crafted through the particulars of its contemporary political moment. In other words, this chapter allows the reader to gain some understanding of the context through which the military–peace complex is shaped.

The second chapter is focused especially on performativity, exploring three key groups of actors within the military–peace complex: civilian peace/statebuilders, counterinsurgency soldiers and private military security contractors. The chapter focuses on how these actors operated in tandem and in parallel, entangled in various ways, to produce the performative practices of the military–peace complex. It highlights three key logics centring on liberalism, security and gender that intertwine different actors and continually reproduce the category of the international (in opposition to the local). This is a central focus that continues into Chapter 3, where I focus on material and spatial practices to elucidate non-traditional modes of slippage between peace and war work in Afghanistan. Again, I draw on particular examples in the material and spatial domain to understand the disaggregation between international and Afghan bodies within the overarching military–peace complex, and to highlight the ways that everyday and unnoticed elements contribute to the politics of intervention and statebuilding. Finally, in Chapter 4 I return to consider gender as a central organising theme within the military–peace complex. I focus on women and the female body, exploring how the idea of gender, especially that of women, was instrumentalised within both peace and war-making praxis, how both depended on the foil of the 'average third world woman' (Mohanty 1984) and how international women in both spaces were liminal figures, generative of unease.

I conclude by addressing some final points: I highlight what we gain from the military–peace complex framework, I note my reflections on questions of intentionality, imminent critique and, finally, the possibility of an alternative, hopeful, and care-oriented and solidarity-focused approach. I bring the book to a close by positing the importance of the military–peace complex as an idea and suggesting what might be gained from drawing upon it in other contexts and other ways as well.

Taken together, these chapters aim to offer a new lens through which to view the international project in Afghanistan. Building particularly on feminist international relations, critical peace studies and critical military studies, it elucidates modes of slippage and entanglement that normally sit outside the gaze of international relations and war studies. It provides an unorthodox way of viewing interventions, one that is primarily focused on those ideas of disjuncture and layering that I highlighted at the beginning of this Introduction. My contribution here is to offer a window through which to see and think differently about the international project in Afghanistan, and the tangled links between the everyday, embodied, gendered, spatial, material and geopolitical. As you, the reader, progress through the book, I hope you will find familiar actors framed anew, and small, unnoticed relationships made central in interesting ways. It is only by offering such a lens, though it is certainly still a partial view, that, I argue, we can see another, crucial side of the whole picture.

Notes

1. These include documents from the Lessons Learned Project, a set of internal interviews conducted on behalf of the US government in relation to Afghanistan, and from the WikiLeaks Afghan War Logs.
2. I use the term civilian in a relational sense here to refer to anyone who was not in the military at any stage in their career, with the exception of private security contractors who I identify as such when making reference to them.
3. Astri Suhrke (2011: 46) makes the point that counterinsurgency was in fact central to the NATO approach and the strategy of European military actors much earlier than 2009.
4. Despite the fact that this book incorporates a strong focus on gender, peace and conflict, there are few substantive references to United Nations Security Council Resolution (UNSCR) 1325. The reason for this is twofold. First, there is already a significant amount of feminist engagement with UNSCR 1325 and so it is a well-covered topic. Second, UNSCR 1325 was mentioned very rarely by my interview respondents in relation to Afghanistan, and my analysis subsequently reflects that relative absence.
5. For a specific exploration of the intersections between critical peace studies and feminist work, see *Peacebuilding* 7(2) (2019).

CHAPTER 1

Afghanistan in Context

Having outlined some of my conceptual tools and core arguments as well as my approach to my material in the Introduction, I use this chapter to discuss Afghanistan more specifically, providing a brief and limited engagement with its recent history and the socio-political shifts that have accompanied that history, especially in relation to conflict. It is impossible to fully understand the post-2001 international engagement with Afghanistan without understanding the country's history and geopolitical trajectory and the account I give here is still too restricted by scope for depth of historical understanding. This chapter is simply a small attempt to offset the 'disease of ahistoricity' (Ndlovu-Gatsheni 2009: 179) or, more commonly, a narrow and parsimonious historicism prevalent in mainstream representations and politics. Yet while it is vital to recognise the role of the past, I do not wish to assert Afghanistan's path dependency or atemporal fixity (see Manchanda 2019). Unquestionably, stories of external interference and conflict are only one facet of the country's past, and they do not predetermine its future. In discussing some fragments of history, I do not intend to reify dominant narratives about Afghanistan as a 'graveyard of empires', an always already harsh, hostile and innately warlike land (see Manchanda 2019), and my exploration will necessarily be partial and come with caveats. However, it will give an indication of some core issues and events framed in such a way as to be salient to the discussions that follow in this book and in order to give the reader a general sense of context.

War and Peacebuilding since 2001

I want bin Laden's head shipped back in a box filled with dry ice. I want to be able to show bin Laden's head to the President. I promised him I would do that . . . Have I made myself clear?

– Cofer Black, director of the CIA's Counterterrorism Centre, briefs first CIA team to enter Afghanistan (cited in Bird and Marshall 2011: 73).

There was a kinetic phase and then an ideological phase based on using the idea of freedom and democracy as an alternative vision to terrorism and to counter the appeal of al Qaeda.

– Stephen Hadley, National Security Advisor under President George W. Bush, interviews for the Lessons Learned Project ('Stephen Hadley, Lessons Learned Interview', 2015)

When Osama bin Laden planned an attack on the United States, carried out with devastating brutality on 11 September 2001, there is a chance he expected America to respond as it did (Allin 2011: 49). Those with experience fighting in Afghanistan's wars might have gained some insight into the mechanisms through which to engage (and fight) a superpower (Duncanson 2016: 83; Barfield 2010: 255). Bin Laden did have that experience, having fought against the Soviet occupation alongside the Mujahideen in 1987 (Roy 2015: xix). The fact that al-Qaeda assassinated Massoud, a leader of the Northern Alliance, two days before 9/11 might suggest that they possibly pre-empted attempts to rekindle American-Mujahideen partnerships as part of an Afghan conflict (Nicoll 2011: 25; Joya 2009). Yet, regardless of whether bin Laden expected the United States to invade Afghanistan or not, it would seem that their decision to do so helped his cause in some ways, providing a recruitment rationale for anti-Western militancy, and setting the stage for a focus on extremism, of both the (so-called) Islamic and Islamophobic kinds, that still shapes global political dynamics today (see Duriesmith and Ismail 2019; Eroukhmanoff 2015; Jiwani and Dakroury 2009; Razack 2008; Wekker 2016).

While based in Afghanistan, Osama bin Laden and al-Qaeda, the terrorist network he fronted, claimed responsibility for the infamous 9/11 attacks and the deaths of almost 3,000 people. President George W. Bush and his administration gave Afghanistan's Taliban government an ultimatum. They were required to hand over bin Laden or face war. Mullah Omar, the Taliban leader, refused, and thus the initial stage of international engagement in Afghanistan began (see Duncanson 2016: 84). The idea that the war in Afghanistan was a result of 9/11 helped to shape the motivations for and approach to the conflict from the outset, especially on the part of the Americans. One former military respondent explained to me that:

> [T]he Americans were sent here with a clear task to disrupt al-Qaeda and Taliban and to make sure that a thing like 9/11 will never happen again, and if some officers of them took a decision, to get a big Taliban guy or even to find out, or disrupt anything linked to foreign fighters . . . they always justified it with look what those guys did to us in New York 11th September 2001.

His words and the quotation that began this section highlight an element of revenge within some military motivations and a need to demonstrate success, especially at the start of the conflict and on the American side.

Indeed, the first and most clear-cut warfare-based stage of this contemporary Afghan conflict was quite a rapid affair. The US and the Northern Alliance overthrew the Taliban militarily in three months. Only 102 days after the invasion of Afghanistan, on 5 December, the international community was facilitating peace talks for the 'post-conflict' country (Harsch 2015: 107; Dodge 2011). These talks, which resulted in the Bonn Agreement, were unusual in that they did not include representation from the defeated party, the Taliban (Harsch 2015: 107; Suhrke 2011: 14). The agreement laid out a plan for 'charting the post-2001 transition period' in Afghanistan (Suhrke 2011: 14). It mandated a Pashtun from the Rome Group (a faction of political exiles in Rome) named Hamid Karzai, who was linked to former ruling elites, to form an interim government. He was to lead a thirty-member interim administration to facilitate the holding of a *Loya Jirga* (a 'Grand Assembly' (Abirafeh 2009: 17) that brings together representatives from across different communities) and preparation for elections (Nicoll 2011: 26; Suhrke 2011: 25).

Looking at the military engagement, this phase of the Afghan conflict can be defined in terms of its attempted minimalism (Suhrke 2011: 24). In his election doctrine and initial response to 9/11, President George W. Bush contrasted his conservative military ideologies and global aspirations with the liberal humanitarian campaigns of the 1990s. He claimed: 'I don't want to nation-build with troops' (Dodge 2013: 1190). The Bush administration and various other neoconservatives in positions of power at the time had a specific understanding of how they wanted the invasion to unfold (Nicoll 2011: 27). It was based around the idea of a light footprint, minimal engagement, substantial airpower and thus less risk of loss of life and wasted resources on the American side. Moreover, the thinking within the administration was that 'the execution of nonmilitary tasks undermined the military's morale and readiness' (Harsch 2015: 108). Bush advisor Condoleezza Rice flippantly encapsulated this perspective by stating at the time: 'We don't need to have the 82nd Airborne escorting kids to kindergarten' (Allin 2011: 53–4). There was a prevalent desire within the Republican administration to 'use American military power for decisive effect' while 'leaving responsibility for the aftermath to Afghanistan' (Nicoll 2011: 27). To an observer at the time, the Afghan war might have seemed like a resounding victory for American military power by December 2001. With the benefit of hindsight, however, it is clear that the international engagement with Afghanistan was only beginning at this stage.

These early years, as it were, brought key players onto the Afghan stage – militarily these were the International Security Assistance Force (ISAF), led by the British, and NATO, with multiple contributors but largely guided by American desires, at least initially (Allin 2011; Dodge 2011; Suhrke 2011). NATO took over responsibility for the war in Afghanistan, despite the reservations of member states, arguably in part as a rehabilitation strategy for the security organisation, whose purpose and raison d'être at the time was unclear. The compartmentalised nature of these bodies, made up of different elements and national contingents, fostered multifaceted and non-linear chains of command and a lack of cohesive overarching strategy. Tim Bird and Alex Marshall (2011: 5) reinforce this point:

> [w]hether on the subject of poppy eradication, counterinsurgency tactics, the desirability of negotiating with the Taliban, developmental policy, the approach to corruption within the Afghan government, policy towards Pakistan, Afghan security sector reform or a myriad of other issues, different national preferences within the intervening coalition have prevented a unified and coherent approach.

In the thirteen years of international engagement, different national governments had to answer to the differing expectations and normative parameters of their domestic populations and were required to sell their military strategy in different ways to voters (Bucher et al. 2013; Holland and Aaronson 2014), resulting in politically contingent, and often divergent, practices (see Suhrke 2011).

In terms of civilian actors, the United Nations Assistance Mission to Afghanistan (UNAMA) was established in 2002, and was designed to facilitate the achievement of the roadmap set out by the Bonn Agreement, 'including the organization of the emergency and constitutional *Loya Jirga*, elections as well as the promotion of human rights, the rule of law, and gender equality' (Harsch 2015: 109). The United Nations (UN) was also present and active in other forms such as the United Nations Children's Fund (UNICEF) and the United Nations Development Programme (UNDP), and there was a blossoming army of NGOs, international organisations (IOs) and everything else in between. Their work was and remains disparate in nature, and they formed an extensive and well-resourced network of service provision, paralleling or supplementing government structures (Goodhand 2013). Often the lines between military and civilian interveners and their activities and mandates were blurred in practice, a phenomenon which I explore in greater detail throughout the book (see Nicoll 2011; Azarbaijani-Moghaddam et al. 2008). Thus, in sum, this early phase can be characterised by military 'victory', short-sighted military and strategic engagements, and the growth of an international aid industry in Afghanistan (Dodge 2013: 1207).

After a few years the international involvement with Afghanistan morphed into a much more ambitious engagement focused on substantial restructuring of the Afghan state. Toby Dodge argues that 'minimalist commitment' to statebuilding was dropped and replaced by a 'Liberal Peacebuilding approach given ideological coherence by the four major categories of neoliberalism, the individual, the free-market, the role of the state as guarantor of the rule of law, and the imposition of a democratic system' (Dodge 2013: 1207). On the civilian side this meant a greater focus on institution-building, the push for elections, attempts at strengthening central government, training and capacity-building for indigenous civil society, and shaping and expanding the army and police force (these latter aspects fell to foreign militaries as well).

On the military side, this manifested in work such as partnering and advising (pairing with and training Afghan troops and police units) (Hakimi 2013; Welland 2015) and the apparent quest for securing the 'hearts and minds' of the Afghan population as a military technique (Khalili 2011). It is telling that counterinsurgency was once referred to as 'armed social work' by David Kilcullen, one of its intellectual influences (Dyvik 2013: 420). The 'hearts and minds' strategy of counterinsurgency policy which became dominant in Afghanistan falls into three categories (Egnell 2010: 282). Firstly, it incorporated the undertaking by military personnel of certain humanitarian-style activities (building schools and bridges, for example) designed to gain popular support. Secondly, it was an approach to military operations that relied on less invasive force protection and much more on a general attempt to integrate with the populace (and benefit from so-called 'human intelligence': information gathering theoretically generated through trusting relationships). Finally, 'hearts and minds' referred to the attempt by military institutions such as NATO and ISAF to control the narrative around their presence and their specific activities (Egnell 2010: 283; Khalili 2011). An international respondent who worked in military media in Afghanistan described to me this last aspect of the hearts and minds approach as follows:

> [T]hey [the international military] implement or they develop some media, usually a newspaper or radio station . . . in order – I basically quote now – to inform the local population on the mission of ISAF. So, what is behind it, it is pure PsyOps [Psychological Operations], it is psychological operations, it is this general kind of idea to say to people – we are the good guys don't shoot at us.

In addition to this media-based aspect, knowledge production was also important in forming the 'cultural' backdrop to this approach, and, as such, social scientists were employed to gather knowledge on the 'human terrain' of the counterinsurgency site (Zehfuss 2012).

This COIN strategy in Afghanistan is associated with two key military figures, General David Petraeus and General Stanley McChrystal. McChrystal was placed in command of ISAF forces in 2009, and Petraeus was, at that time, the head of Central Command, the 'regional military command for the Middle East and Central Asia' (Allin 2011: 44). McChrystal, influenced by the approach Petraeus had developed based on his experiences in Iraq, argued that counterinsurgency was as much socio-political as it was military. Since (in this view) insurgents relied on social capital and support from the population, it was this same population that had to be convinced to turn against them. He suggested, in an ISAF memo leaked to the *Washington Post*, that foreign military in Afghanistan needed to become 'credible to . . . Afghans' (Nicoll 2011: 44; Khalili 2011). This meant greater contact with the population, the establishment of closer relationships with communities, the reduction of distancing security measures, and the undertaking of the non-military style humanitarian projects that the Bush administration had been so against in 2001.

Thus, in this second phase of the international project, billions were spent on so-called reconstruction projects, the security sector was fostered further and mechanisms were put in place to engage with Afghan communities in order to gain support and enhance military effectiveness (Gilmore 2011; Hakimi 2013; McBride and Wibben 2012). One notable aspect of this strategy was the development of Provincial Reconstruction Teams (PRTs) designed as a kind of hybrid between militaries, development workers and peacebuilders. In nationally structured units, these PRTs as part of wider efforts that also included all female units – the Female Engagement Teams – set about conducting development projects and promoting the authority of central government, within a broader security and COIN-oriented agenda (Allin 2011; Azarbaijani-Moghaddam 2014; Dyvik 2013; Farrell and Gordon 2009).

Thus war-fighting took place alongside peacebuilding or peace promotion work to varying degrees, and international actors flooded into the country to participate in this work after the apparent defeat of the Taliban in 2001. Goodhand and Sedra suggest that '[t]he US was in the beginning a reluctant statebuilder, but this position changed over time as statebuilding came to be seen as the vehicle for stabilization, re-election for President Bush in 2004, and the achievement of an exit strategy' (2013: 241). Zubeda Jalalzai and David Jeffress argue that the perception of the intervention in Afghanistan as successful, and as ushering in a 'smooth transition to democracy', helped to provide legitimation for the subsequent war in Iraq (2011: 10). Arguably, one component of President Obama's 2008 election campaign centred on framing Afghanistan as the 'good' war against Iraq as the 'bad' (Williams 2011) and thus there was a varied but consistent set of domestic political pressures behind American decision-making processes in relation to the intervention and peacebuilding project. Similarly, domestic political challenges and shifting justificatory framing shaped the nature of the involvement of NATO countries in the Afghan peacebuilding project, for instance in Germany, where public opinion trended away from war-fighting practice and rhetoric and politicians need to demonstrate an acknowledgement of this in their foreign policy choices (Bucher et al. 2013: 528). In another example, in Denmark, private security actors were a politically sensitive issue, and thus were left out of policy documents on civil–military cooperation in Afghanistan (Stepputat 2012). In another context again, Suhrke (2011: 33) argues that British engagement was shaped by Tony Blair's firm belief in 'military intervention as a tool of liberal internationalism' demonstrating the different intersections between national political frameworks and military choices.

On the civilian side, the idea of 'civil society' that emerges in the context of liberal peace interventions such as in Afghanistan is often driven by external mandates, goals and funding and has a large international sector. As Richmond suggests, in liberal peace interventions, 'international aspirations often create a "civil society" that effectively floats far above the ordinary individual and the "local" where everyday life occurs' (2009b: 325). Afghan civil society actors in the post-2001 context are often (though not always) bound or impacted by dominant international ideas around statebuilding, since international donor institutions hold the key to accessing funding streams and have the capacity to influence areas of priority focus. For the time period in Afghanistan that is my focus in this book, those dominant ideas largely mapped onto the liberal peace framework.

The liberal peace paradigm is a particularly fluid and all-encompassing approach to governance and the pursuit of peace which centres on and promotes neoliberal economics, Western style institutions, democratic elections and international intervention, military and otherwise (Duffield 2001; Goodhand and Sedra 2013; Richmond 2009b; Suhrke 2011). A paradigm that emerged after the Cold War (Paris 2010: 337), Goodhand and Sedra define liberal peacebuilding as 'the simultaneous pursuit of conflict resolution, market sovereignty, and liberal democracy' (2013: 239). It is undertaken by military and civilian actors, both state and non-state, and is collapsed into, and symbiotic with, the practice of statebuilding (Duncanson 2016; Goodhand and Sedra 2013: 240). There is a specific set of institutions and bodies that are understood to make up the core liberal peacebuilding actors, primarily the United Nations (UN), the North Atlantic Treaty Organisation (NATO) in some cases, and a dynamic set of national state bodies and NGOs (Duffield 2001; Higate and Henry 2009: 9- 11). Roland Paris refers to this 'apparatus' as a 'sprawling network of governmental and nongovernmental agencies' (Paris 2013: 538), and Goodhand and Sedra suggest that many within this apparatus are linked by 'complex sub-contracting arrangements' (2013: 240).

The liberal peace provides a particular narrative frame of legitimation which centres on notions of democracy, free markets, modernity, individualism and progress, and understands peace to be a product of and a requisite for these ideologies (Richmond 2009b). According to Paris, this discourse and the actions it justifies lead to a particular type of globalisation – 'a globalization of the very idea of what a state should look like and how it should act' (Paris 2001: 101). The liberal peace can be understood as a mechanism to introduce fundamental social engineering, rights provision and reorganisation in order to recover from and prevent the resurgence of conflict. It can also be understood as a product and a tool of a deeply unequal world, 'divided between liberal interveners (with liberal agendas) and non-liberal and a-liberal recipients (who do not share or resist these forms of alien imposition)' (Campbell et al. 2011: 2). In this latter vision the liberal peace project mirrors the colonial one in some ways and equates the pursuit of Western-style modernity with progress, perpetuating certain power relations, and structural inequalities in the international system in service of a disingenuous liberal universality.

The liberal peace paradigm contains certain understandings about what constitutes security (Hehir 2007) and whose security matters most, particularly in the post-9/11 environment, where the dangers of 'failed' statehood include the fostering of terrorist networks (Hudson 2012). Within this mode of thinking development is instrumentalised (see Haastrup 2017; Hudson 2012) since the factors that contribute to poverty and underdevelopment are understood to generate insecurity. The liberal peace project therefore conflates the desire to enhance economic output in a given conflict-affected state with the desire to ensure global 'security', within its own understanding of that term (Duncanson 2016). Thus 'human security' becomes a tool for the achievement of a more traditional conception of militarised security (Henry et al. 2009: 15). Suthaharan Nadarajah makes this argument in relation to humanitarian aid policies:

> driven by the now common, if contested, wisdom that underdevelopment and poverty lead to violence donors have sought to actively use aid to intervene in 'internal' conflicts in order to end on-going violence, ameliorate its perceived causes and, thereby, to 'build peace'. (Nadarajah 2013: 59)

The liberal peace and related interventionary paradigms have many supporters in scholarship and policy domains. Though they often manifest in problematic ways, the idea that conflict should be addressed at the 'roots', that human rights should be respected and that populations should be able to vote for their government do not seem inherently insidious (Paris 2010). Moreover, in contexts such as Sri Lanka, for instance, which have experienced an oppressive 'victor's peace' (Goodhand 2010; Friedman 2016; Piccolino 2019), I have witnessed first hand the sentiment amongst some members of the war-affected population who advocate strongly for more international involvement and greater international institutional oversight. Equally, however, the idea that foreign governments and international institutions should try to reshape a state in the aftermath of conflict has been criticised from multiple perspectives. This is based on the ideals themselves, looking at questions of knowledge production as power within those ideals from first principles (Howell and Richter-Montpetit 2019; Jabri 2013), on the racialised application of peace practices in service of elite, corporate or Western interests and/or on how liberal peace principles manifest in praxis (reliance on private companies, neoliberal economic reforms which further marginalise the vulnerable and so on) and the manner in which template-based, technical, foreign and institutional knowledge and epistemologies in peacebuilding become valued over those kinds of understandings which are contextual, indigenous and complex (Autesserre 2014: l. 4225, l. 4676).

Potentially, this high level of critique has contributed to a 'post-liberal' phase, where interventions are purely military and statebuilding is not attempted (intervention in Libya in 2011 is the prime example of this). More likely, international institutions will increasingly incorporate hybridity – the mixing together of the 'international' and the so-called 'local' to form something distinct (and different from the sum of its parts) – into their mandates to ostensibly offset power hierarchies between external and indigenous approaches (Mac Ginty 2010a). However, what is important for this book is that liberal peace principles were enormously influential in the Afghan statebuilding project and shaped the international engagement with the country (Dodge 2013).

The doctrine of counterinsurgency along with the principles of an 'integrated' and 'comprehensive' approach within the overarching remit of the liberal peace framework marked the blurring of boundaries between civilian and military work (Azarbaijani-Moghaddam et al. 2008; Suhrke 2011). Boundary-blurring activities included the use of social scientists to produce 'cultural' knowledge (called the Human Terrain System), the building of local government capacities, community and development projects, the promotion of education and healthcare, and activities designed to bolster the legitimacy of central government in the provinces (Goodhand 2013; Zehfuss 2012). As I progress through this book, I do not suggest that anything about this approach in Afghanistan was radically new. I do, however, suggest that it is important to recognise the multitude of ways – especially, in this book, the less traditionally recognised ways – in which the liberal peace promotion agenda and the statebuilding and stabilisation paradigm have evolved in practice in Afghanistan to mean that military and civilian activities are dual components of an entangled agenda, and are interwoven and complementary as well as complex and contradictory.

History of Interference

Shaped as a state in the Westphalian sense by British imperial exploits, Afghanistan is home to multiple ethnicities and peoples and has been burdened with an extensive history of conflict. Much, if not all, of that conflict has been inseparable from wider geopolitical and regional shifts and has been tied to external interference. The country has a long history of (semi-)colonial and regional interference. In the nineteenth and twentieth centuries, Britain's attempts to gain control over the territory of Afghanistan as part of the 'Great Game' power struggle with Russia resulted in three Anglo-Afghan Wars, 1839–42, 1878–80 and 1919, with the Afghans winning 'independence' from a 'war-weary Britain' in 1919 (Harsch 2015: 105). Nivi Manchanda (2019: 312) notes that at this point 'rather than some sort of concession to the "unruly" Afghans, it suited the British to keep Afghanistan semi-colonized, which often boiled down to control without investment'.

Indeed, upon invading the country in an attempt to secure their interests in 1839, the British 'pursued an agenda of imperial paternalism which was to become paradigmatic' (Cronin 2011: 52). Not 'attempting the full-scale military-political administration' of the country at any point, Afghanistan was nonetheless seen as a political tool caught between the Russian and the British empirical territories (Bird and Marshall 2011: 11). This is not to imply a lack of agency and complexity within Afghanistan's socio-political arena. Political and military interests within the country were key to how events unfolded in the nineteenth and early twentieth centuries (as they are now). Some key political and military leaders supported the idea of British involvement and even the Amir Dost Muhammad Khan who had fought against the British in the First Anglo-Afghan War accepted British recognition and good relations by the mid-nineteenth century in order to help stabilise his rule (Lee 2018: 316–17). However, the presence and actions of the British also caused social and political problems and generated great resentment. For example, in the late 1830s the addition of 30,000 foreigners (military and civilian), based in Kabul, hugely inflated food prices, especially that of bread, Afghanistan's staple food (Lee 2018: 260–80). This and other socio-economic factors contributed to the 1841 'uprising' in Kabul:

> The uprising in the capital, which began in early November 1841, was the culmination of months of resentment at the presence of alien, non-Muslim forces on Afghan soil, British interference in the king's internal affairs and . . .

fiscal and military reforms, which had undermined the power and wealth of both the king and his courtiers. For this reason the hatred and resentment was particularly directed at the British political establishment. (Lee 2018: 272)

The defeat of the British in this First Anglo-Afghan War contributed to Western framing of Afghanistan as an uncivilised and barbaric place as part of efforts to assuage Britain's sense of national humiliation. Individuals instrumental in the catastrophic events 'were recast as martyrs to the Imperial cause, men who gave their lives trying, in vain, to extend the benefits of civilization to an ungrateful, "savage" and "treacherous" people' (Lee 2018: 304). Though sometimes attributed primarily to the influence of conservative Islamic politics and ever closer ties with Russia, it is important to note that this reframing, the election of the Conservatives in Britain and the subsequent political prominence of an interventionist and pre-emptive approach called the 'Forward Policy', contributed greatly to the outbreak of the Second Anglo-Afghan War (see Lee 2018: 362). Largely, the Second and Third Anglo-Afghan Wars were successful enough for the British (though in the case of the third war, this is more ambiguous) and other reasons were involved in imperial disengagement. Overall, as Manchanda (2019: 312) points out,

> the reason Afghanistan never was fully colonized – as the pattern of British incursion and retreat demonstrates – owed as much to British indecisiveness and lack of interest in the country as it did to any ineradicable difficulties in conquering the country or to the Afghans being a particularly formidable enemy.

Within more recent history, Afghanistan has been seriously impacted by external interference, tumultuous internal politics, elite actions and decades of conflict since the so-called Saur (April) Revolution in 1978 (Siddiqui 2014: 629), when the pro-Soviet communist political party, the People's Democratic Party of Afghanistan (PDPA), staged a coup, attempting dramatic political transformation and provoking an insurgency (see Wahab and Youngerman 2007: 129–70; Cronin 2011: 47). In the face of a pending PDPA defeat, the Soviets invaded in 1979 in support of the communist factions and within the broader political powerplays of the Cold War (Siddiqui 2014). The US and Pakistan supported the anti-Soviet Mujahideen in their continued military efforts, supplying them with weapons and financial resources, something that would have far-reaching implications for stability in the region (Wahab and Youngerman 2007: 157; Cronin 2011: 47). It was in part external

backing that created a coherent Mujahideen from the seven fairly disparate Northern Alliance factions (Nicoll 2011). Sponsored by Pakistan
and the US, the Northern Alliance, a group of militia originating in
the northern regions of the country (Nicoll 2011: 34; Mahmud 2010),
would come to be another major Afghan player in the conflict dynamics
that characterised Afghanistan post-1978 and a focal point of opposition to the Taliban (Goodhand 2002: 838; Joya 2009).

Like the wars with Britain decades before, this war had a devastating
impact on the infrastructure, agriculture and population of the country,
with the rural communities often bearing the brunt of the suffering and
damage caused by military retaliations (Siddiqui 2014: 626). Facing military stalemate in Afghanistan and increasing domestic and international
pressures, the Soviets withdrew in 1989, leaving what Barfield terms a
'client regime' under Najibullah in place (Barfield 2010: 5). Najibullah's
government survived and demonstrated unexpected levels of resilience
while it was able to rely on financial support from the Soviets (Smith
2014: 308). When the USSR collapsed and the money flow was cut off,
in combination with ongoing internal pressures, Najibullah's government also collapsed and a period of civil war followed (Barfield 2010:
6; Suhrke 2011: 21). Malalia Joya (a renowned Afghan politician and
activist) describes the de facto rule of the Mujahideen between 1992 and
1996 as harsh and violent: 'At first the people celebrated their victory,
but soon their hopes turned to ashes when these extremists proved that
they could be even worse than the Soviets' (2009: 25). For Joya, the
Taliban were not a radical departure from what came before, but rather
operated on a continuum of harshness towards the population.

Coming to power amid civil war and internal uncertainty, the Taliban
took over in 1996 and governed as a repressive, totalitarian regime.
Though bin Laden, the Taliban and Afghanistan were a US and UN security concern (see Kakar 2011: 2; Suhrke 2011: 22) the internal dynamics
of the country were not firmly in the international spotlight until 2001
when the 9/11 attacks provoked an American-led intervention. Marking
the start of the so-called 'global war on terror', the intervention, as
outlined above, also heralded the attempted promotion and implementation of liberal peacebuilding structures by foreign military and
civilian actors (Dodge 2013) and a special focus on 'saving' Afghan
women from oppression (Abu-Lughod 2002; Ferguson 2005; Khalid
2011) which I will discuss in Chapter 4.

Intervention in Afghan affairs has historically been a regional preoc-
cupation as well as a global one. When the West was not as central an
element in Afghanistan's geopolitics as it is today, such as between 1989

and 2001, regional dynamics remained crucially important. Of particular significance then, as now, was the role played by Pakistan (see Abbas 2014; Alimia 2019; Mahmud 2010; Saikal 2010; Yousaf 2019), which maintained its support of the Mujahideen and then backed the Taliban. Pakistan sought a pro-Islamabad government in Kabul, primarily as a barrier to Indian influence in Central Asia (Roy 2015: xviii–xix). India has also historically sought to build relations with Kabul (Roy-Chaudhury 2011). Pakistan, seeking to curtail India's influence and attain 'strategic depth' in the region, has frequently played an instrumental part in Afghan affairs (Roy-Chaudhury 2011). The relationship between Afghanistan and Pakistan has been one defined by bet-hedging, patronage, border politics and resistance (Bird and Marshall 2011: 185–215; Mahmud 2010). Roy-Chaudhury argues that: '[a]lthough the violence and instability in Afghanistan adversely impacts Pakistan's domestic politics and security, Pakistan's interventionist policies towards Afghanistan for the past 32 years have decisively influenced the volatile security environment in Afghanistan' (2011: 167). Similarly, Bird and Marshall (2011: 2) point out that these two countries are 'inextricably linked'. Moreover, while the details are too extensive to do justice to here, other states such as China (Le Miere et al. 2011), Iran (Hokayem 2011a), Saudi Arabia (Hokayem 2011b) and Russia (Antonenko 2011) have at various times engaged with patronage networks, supported favourites, been supported by political forces within Afghanistan and had key roles in Afghan political and security trajectories.

Legacies of War

The legacies of historical and ongoing violence in Afghanistan have been many and varied, some more direct than others. The cost of war has been high throughout Afghan history. For example, according to Michael Harsch, 'from 1978 to 2012 approximately 335,000 combatants were killed in armed clashes that, when considered collectively, become the second-most deadly conflict since World War II' (Harsch 2015: 103). According to Siddiqui, from 1979 'Soviet bombing destroyed entire villages, crops and irrigation, leaving millions of people dead, homeless and starving' (Siddiqui 2014: 626).

Key actors, groups and persons in Afghanistan have histories inseparable from the histories of conflict. The Soviet War saw the displacement of millions of Afghans who sought refuge from the violence in neighbouring Iran and Pakistan. Thus, thousands of male Afghan children received their education within the refugee camps, in religious schools called *madrasas*, which often excluded females, and 'where teaching was based on a strict interpretation of the Koran' (Nicoll 2011: 35). There were exceptions, such as a school sponsored by the Revolutionary Women's Association of Afghanistan which also taught girls, as well as secret schools within Afghanistan (Joya 2009: 19). Yet the *madrasas* were in the majority and it was from these schools that the Taliban recruited many of their members in the 1980s and 90s. It was within this conflict-created demographic, with a majority Pashtun ethnicity with links to Pakistan, conservative religiosity and in intervention-based exile, that the Taliban sought to attain social capital and support (Abbas 2014; Rubin 2013: 54). Moreover, it was precisely because of the chaos wrought by the war with the Soviets and the subsequent power vacuum that followed the dissolution of the government that the Taliban gained such traction, coming to represent a modicum of order and stability (Kakar 2011; Nicoll 2011: 34) as well as being backed by Pakistan as an alternative to the Mujahideen (Lee 2018: 631; Joya 2009).

In contemporary times Afghanistan has produced up to 90 per cent of the world's opium supplies, meaning that drug traders and criminal organisations mesh with local dynamics and leadership structures (Bird and Marshall 2011: 7). Poppy cultivation has spiralled in the context of war and military governance since the American-led intervention in 2001. Dodge (2013: 1205) has argued that neoliberal economic policies pushed by the World Bank and IMF post-2001 as part of the liberal peace framework may have made opium production more likely, since crops such as cotton were discouraged due to lack of market potential. In many cases farmers grow poppies out of necessity and are not accessing any of the real wealth of the drug trade themselves. Poppy cultivation has become intertwined with the war economy, in which both internal and external parties were complicit, and was increasingly a focus of the international military agenda:

> Coalition forces initially turned a blind eye to poppy cultivation and trafficking, fearing that counter-narcotics efforts would upset the fragile political coalition that had been forged to pursue the 'war on terror'; but between the Bonn Agreement of 2002 and the Afghan Compact of 2006, counter-narcotics rapidly rose up the policy agenda, based on the growing perception that the opium economy was a significant driver (as well as a symptom) of insecurity and bad governance. (Goodhand 2008: 405)

In the latter years of the recent (and arguably ongoing) war Astri Suhrke characterised Afghanistan as a 'rentier state' reliant on sources of external funding (2013). The picture that Suhrke paints is of an economy dependent on external aid and the drugs trade and a generation of elite politicians unaccountable to their population. Jude Howell and Jeremy Lind find that in the Afghan context 'the securitization of aid has not only nurtured a "rentier" civil society, comprised of an assortment of donor-funded NGOs, but also promoted a particular model of state-civil relations that prioritizes service delivery over the deliberative role of civil society' (2009: 719). Both of these arguments suggest that the structural and economic issues Afghanistan faces are bound up with the legacies of war and international involvement.

The American-led war in Afghanistan was never 'won', and military optimism in the initial months proved unfounded. By 2010, the situation in Afghanistan was becoming increasingly difficult for the population, the Afghan state, and Afghan military and civilian internationals: '[c]onflict-related civilian casualties increased by 15% in 2010, as did the number of bomb explosions and suicide attacks carried out by Taliban insurgents' (Abbas 2014: 1). A decade after the declaration of victory over the Taliban in 2001, it had become crystal clear that they were not defeated and remained a regenerating, significant and violent force in Afghan affairs (see Kakar 2011). In 2013 alone, for example, they claimed the lives of almost 3,000 Afghan and international security personnel, and were clearly resurgent in Pakistan as well as Afghanistan, mounting attacks in both countries (Abbas 2014: 1). From 2010, this situation was increasingly acknowledged by the international community, and there was a shift towards ending engagement and transferring total responsibility to Afghans. Meeting in Lisbon, various international actors decided that it was time to start a process of disconnection, and they set a timescale for troop withdrawal to be completed by the end of 2014 (Nicoll 2011: 21).

Afghanistan saw its first democratic transition of power in 2014 Afghanistan (Nasimi 2016). The elections were controversial, tainted as on previous occasions (the presidential elections in 2009 were marred by allegations of ballot stuffing and other practices) by accusations of large-scale fraud (Coburn 2015). Karzai was constitutionally prohibited from running; the two front-runners were Abdullah Abdullah, who had been the primary challenger to Karzai in 2009 (Dodge 2011: 82), and Ashraf Ghani, who was inaugurated as President on 29 September 2014 (Coburn 2015). After the first round of elections in April, the results were indecisive, and accusations of fraud and bad practice abounded (Coburn 2015). There thus followed a second round after which, with the help of intensive political negotiations, Ghani was declared victorious and Abdullah was given the newly created position of Chief Executive Officer (Waldman 2015: 7), ending the stalemate with an improvised power-sharing agreement (Coburn 2015: 2).

Despite the legacies of war, Afghanistan has an incredibly strong tradition of activism and resistance of different kinds. Huber (2014) noted the peaceful protests over the 2014 election results that went almost unnoticed but are, she suggested, hugely important in high-lighting civil participation and peaceful resistance. Afghan women have always continued to organise, especially around the provision of girls' education, regardless of the dangers and extensive restrictions in place under the Taliban (see Abirafeh 2009; Rostami-Povey 2007; Joya 2009). Malalia Joya writes of a society bound by solidarity, and a collective painful history where women often receive male allyship and a huge majority of the population support each other in any way they can (see also Rostami-Povey 2007).

Myths, Tropes and Identities

Though they can signal factors to consider, there is a tendency for evaluations of the context of Afghanistan to overly foreground the demographic and cultural (Abu-Lughod 2002) – the rural/urban and religious/secular divides and 'tribal' praxis, for instance – at the expense of a more complex understanding (Barfield 2010: 13; Nasimi 2016; Manchanda 2018). The reality has always been nuanced and, as Barfield suggests, between the different groups and actors, 'positions differed depending on the issue involved' (Barfield 2010: 13). Moreover, the ideas of 'tribes' and 'tribalism' in Afghanistan, as outlined particularly by Manchanda (2018: 168), are associated with imperial perceptions of perceived 'primitive' communities and are often a mechanism through which political sense is made of nation-building aspirations: 'often in support of "nation-building" projects, tribes have been understood as the "other" against which the nation-state – still the prime unit of analysis for political scientists and international relations scholars – is posited'.

Thus, the idea of the 'tribe' should usually be viewed with caution when it appears in Western discourses on Afghanistan. Moreover, it is important not to consider ethnic, religious or cultural dynamics as somehow innate to Afghanistan or discrete from its politics, geopolitics and history. Yet, forces such as ethnicity are, as articulated by Rabia Nasimi, 'powerful enough to mobilise people' (Nasimi 2016) and thus a feature to highlight briefly. According to Alexander Nicoll, 'Pashtuns are estimated to make up some 42% of Afghanistan's present population, Tajiks 27%, Hazaras 9% and Uzbeks and Turkmens a total of 13%, with smaller groups making up the remainder' (Nicoll 2011: 29). Yet, Nasimi (2016) suggests that 'the exact proportions of each ethnicity continue to be questioned, as it is politically sensitive and considered relevant to political discussions in Afghanistan'. Ethnicity and religion cross-cut Afghan history and political structures in various ways and with varying degrees of fidelity to their ideological origins. Narratives that reify religious or ethnic dynamics often do so in service of parsimony or to adhere to implicit ideas of Western rationality and enlightenment progress. Malalia Joya emphasises that when she was growing up, ethnicity was not an acrimonious part of Afghan identity (2009: 9). When asked to describe her ethnic background by reporters, she tells them 'I am Afghan . . . ethnic groups are all the same for me' (2009: 8).

Echoing this, Barnett Rubin also argues that Afghan national identity is 'multi-ethnic' as well as Islamic. Bird and Marshall suggest that cohesion is facilitated by defining Afghan identity against that which is foreign, or non-Afghan, reflecting the country's history of invasion (Bird and Marshall 2011: 6). Historian Mohammad Hassan Kahar makes a similar point about the idea of Afghan-ness as an identity (2003: 1). Rodney Stewart suggests that it is the Islamic anchor which holds the identity structures of the nation together, providing a 'unity' around which collective ideologies can be built (Steward 2011: l. 1061). These perspectives form part, but not all, of the picture and illustrate the complex and shifting realities at play.

It is true that ethnic and religious components are to some degree inseparable from Afghanistan's history of conflict, insofar as they have so frequently been wound into narratives, perceptions, justifications and rationales of and for violence in the country (Barfield 2010; Bird and Marshall 2011; Joya 2009; Nasimi 2016; Rubin 2013). As much as religiosity is mythologised, politicised and tied to notions of tradition, especially when it comes to reductionist views of the Islamic faith in the West (Razack 2008; Said 1979; Wekker 2016), equally the vilification of issues such as women's rights as foreign and un-Islamic can be just as politically motivated and does a disservice to the religion and the dynamism of a society like Afghanistan's (Ahmed 1992; Ahmed-Ghosh 2003; Billaud 2015; Joya 2009). Contrary to this it was highlighted to me by Afghan women's rights activists that Islam and its organisational mechanisms in Afghanistan offered opportunities for supporting women and ensuring their rights and freedoms (see also Billaud 2015;

Joya 2009). Unfortunately, both fundamentalist conservative forces and Western 'liberals' have associated religiosity in Afghanistan with an automatically restrictive environment, playing into wider racist tropes and myths (see Pratt and Richter-Devroe 2011; Wekker 2016).

Additionally, over time, ethnicity, religiosity and violence have been collapsed into one another in various ways in the Afghan context. For example Islam in Afghanistan has been filtered through ethnic identity and pre-Islamic Central Asian culture, creating more localised systems of belief (Barfield 2010: 6). Hazaras (often Shia Muslims) have historically been persecuted by the Taliban, who follow Sunni Islamic teachings and adopted the promotion of Sharia law, a strict interpretation of Islamic code, and Hazaras were again targeted in recent ISIS attacks (Rasmussen 2016b). At the same time, while 80 per cent of the Taliban are ethnically Pashtun, the majority of Pashtuns in Afghanistan are not Taliban supporters (Roy 2015: xvi–xvii). Part of the link between ethnicity, kinship structures and religion has also been generated by the specific formation of Islamic groups over time. Islam is the central pillar of political and social cohesion in Afghanistan but in fact even the so-called 'Islamic parties', such as Jamiat-e Islami and the Hezb-e Islami, actually have organisational structures 'largely influenced by ethnic affiliations' (Cronin 2011).

The notion of religious identities, as contrasted to secularism, has been a rallying point for political divisions and grievances in Afghanistan at various stages, and certainly there have been drives towards secularisation that have had powerful implications for the country in the past (Cronin 2011: 68; Manchanda 2019). This is particularly true in relation to the communist tendencies that developed in Afghanistan in the 1970s. Many army officers and urban intelligentsia were attracted to the secular ideologies of the Soviets. In the case of the army officers, this had been fostered by the increasing involvement of the USSR in the training, education and development of the Afghan army in the post-Second World War period. Manchanda (2019: 312) articulates how one faction of the PDPA gained dominance and 'instituted radical land reform, made drastic changes in family law and transformed the education system. Their allegiance to Marxist political ideology also saw them launch a wholesale attack on Islam, one that alienated large portions of the Afghan population.'

Thus, while, as evidenced, ethnicity and religion have been important aspects of Afghan history and culture, their role cannot be extrapolated from discursive constructions of power and enmity, wider questions of ideology and the way they have played out on a worldwide scale (Abbas

2014: 2). In particular, the relationship between Islam and extremism in the country has been shaped within a broader global narrative (Razack 2008; Wekker 2016). As Abbas suggests, when analysing the Taliban 'the fashionable diagnosis in some Western circles was that the problem was Islam itself, the professed religion of these extremists and terrorists' (Abbas 2014: 2). Any discussion of Afghanistan's religious dynamics should thus be coloured by its position on the global stage and within discursive geopolitical shifts in recent times.

Women's Rights and Freedoms

I have often heard that Afghan women are not political. That peace and security is man's work. I am here to challenge that illusion.

– Jamila Afghani, Afghan women's rights activist (cited in Taplin 2014)

As feminist scholars have highlighted, it is important not to feed into predefined narratives about Afghan women who lack agency and are perennial victims of men and circumstance. As such, it is vital to pay attention to the diversity of experiences and power differentials between, say, younger and older women within the family; women who have high levels of education and professional status and women who do not; married women whose marital relationship is harmonious and loving and married women who experience domestic violence; and of course endless variations and multiplicities (see Billaud 2015). Indeed, Maliha Zulfacar (2006: 27) suggests that 'the term "Afghan women" covers a multitude of traditions, ethnicities . . . allegiances, regions, etc. The term as a socio-economic entity is so broad as to be almost meaningless.' As Chandra Mohanty (1984: 344) pointed out, 'women are constituted as women through the complex interaction between class, culture, religion and other ideological institutions and frameworks' and cannot be treated as a single category of analysis in any nation. While much of this complexity falls outside the scope of this book to explore, the chapters that follow do call upon different vocational experiences and expert ideas shaped by those experiences that are expressed by different Afghan women within different contexts.

However, while rejecting false universality, it is also important to recognise the patriarchal restrictions that many women in Afghanistan have faced and to recognise that patriarchy as a social and cultural framework has been influential in the country. Moghadam has argued that Afghanistan constitutes part of a so called 'belt of classic patriarchy' which is 'characterized by male domination, son preference, restrictive codes of behaviour for women, and the association of family honour with female virtue' (Moghadam 2004: 143). She suggests that community structures have developed along patriarchal lines as a perceived survival tactic linked to cohesion (through arranged marriages for instance) and 'notions of common patrilineal descent' (Moghadam 2004: 143). In reality practices associated with patriarchal norms such as gender-based violence or low levels of female literacy (see Alvi 2012), among others, are intersectional, and experiences of these vary enormously in Afghanistan, and in ways beyond which the scope of this book can address. Women can navigate patriarchal constraint in different ways depending on life circumstances. Yet patriarchal frameworks can mean behavioural restrictions that intersect with other aspects of life such as poverty and conflict within an unjust gender order, and that women are shielded from the outside world in a way that might negatively impact their rights and freedoms – an approach designed to uphold family honour – rather than necessarily for the sake of women themselves.

Concepts of masculinity play a role in gendered orders within the Afghan context: '[m]any men participate in the maintenance of unjust gender relations and sexist practices, becoming gatekeepers of the gender order and using social constructions of masculinity and male identity to justify it' (Azarbaijani-Moghaddam 2012). Yet it is important to note that fixed ideas about men and masculinity in Afghanistan, especially those that circulate through Western media and policy thinking, can preclude a recognition of the fact that Afghan men act, and have always acted, in solidarity and collaboration with women and that 'many Afghan men oppose traditional ideologies of male superiority and dominance' (Rostami-Povey 2007: 7).

My respondents who worked on gender issues did regularly critique an ideology of patriarchy that impacted many in Afghanistan and intersected with the circumstances of women's lives especially. For instance, different Afghan civil society actors suggested to me that the idea of 'protection' was a way of removing women from the public sphere and attempting to deny them agency and involvement in decision-making processes. This conceptualisation of protection was outlined by one respondent as follows:

> That protection is really a sort of indicator of the patriarchy that is going on in this society, and we girls, women, daughters, wives, we are considered as the saviour of family's name . . .

We women are kind of considered as the saviours, or the safeguard, of family's honour. No matter what men in the family does, that doesn't matter, but a women, for example, if she works, if she studies, something wrong happens to her or she for example makes a mistake then it is all, like the family loses honour and the family's man is mandated to actually do something to protect that honour . . .

So that's why when they say that we are protecting our girls, we're protecting our honour. And that protection is actually encircling her so that she is not able to move anywhere, she's not able to speak out . . .

And that's what they the think protection is all about in this society, because it's really I think it's caging rather than protection, so that she is caged, she is shamed, she is not able to make a decision, whoever she wants to marry she has no right to even say. It is us the family who will decide whom she will marry, what she will do, where she will live . . .

So this whole notion of protection is actually caging her, chaining her because there is this understanding if a woman is free she will be immoral, she might become a prostitute, she might do something very bad, and then we as family bear the responsibility so we should actually be, we will be ashamed in this society. (Asal, Afghan activist)

Consistently, women and male allies push back against any restrictive environment (such as that cited by Jamila Afghani at the top of this section and by many of my respondents), but priorities of course differ for different people as with any society. While being able to participate in education, politics and public society is crucially important for some Afghan women, others struggle more directly with issues related to everyday life and survival (see Abirafeh 2009; Billaud 2015; Burki 2011; Rostami-Povey 2007; Zulfacar 2006). The Afghan women I interviewed for this book were almost all privileged (to differing extents) by education, status, resources and, in some cases, family support, and their concerns ran a full spectrum from what might be called the everyday to the geopolitical (though these two dimensions often intersect). In research for an Afghan NGO, EQUALITY for Peace and Democracy (EPD), Marie Huber and I (2014) noted that women community leaders and organisers in the provincial regions around the country were equally concerned with infrastructural issues, such as roads and economic opportunities (the availability of skills training and employment, for example) as they were about classic first-generation rights issues and political enfranchisement and that they mobilised human rights discourses across a spectrum of concerns.[1] Additionally, in the same report, we note that the key question of negotiating with and reintegrating the Taliban provoked significant variation in perspective. Even within my still limited research experience, there was of course an enormous and complex variety of gendered lifeworlds and political perspectives in evidence.

The symbolic and justificatory power of Afghan women's rights for Western governments became a global concern after 2001 (Ferguson 2005). The Taliban coming to power in 1996 was not overly noted within the international community, although in time some attention was paid to the suppression and treatment of the population (Roy 2015: xix). Joya argues that the brutal treatment of women (and the population generally) by the Mujahideen prior to the Taliban takeover went largely unnoticed (2009: 27). However, when the power of the initial terrorism-based rationale for intervention stated to fade away post- 2001, and as a softer supplement to it from the outset (Abu-Lughod 2002; Abirafeh 2009; McBride and Wibben 2012; Wright 2019), 'Western governments "sold" their involvement in Afghanistan as a way of "freeing" Afghan women from their exclusion from the public space – exclusion embodied by the *burqa*' (Roy 2015: xx). This liberal feminist concern for Afghan women was typified by Laura Bush's radio address to the nation in 2001 and signalled a utilitarian co-option of Afghan women in service of both a conventional security (Ferguson 2005) and a broader neoliberal peacebuilding agenda (Billaud 2012; Fluri 2009a, 2009b). An example of the duality at work around Afghan women is evident in the fact that, while Laura Bush spoke of their plight, the US chose a strategic partner in the form of the Northern Alliance, with no heed whatsoever paid to its 'record of disregarding women's rights' (Charlesworth and Chinkin 2014: 602; see also Joya 2009). The association between the West and the championing of women's rights had complex implications. An orientalising focus on Afghan women as vectors of modernisation has a circular history, as I discuss below (see Zulfacar 2006), and links to wider traditions of a certain type of white or liberal feminism (see Henry 2018; Howell and Richter-Montpetit 2019; Thobani 2007) which I discuss further in Chapter 4.

Modernisation vs Tradition

The very concept of modernisation is loaded; it comes with racialised associations and a temporal privileging of the mechanisms of industrialised societies. Depictions and understandings of Afghanistan in the West can create a false dichotomy between the forces of modernity and those of tradition (see Billaud 2015; Manchanda 2017). In fact, these two frames of reference and associated ideologies have been crafted in dialogical interaction with each other. In practical terms the tug of war between these forces has had serious implications for the population, especially for women in Afghanistan whose bodies have been co-opted repeatedly as symbolic vectors of traditional or modern praxis (Burki 2011; Joya 2009; Khalid 2011). With each cycle of 'modernisation' there has come violence, and with each resultant backlash, there has come further violence. As such, like the 'local' and the 'international', these categories (traditional and modern) might be understood as social constructs, with little innate meaning outside their contextual relationality and certainly no intractable connections to certain groups of people, who are always already one or the other.

In the early twentieth century King Amanullah, with the help of his wife, Queen Soraya, implemented a programme of reform. They looked to the West as a barometer of statecraft and nationhood and identified veiling practices in particular as being a symbol of anachronism. On one occasion Amanullah's government staged a scene of unveiling, whereby a group of women (the wives of government ministers) removed their veils in front of a council of elders (Burki 2011: 49). A diplomatic tour of Europe complete with images of the controversial and outspoken Queen Soraya, variously unveiled, in Western-influenced clothing or being kissed on the hand by the French head of state, simultaneously destabilised the domestic rule of her husband, provoking violence and turmoil, and earned the regime, and state, a degree of (racialised) legitimacy abroad (see Edwards 2006). Other aspects of reform pushed by this king included a new currency and issuing of banknotes, infrastructure projects such as dams and irrigation schemes, and a legislative council to update the country's legal framework (Lee 2018: 470, 472, 473). Amanullah also increased taxes (Lee 2018: 469). The backlash to these reforms in the form of violent resistance organised against the king ended with his removal from power and flight from Afghanistan, after which his modernisation attempts were effectively reversed, including the backsliding and political manipulation of women's rights and status by more conservative elements in society (Burki 2011: 49–50).

The pro-Soviet PDPA, which came to power through military coup in 1978 (Cronin 2011: 68) and subsequent Soviet intervention force, also implemented a modernisation effort and, again, much of this centred on women, their bodies, freedoms, opportunities and veils (Zulfacar 2006). Under the Soviets, women in urban centres could attain a secular education and seek professional employment, predominantly in the state sector (Rubin 2013: 54–5). This shift in women's rights and status was therefore associated with the Soviet regime so deeply hated in some quarters, and was a phenomenon disconnected from the rural population (Rubin 2013: 55).

More generally there was a large divide between the urban and the rural reception of the PDPA and Soviets, part of which was linked to religion, with the explicit secularism of the PDPA stirring opposition (see Manchanda 2019). It was also linked to questions over who benefited from Soviet links and the violence the Soviets meted out to any opposition (Lee 2018). Massive privileges were afforded to the officer class in the Afghan army by the Soviets prior to 1978, with this group totally disconnected from the realities and needs of the rural population (Cronin 2011: 68). This divide was then fostered by the American and Pakistani sponsorship of the anti-Soviet Mujahideen forces during the war that followed, and equally cemented by the 'modernising' ambitions of the Soviet occupation, which saw Kabul and the urban hubs become more and more differentiated from the rural population. These modernising efforts came to an end when, despite demonstrating some substantial successes and resilience to opposition forces (Ward et al. 2011: 253), Soviet financial assistance to the Najibullah regime was cut off and the centralised government collapsed, pushed out by Mujahideen militias. There is, of course, great historical irony in this Western support for forces that Joya (2009) considers as socially conservative and politically repressive as the Taliban, while they fought against a Soviet invasion promoting secular social fabric and principles of modernisation, given that the West would one day come to promote similar principles and be faced, in turn, by conservative opposition.

In the war in Afghanistan to oust the Taliban government in 2001, women's rights and gender mainstreaming were once again a central concern and reference point of political rhetoric and concepts of modernisation. As referred to above and most famously, Laura Bush announced that 'the fight against terrorism is also a fight for the rights and dignity of women' (Ferguson 2005: 22). This framing of Afghan women as both victims and liberal subjects awaiting liberation set the tone for the peacebuilding project to come. Mainstream rhetoric seemed to understand Afghan women as helpless and lacking agency, hidden beneath burkas and waiting to be granted their rights (Abu-Lughod 2002).

It is a cautious balancing act to consider the issue of women's rights in Afghanistan.[2] On the one hand, as in many contexts, ideas based on the country's highly conservative principles can lead to suffering, and especially the suffering of women. Yet, on the other hand, forced modernisation efforts in the past have only resulted in backlash and the entrenching of conservative visions for society, and there is a distinct

Orientalist undertone in much of the rhetoric about Afghan women's lifeworlds.[3] Afghan activists and NGO workers I engaged with formally and informally often saw their society as an Islamic one and wanted to craft space for themselves within the remit of a clearly socially egalitarian identity, by respecting, rather than rejecting, religion and avoiding any reification of Islam as somehow overly traditional and inflexible (see also Billaud 2015). Moreover, 'modernisation' efforts driven from outside Afghanistan have been undercut by war, by a violent brutality against dissenting forces (such as under the Soviets), by civilian collateral damage and by the championing of political elites with a history of violence, undermining any attached moral claims, especially those relating to gender equity and women's rights.

Overall, the ideas of tradition and modernisation have mapped onto ideas about appropriate Afghan custom and socio-political order jeopardised by foreign-imported principles and forced change. They are, in addition, bound up with an orientalising exceptionalism that represents Afghanistan as somehow entrenched in inflexible tradition, a narrative that negates complex levels of complicity by the very modernisation projects which are often depicted in turn as doomed to fail because of the country's innate and intractable conservativism (Billaud 2015; Manchanda 2019).

The State

Linked to this idea of modernity vs tradition are conceptions of the state and government and what these should look like.[4] It is often suggested that the very idea of the state does not suit Afghanistan for multiple reasons – geographical, historical, cultural (see Kakar 2003). While this may be true in a sense, it is also true that the notion of the 'state' is derived from Western conceptions of political community and this conception has been transposed onto Afghanistan as part of a racialised 'failed state' narrative (see Howell and Richter-Montpetit 2019). As such, Afghanistan has been framed as a 'failed state' arguably from the point it was conceived of as a 'state' at all. The country's modern historical trajectory is framed as chequered by repeated so-called 'failed state-building' attempts (Cronin 2011: 47) and a regularly resurfacing perception of a 'long political-economic record of profound ungovernability' (Bird and Marshall 2011: 11). The idea of 'ungovernability' here has distinctly colonial connotations linked to ideas of barbarism and is implicitly compared to the stability of 'good' states (Howell and Richter-Montpetit 2019; Manchanda 2017).

The idea of the state in the contemporary imaginary requires some degree of centralised power, capable of governance and revenue collection as well as wielding the 'legitimate' (though this is definitely a contested point) use of violence (Arendt 1970; Fanon 1986). There have been some distinct drives towards centralisation of power and governance in Afghanistan, often – though not always – externally linked. One key example is Abd al-Rahman Khan, who came to power in the late nineteenth century, at the end of the Second Anglo-Afghan War. His 'ambition was to remodel Afghanistan along Tsarist lines by concentrating all power in his own hands, which meant destroying and dismantling all competitive power structures' (Lee 2018: 384). This centralisation process was undoubtedly violent and is again wrapped up with British imperial exploits and their consequences as well as the complex legacies of Afghan political claims and power shifts (Lee 2018; Omrani 2014).

Overall the state in Afghanistan has been a difficult notion, bound to racialised logics and particular visions of progress (Billaud 2012; Manchanda 2017) and practically unstable (Nicoll 2011: 29). In fact, it is perhaps best simply to think in terms of a 'frontier' space, a space that has been constituted within (neo)imperial imaginaries. As Manchanda writes (2017: 387), 'the "frontier" has played a formative role in defining Afghanistan as a state and space and this plays out in how we interact – through representation, policies, and intervention – with the state in the global realm today'.

Another recurring theme related to the notion of the state is the idea of disparate aspirations and ideologies between an urban, often foreign-supported, governing elite and a disconnected rural population that falls back on ethnic and kinship linkages in the absence of effective centralised governance structures. There is no natural or simplistic always pre-existing divide between rural and urban in Afghanistan, and these populations cannot be seen as a homogeneous unit, but some dissonance has occurred. The narrative goes that foreign powers intervene, often bolstering the elite grouping of choice (at least initially) but as they and their Afghan partners become mired in the complexities of governing, or as foreign support is withdrawn, rural or provincial militias and the so-called 'strongmen' that head them up are called upon to guarantee power maintenance (Cronin 2011; Omrani 2014). There is some truth to this, though it is important to be cautious about reifying narratives of warlords and tribalism as I have articulated above and to note the complicity of foreign powers in terms of reliance on, funding of and support for non-state militias (Mac Ginty 2010b),[5] as well as recognising the modes of knowledge production which tie sets of racialised expectations to labels like 'warlord'.

In recent times governance issues have hampered the central government in Kabul. Decision-making interests have often sought to bypass local and regional government levels and have reified personalities over processes (see Dodge 2011; Burki 2011). Hamid Karzai, appointed initially to lead an interim government in 2001 and subsequently elected President in 2004 and (controversially) in 2009, exemplified this tendency. He used his position to issue decrees, appointed to government positions those he favoured, his family or those he needed to placate, was ambiguous and utilitarian on women's rights legislation (Heath and Zahedi 2011: 297) and at one point was found to have amassed huge sums of money for use in political pay-offs (Dodge 2011: 86). For these and other reasons, '[d]oubts about his ability to handle this level of authority became widespread after his election in 2004' (Dodge 2011: 86). Importantly, Karzai was often torn between the need to placate conservative forces within Afghan politics on the one hand, and foreign governments and military commanders on the other, and those forces are complicit in his actions.

Geography and Borders

Related to the idea of the state in material terms and worth mentioning very briefly are questions of borders and geography. Afghanistan does not 'have natural geographical borders' as such (Wahab and Youngerman 2007: viii) though border politics has been and remains deeply significant. Afghanistan is a landlocked country that borders the former Soviet republics, as well as Iran, Pakistan and China (Bird and Marshall 2011: 7). Borders, as ever, prove permeable. In the late nineteenth century, after the Second Anglo-Afghan War, the British remained preoccupied with Afghanistan's 'poorly defined and poorly defended north-western frontier' as a possible geographical foothold for Russia (Lee 2018: 386). Refugees have moved across Afghanistan's borders at various points in recent history, fleeing intervention and violence. Drone warfare has blurred the boundaries between Afghanistan and Pakistan in the pursuit of the war on terror (Agius 2017). The Taliban made use of the border with Pakistan in 2001 to escape the US military, and their familiarity with the landscape offered military advantage throughout the war. In fact, Pakistan's support for the Taliban when it first emerged as a coherent organisation was linked in part to economically grounded geographical aspirations across its borders:

Benazir Bhutto, who had been returned as Pakistan's prime minister in 1993, also hoped the Taliban would restore security on the Chaman–Kandahar–Herat highway and open up a potentially lucrative trade route between Pakistan, Turkmenistan and Uzbekistan. This would offer the possibility of the construction of a pipeline from Turkmenistan, which could provide Pakistan with cheap gas and oil. (Lee 2018: 631)

Many of the tensions and shifting support networks that exist between Pakistan and Afghanistan today are linked to the point where British colonial officer Durand drew a border between Afghanistan and Pakistan in 1893, straight down the middle of the Pashtun community (Cronin 2011: 65–6; Mahmud 2010). Manchanda (2017: 391) highlights that 'the Durand Line deliberately followed a topographic ridgeline that could be held at strongpoints blocking mountain passes that the British ascertained as crucial to the defence of their empire'. When the 1947 partition of India resulted in the creation of modern-day Pakistan and the solidification of the border between the different sections of the Pashtun community, Afghanistan refused to recognise its legitimacy. It was partly because of this political sticking point around territories that Afghanistan and the USSR grew closer. Not only did the Soviet Union support the Afghan desire to unify the Pashtun territories (the so-called Pashtunistan issue), but a punitive arms embargo (imposed by the West) enforced on Afghanistan as a result of its stance drove the Afghan government to seek military aid from the Soviets (Cronin 2011: 65–6).

Bordering practices, then, imposed by empire and (neo)colonial forms of governance, are, as with so many other contemporary states, core to the trajectory of Afghanistan. Bordering practices and the production of geographical imaginaries that shaped Afghanistan's past continue to produce particular forms of spatial and conceptual knowledge about the country. As mentioned above, Manchanda (2017: 394), discussing imperial knowledge production on Afghanistan as a space and territory, highlights the role of the 'frontier' as a definitional concept, pointing to a site that 'remained a space of exclusion from power and a place of "subjugated knowledges" (Foucault 2003: 11) in which the British comfortably rendered some peoples less governable than others'.

As I outline, this idea of (geographically influenced) ungovernability is still pervasive. The conceiving of Afghanistan geographically, especially in the West, has been a political form of knowledge production. Additionally, geographical features and landscape have played a role in questions of stability (for instance in relation to securing road travel; see Kakar 2011) and violence (the significance of the destruction of the

Bamiyan Buddhas is one example here; see Hamdouni Alami 2011). Significantly for this book, and something I will return to in Chapter 3, aspects of the landscape are marked by their relationship to war-making, indeed histories or layers of war-making. Fundamentally, though much of the detail falls outside the scope of this book, border politics and geographic ideas, histories and imaginaries play a role in both conceiving Afghanistan and understanding its war past and contemporary context.

The Taliban

The Taliban first came to power in a violent takeover, led by Mullah Omar, who was perceived to have significant 'spiritual legitimacy' (Lee 2018: 634) and signalled a movement towards more regimented governance. Mohammad Hassan Kakar (2011: 2) writes, in relation to the Taliban assent to governance, 'what helped the Taliban most was their program of disarmament, prohibition of poppy cultivation, and the establishment of peace and security'. Once in power the Taliban implemented totalitarian rule, banning TV and music, enforcing a rigid dress code, closing down girls' schools and putting in place strict gender-segregation regulations that had disastrous implications for women's healthcare provision and other sectors (Lee 2018: 636–7).

In the contemporary context the Taliban are not in fact a unified entity with a linear mandate. David Kilcullen suggested from a military perspective that the Taliban were a 'highly adaptive social movement' and defied attempts to articulate a unified operational logic (Nicoll 2011: 37). Equally, as the post-2001 conflict progressed, the Taliban became hybridised. They maintained an ideological reputation, one that was adhered to and fostered by its leadership; however, within the group there were those who demonstrated criminality and lacked any overarching socio-political motivation beyond survival or personal gain (Johnson and DuPee 2012). Equally, the rank and file, as it were, could just as easily be so-called $10 Talibs (seasonal fighters paid $10 a day to join the Taliban during times of the year when there is less farming work to be done and driven to violence by the need for a wage) as ideologues driven by fundamentalist aspirations (Abbas 2014). Thus, any process of negotiation or reintegration of Taliban combatants has to manage the disparate forces and grievances at work (see Coomaraswamy 2015).

With the discovery in 2015 of Taliban leader Mullah Omar's death, there was a change in Taliban leadership. In the current context, in light of recent talks and the US–Taliban agreement noted below, there is certainly unease and fear around the possibility of a Taliban return to governance,[6] yet both the outcome and the implications of this process are unclear. Ambiguity on this issue was encapsulated by Afghan academic, street artist and activist Shamsia Hassani in an interview (cited in Geranpayeh 2019): 'This is the land of strange and unpredictable events. If the Taliban return, perhaps things will get worse, maybe they will stay the same and maybe they will improve. We don't know what will happen.'

Contemporary Afghanistan

The year 2014 was an important one for Afghanistan. The drawdown of international troops took place in 2014 while the symbolism and actual marker of civic participation illustrated by millions of people, including women, voting in the national elections resonated around the world (Coburn 2015). President Ghani included women in the nominees for government positions and there has been a focus on building the capacity of female police officers. Yet violence against women remains endemic and underreported (Amnesty International 2018); *The New York Times* reported that the sexual abuse of children by US-backed Afghan militia commanders was known about and ignored by their American military partners (Goldstein 2015), and much of the rhetoric around gender equality and participation that defined international engagement with Afghanistan did not manifest in reality (Billaud 2015).

Due to the stepping up of violence, there have been growing numbers of refugees and internally displaced peoples forced to flee their homes (Blomqvist 2016). In Internally Displaced Persons (IDP) camps the conditions are often difficult and dangerous (Blomqvist 2016). Competition for food and aid has increased in the last few years as numbers of displaced peoples exceed the already stretched available resources and the international donor community loses interest in Afghanistan (Blomqvist 2016).

The 2017–18 annual report from Amnesty International stated:

> An increase in public punishments of women by armed groups applying Shari'a law was reported. Human rights defenders received threats from both state and non-state actors; journalists faced violence and censorship. Death sentences continued to be imposed ... Members of the Hazara minority group and Shi'a continued to face harassment and increased attacks, mainly by armed insurgent groups. (Amnesty International 2018: 66)

Recently, negotiations took place in several phases between the US and the Taliban in Doha and resulted in an agreement on 29 February 2020 whereby US/NATO forces are to fully withdraw over the course of fourteen months, while the Taliban agree not to allow any 'extremist' group, such as al-Qaeda, to operate within the territory under their control (*BBC News* 2020). This series of peace talks did not include the Afghan government and were also conducted in light of significant Taliban military strength and control over large sections of the country.

In 2019 a *Loya Jirga* was held; it involved around 3,500 participants, just under a third of whom were women. This called for a ceasefire between the government and the Taliban, while participants also expressed concern about the need to hold onto political and social changes such as those in the area of women's rights. Afghan activist Wazhma Frogh (interviewed for *Council on Foreign Relations* 2019) commented:

> The jirga is very positive, even just in terms of bringing people together. 3,500 people have come together. And 30 percent of them are women. And ultimately it mandated that the government push for a ceasefire in any peace talks. People are demanding the end of bloodshed. So, I think that's a positive impact.

She went on to say of the ongoing peace process:

> Women are pushing to be included in the process. They are very strong. The challenge is always that they are told this is not the time for women. When we ask the U.S. envoy why women are not part of their talks, he says he's only talking to the Taliban about the U.S. withdrawal, and that when Afghans talk with the Taliban, then women's rights can be discussed. So, that's the major challenge, that we do not have the opportunity yet.

Meanwhile, leaked documents from the Lessons Learned Project, a series of interviews with high-level US officials involved in the war and statebuilding in Afghanistan at various stages, published by the *Washington Post* in late 2019, highlighted mismanagement, lies and failures within the conduct of the US-led military and statebuilding project (Whitlock et al. 2019).

Between 2009 and 2019, the UN recorded 100,000 civilian deaths as a result of the conflict at the hands of ISIS, the Taliban, the Afghan military and international military forces. The UN Assistance Mission to Afghanistan remains operational, and foreign troops remain in the country, though US President Trump is aiming for a full withdrawal. Afghanistan continues to receive huge amounts of foreign aid. Activists, artists, legislators, NGOs and others in Afghanistan continue to work to enhance human rights protection within the legal system, as well as political and social practice, and to continue improvements in health-care and educational provision. President Ghani, emerging victorious from the latest round of elections in 2019, along with the rest of the government, faces governance and security challenges of multiple differ-ent kinds and a deeply contentious and difficult process of peace talks with the Taliban ahead.

Conclusion

This chapter has provided a brief and narrow engagement with the context of Afghanistan in order to support the understanding of readers as they progress through the rest of the book. There is much more to discuss in terms of Afghanistan's rich and fascinating history and that history is much more than a history of conflict. However, a survey of conflict, peacebuilding and themes within recent history highlights the connections between the past and the present, and the complexity and nuance of this political and social lifeworld. This lays the foundations for an understanding of some of the mechanisms of the military–peace complex in Afghanistan, how it drew upon familiar stories of modernity and women's emancipation, and how it echoed past attempts to influ-ence Afghan politics via military means.

In articulating context in this chapter, I have flagged up key areas that help to make sense of my analysis. For instance, highlighting the contestation around notions of the state, as well as the false binary of traditionalism and modernity, brings into greater relief the disjunctures surrounding the liberal peace framework in Afghanistan which I engage with in the chapters to follow, while recognising the long cycles of polit-icisation around gender and women's rights in particular helps to his-toricise my analysis of instrumentalisation in Chapter 4. Additionally, though I only briefly note questions of geography here, I take up the theme of materiality and space in much greater depth in Chapter 3.

One thing this chapter has done is elucidate the ways in which the military–peace complex, as I outline it, is very much bound up with the narratives and histories that circulate around Afghanistan. Though the military–peace complex as an idea is salient in other contexts where military–peace work entanglements manifest in everyday ways, this chapter helps the reader recognise the role that Afghanistan, as an ide-ational concept, as a state, as a territorial imaginary, played in shaping international engagement and the multi-layered entanglements, logics and performances that I am interested in exploring in this book. In the next chapter, I focus on these entanglements and performances directly, outlining key groups of actors within the international project as I see it, and positing certain key logics that shape the military–peace complex and my analysis of it.

Notes

1. This project consisted of nine consultations with seventy-four women from twenty provinces – Nangarhar, Logar, Bamyan, Herat, Kandahar, Helmand, Uruzgan, Khost, Paktia, Faryab, Badakhshan, Kunduz, Takhar, Baghlan, Jawzjan, Sar-e Pul, Samangan, Balkh, Parwan and Kapisa – in late 2013. Marie and I used English language translations of these consultations to write the report.
2. For a detailed history of key debates around gender within Islam and discussion of issues such as the veil see Ahmed (1992).
3. It is important to note that the 'modernisation' of aspects of Afghan society has historically not been solely an externally driven project. For instance, in the early twentieth century there was a push from within Afghanistan to reform the education system. These efforts also faced conservative pushback and required negotiation. Lee (2018: 420) writes: 'Afghanistan's first tentative steps towards modernization of its educational system thus involved a delicate balancing act between Islamic conservatives and a small coterie of young, foreign-educated, urban reformers, known as *roshanfikrs*.'
4. For a discussion of the coloniality of the nation-state see Gani (2019).
5. Indeed, recent documents from the Lessons Learned Project highlight the centrality of 'warlords' to international strategy (see Whitlock et al. 2019).
6. I do not discuss the Taliban in detail in this book, as my focus is primarily on the international project in Afghanistan. It must be recognised that the Taliban use terrible violence, including against the Afghan civilian population, and though I do critique logics of security and risk in the international domain of this book, I also note here that the Taliban are participants in a war just as much as foreign militaries.

CHAPTER 2

Performing the Military–Peace Complex: Logics that Entangle

In this chapter I introduce and explore the practices of the three major groups of actors within the category of the 'international' that I wish to explore in this book – civilian actors operating broadly within the remit of the liberal peace, the counterinsurgency military and private military security contractors. I discuss how they intersect, are symbiotic and share or collectively produce certain modes of encounter with Afghanistan and the Afghan population. I outlined in the Introduction the way in which the military–peace complex in Afghanistan operates within the logics of the liberal peace, broadly conceived. In this chapter I am interested in the core themes which help to delineate and gain an understanding of the military–peace complex: distance from and securitisation of Afghan bodies; intensive security practices; gendered logics that render everyday practices and broad ideologies and doctrines intelligible; and neoliberal drivers and ways of seeing both the state and individual in market/consumption-centric terms. In order to explore these themes, I break the chapter down into sections that map onto overarching 'logics', and these continue to be central to my examination throughout the book. I argue that these logics, while distinctly not representative of all international workers, are potent enough to constitute the 'international' as a social category defined against the social category of the 'local'.

As I make extensive reference to the security environment in Afghanistan in this and following chapters it is important to note that this environment changed over time. In terms of international civilian life, broadly speaking, there was an earlier stage up to around 2012 where security was comparatively more lax, though civilian entities were being targeted regularly by the Taliban (Suhrke 2011), and a later stage where even more rigid security measures kicked in, and life became more heavily restricted. These increased restrictions were often as a result of attacks on foreign NGO or IO staff. Not all organisations operated with rigid security mechanisms in place – for some, low-key security measures were preferable – but an extensive security environment was nonetheless a feature for many. For the military, there were often different phases as well; for example, according to one of my respondents, the German forces in the North did not have to deal with a full-scale insurgency until around 2012, while the South was experiencing a lot more 'kinetic' activity before this. Moreover, counterinsurgency, which I explore and unpack below, took hold most officially between 2006 and 2009, and became the overarching doctrine along with an ostensible reduction in remote security logics.

Embodied Performances

Embodied, repeated performances help to delineate the military–peace complex as a praxis. In this book I am interested in how performances are enacted through bodies and rendered political in everyday ways. One of the most important scholars to have written on performance and performativity is Judith Butler, and her work frames subsequent interpretations (Butler 1999). For Butler '[p]erformativity is not a singular act, but a repetition and a ritual which achieves its effects through its naturalization in the context of a body, understood, in part, as a culturally sustained temporal duration' (1999: xv). This illustrates the everyday and repetitive quality of embodied performance.[1] For Butler, as for other feminist scholars, gendered ideas are always a component part of embodied performances and '[t]he identity of the biological body itself is always already interpreted through the culturally specific "matrix of intelligibility" that determines the limits of gender' (Shepherd 2012: 5). Shepherd argues that it is only through understanding the inter relationship between performativity and gender that 'we understand how constellations of practices (in which power is inherent) constitute the identity of the individual, rather than the identity of the individual being read from the biological body' (2012: 5). Higate and Henry (2009) draw on Butler (1999) and Erving Goffman (1959) to conceptualise a performativity with 'far-reaching effects imbued with power and authority' and the capacity to impact upon 'the conditions of possibility by which normality itself is constituted' (2009: 102), and I draw on their framework in this chapter

Performances enacted in relation to conflict-affected space are particularly politically significant. Autesserre argues that the performative practices of statebuilding actors in a conflict-affected environment 'simultaneously embody, act out, and possibly reify background knowledge and discourse in and on the material world' (Bourdieu 1972, 1979; Autesserre 2014). Thus, 'performative infrastructure' in war and conflict-affected spaces is a domain of praxis where 'meanings are produced, identities constituted, social relations established' in an everyday sense, while simultaneously allowing for 'political and ethical outcomes [to be] . . . made more or less possible' in a systemic and structural sense (Bialasiewicz et al. 2007: 2).

As I progress through this chapter, I articulate how the military–peace complex was rendered through performative praxis, enacted through various bodies in various spaces, shaping the ideas of the international and the local as logics.

Civilian Actors and the Liberal Peace

The liberal project is broadly conceived in this book as a transformational social engineering project with a focus on liberal democracy and the free market (Goodhand and Sedra 2013: 239). Moreover '[t]his transformative agenda is operationalized through a range of interconnected initiatives, including security sector reform, constitution writing, good governance and rule of law initiatives, macro-economic reforms, reconstruction, rural development, and so forth' (Goodhand and Sedra 2013: 239). As well as this expansive set of activities, the actors that are engaged in the liberal peace are diverse, 'composed of state and non-state, for-profit and non-profit organizations involved in complex sub-contracting arrangements' (Goodhand and Sedra 2013: 240). Walter (2016: 273) argues that though there were parallels between the post 9/11 project in Afghanistan and previous externally mandated 'modernization' efforts, 'what differentiates this contemporary state-building programme from previous modernization schemas is the highly neo-liberal economic character of development efforts as well as the heavily securitized nature of their implementation'.

Though I consider all internationals operating in Afghanistan as part of militaries, PMSCs, NGOs, IOs and so on to be linked to the over-arching framework of the liberal peace project in most cases, civilian personnel are a particularly vital vector of the ideology and praxis of liberal peacebuilding because they operate across different kinds of space, within different degrees of conflict, and their presence is more visible to host populations than military actors in some cases (Autesserre 2014: l. 962). They are also more varied in mandate and approach, more fluid and hybridised in their activities, and have a more explicit and generally unquestioned relationship to peace promotion than military personnel (Autesserre 2014: l. 5487–774). Smirl argues that the 'spatial and material practices of the international aid community' and the 'highly visible bodies and physical environments of aid workers', in a post-crisis or peace operation context, are an 'essential aspect in international political affairs' with vital implications for the 'way particular categories and relationships are constructed' (Smirl 2008: 237). Moreover, the nature of much civilian peacebuilding work in conflict-affected Afghanistan is such that a significant number of foreign personnel seem to become relatively indistinguishable in terms of lifestyle (though this varies geographically, especially between those located in Kabul and elsewhere) and overarching approach, while still differing in specifics like national origin and area of mandate focus (Autesserre 2014: l. 5487–774). Goodhand suggests that, in theory, peacebuilding NGOs 'assume clear boundaries which differentiate them from other types of organisations', yet 'in practice these boundaries are often blurred and contested' (2013: 288).

Civilian actors arrived quickly after the early phase of the war. As Julie Billaud (2015: 12) puts it, 'shortly after the bombings over Afghanistan abated, a humanitarian theatre was added to the military one'. NGO, humanitarian and civilian statebuilding activities in Afghanistan between 2001 and 2014 incorporated a wide range of areas from education to security sector reform, many of which had a strong focus on gender and women's rights, reflecting a wider political and social interest. International civilians working in Afghanistan were often young, between the ages of twenty and forty, and well educated. Many were from Western countries. Their work in this context was tied into a wider aid industry focused on the idea of alleviating suffering in crisis contexts around the world. While humanitarian work in its earlier manifestations sought to be neutral and apolitical, in the post-Cold War context some of the reputational neutrality of the global humanitarian industry shifted. This shift was linked to a number of factors such as a growing disregard for humanitarian norms on the part of warring parties in ever more complex conflict contexts and more numerous attacks on NGO staff and work as a result, as well as the increased concern with the root causes of conflict, which led humanitarians towards more heavily politicised good governance activities (see Spearin 2008). It is within this broad overarching framework that civilian peace promotion and statebuilding actors operated in Afghanistan.

The Counterinsurgency Military

COIN is a very specific military style that was dominant in Afghanistan from 2006 or so to the official time of troop withdrawal in 2014 (Nicoll 2011: 43–51). In order to understand how the American and British militaries in particular operated in Afghanistan and how this feeds into my conception of a military–peace complex, it is crucial to evaluate counterinsurgency both as a doctrinal phenomenon and as an operational practice.

Within the counterinsurgency paradigm, insurgencies – a common phenomenon in warfare throughout history and a particular feature of the 'war on terror' – are defined as groups that use violence as a method but 'seek political change as their primary goal and reflect the socioeconomic, political, religious, cultural, and ethnic schisms within and among states' (Romaniuk and Webb 2016: xiii). Counterinsurgency sets out to address insurgency on multiple levels, in terms of both its violent manifestation and the socio-economic or other grievances that fuel this violence. The initial evolution of counterinsurgency as a method of warfare is located within British military experiences in Malaya, a colonial war against communist insurgents in the 1940s and 50s (Simon 2015: 887), but it was also influenced by other conflict engagements such as those in Northern Ireland (again shaped by colonial histories) and during the peace support operations of the 1990s (Egnell 2011: 297).

With conceptual foundations in ideas around modernisation theory and Western normative conceptions of legitimacy and progress, the premise of counterinsurgency doctrine is that it is militarily desirable to win the support of the local people in a given country and thus to 'drain the sea in which the insurgents swim' (Egnell 2010: 285) – in other words, to remove the support base for an insurgency, by gaining the loyalty of the population and building the legitimacy of the host government. In practice these activities aim to 'win the hearts and minds' of the population through development or social projects – building bridges or schools, running training programmes, supporting national and regional government figures in their work (Egnell 2010: 284). These activities are seen to address the root causes of violent insurgency, which are viewed as stemming from weak government, poverty and underdevelopment. The perceived strategic value of these activities lies in removing support for the insurgency and making it less militarily effective and easier to defeat. The perceived tactical value lies in the ability of the population to provide militarily useful intelligence and facilitate ease of military operation (see Egnell 2010: 289; Farrell and Gordon 2009; Khalili 2011; McBride and Wibben 2012; Welland 2015).

As I have already outlined, the initial approach to military action in Afghanistan was much more traditional war-fighting, particularly on the American end. European militaries were more interested in statebuilding activities from the outset, largely due to domestic political requirements (Davidson 2013) and military styles and, as it became clear that the war had not been won and the Taliban as well as other armed groups were still an active threat, the whole military approach shifted in this direction (Dodge 2013: 1190). Counterinsurgency as a doctrinal favourite came to prominence due to certain 'norm entrepreneurs' (Finnemore and Sikkink 1998)[2] who promoted it politically and within the military. General David Petraeus, who led American operations in Iraq, was a key advocate and an author of the counterinsurgency field manual published in 2006 (McBride and Wibben 2012: 199). Counterinsurgency was tied into political dynamics in the United States from early on in its implementation, being part of the new President Obama's revised strategy in Afghanistan from 2009 that also included a troop increase and corresponding civilian surge (McBride and Wibben 2012: 201).

General Stanley McChrystal was a key figure associated with COIN in Afghanistan. He became central to the war in Afghanistan in 2009, when he was appointed Commander of NATO forces. McChrystal was inspired by the approach taken by Petraeus in Iraq, and came to advocate for a revision of warfare practices in Afghanistan (Nicoll 2011: 43–6). He believed that the war was being lost primarily because it was not addressing the socio-political grievances of the population and neither the interveners nor their plans for the country appeared 'credible' to Afghans (Nicoll 2011: 44). He instigated further reforms in military practice, focusing on population engagement, the minimising of civilian 'collateral damage' and a change in troop behaviour, asking soldiers to get out among the population and win 'hearts and minds' (McBride and Wibben 2012; Gilmore 2011; Khalili 2011; Nicoll 2011).

The counterinsurgency paradigm led to the development of PRTs, military and civilian units which operated under the umbrella command of ISAF (Nicoll 2011: 40; Welland 2013). These teams were 'intended to boost development in particular areas with military support' (Nicoll 2011: 40). They represent an interesting hybrid between military and civilian work, illustrating the collapse between these two categories that took place on multiple axes within the Afghan peace/statebuilding project (see Goodhand 2013; Suhrke 2011). The teams consisted of civilian consultants and military personnel stationed in different provinces around the country. They worked within the NATO or ISAF command structure, but, in the American case particularly, were also responsible to national military leaders directly. As a civilian liaison to the US military outlined to me, development work and community engagement thus became military strategy:

> as based on the idea of the US counterinsurgency doctrine and development of good practices from around the world, of well, we need to get down to a lower level and work more directly with the communities, both for military purposes and for development and social-advancement type purposes (Mike, civilian liaison to the US military).

As stated above, part of the shift towards counterinsurgency approaches directly produced and increased fluidity between civilian and military spaces and mandates by incorporating development-oriented personnel into military spaces. My respondent framed it like this:

> And the intent of the US government was to sort of augment the vast number of troops that were going to suddenly be going into this relatively small area with civilians, development experts, and political field officers, and these kind of things in order that it wasn't seen solely as a military operation . . . So there was a little sort of nucleus, a civilian team that was down there, completely embedded with the military. (Mike, civilian liaison to the US military)

Civilian bodies and less traditionally war-focused ideas thus circulated around and through military spaces in a very pronounced way. Yet, though counterinsurgency brought development and military para-digms into closer proximity, it was also fraught with internal contra-dictions precisely because of this. One of the aspects that came up with respondents in discussions around COIN was the fact that there were inherent contradictions and difficulties in conducting war and peace-building projects simultaneously and in the same place. For example, Mike pointed out that:

> [i]t was difficult for the civil affairs team to come into a village, you know, that had had a special forces night raid the night before, you know, and be like OK we want to do X,Y, Z and the people were like 'Wait a sec, look you came and you took away ten people in our villages last night at gunpoint and we don't know where they are, we're not going to do anything until we have some sort of clarity on where these people are'. (Mike, civilian liaison to the US military)

A former Air Force respondent agreed:

> [I]t seemed like a lot of times we were going into villages and first step raid village, see if they're terrorists, take weapons, interrogate them on the few weapons that they do have, you know they have an AK47 lying around, interrogate them, see if they're terrorists. After this like, you know, storming through their village and knocking down doors, emm we try to sit down with the village elder who I mean [laughs] isn't particularly keen on talking to us at that point. (Ben, former US Air Force)

According to Ben, most soldiers were 'walking there strictly with engagement in mind, we don't have any kind of hearts and minds in our training'. Similarly, one respondent, a former infantry soldier in the British Army, explained that certain phases of training in Sandhurst highlighted complexity and nuance more suited to a population-centric style of warfare. Yet, on the other hand infantry training remained very much about traditional soldiering: 'you went to infantry training school, and this is to teach you to be an aggressive infantry leader, and when I was there, there wasn't that much emphasis on the COIN thing' (former British solider). Jack suggested that adherence to a civilian protection mandate as part of the COIN approach was dependent upon who was in charge of a particular unit, so that 'you may have the type of facilitator that says if you're fired upon you're justified to fire and whatever happens after that happens' (Jack, former US Special Forces).

Talking about making military decisions, Ben argued:

> Those kinds of calls are quite tricky when you have this whole COIN thing in the background of, you know, hearts and minds or whatnot and it comes off as a bit of bullshit at the end of the day. What is our job here? Is our goal getting rid of these guys who are shooting at us, or is it, you know, hearts and minds? At a certain point you realise that every time you go out you get shot at and you are killing bad guys, and you are doing that more often than you are actually [doing] hearts and minds. (Ben, former US Air Force)

What all these comments indicate is that with the counterinsurgency template in Afghanistan, there was a disconnect between what was outlined as an approach within the paradigm, and the reality that was actualised on the ground. Arguably in practice, despite the rhetoric, '[v]iolence is used, often against civilians; troops have less contact with the population than they should; and experts in human terrain often become militarized themselves rather than having the reverse impact upon the units among which they are deployed' (McBride and Wibben 2012: 201).

Robert Egnell points out that despite the nice rhetoric and pictures of soldiers with children and so on, counterinsurgency built on the legacies of colonial wars was still 'primarily conducted to achieve military objectives rather than to achieve development or humanitarian aims' (Egnell 2010: 289). Additionally, because military objectives were always and automatically primary, decisions were made which benefited military objectives in the short term but could hardly be said to have won many 'hearts and minds'. For example, 'the US military cooperated with Afghan warlords and local strongmen who were supposed to guarantee stability in their areas of influence' (Harsch 2015: 108; see also Joya 2009: 66). This cooperation with individuals and groups known for violence against civilians and gendered violence also points to particularly gendered and militarist understandings of power (Mac Ginty 2010b) that are at odds with the (also gendered) 'softer', 'gentler' civilian-focused approach of COIN, which in and of itself was a strategic approach with clear military goals rather than a humanitarian project (Dyvik 2013; Gilmore 2011). Thus the 'development' or 'civilian-oriented' aspects of warfare enacted through counterinsurgency strategy were arguably performative, not in the sense of individual soldiers or intentions being somehow dishonest, but rather in terms of the overarching and collective disjuncture between the shallow theatre of 'hearts and minds' work and the reality of military objectives.

Private Military Security Contractors

Private security is ubiquitous in the contemporary context; contractors do all kinds of work, guarding anything from shopping centres to diplomats, and the umbrella companies that run privatised security operations are involved in diverse facets of society such as migrant housing and control, public health services, prison management, sporting events and so on (see Abrahamsen and Leander 2016: 1).

Private security or private military security companies (PMSCs hereafter) are one of the clearest and most visible connections between civilian and military praxis as well as to broader ideologies of neoliberal governance and economics, one that maps the body and its spatial power onto broader dimensions of economic exchange. Eichler points out that the wars in Iraq and Afghanistan fuelled the 'burgeoning demand for private military and security services' where 'contractors outnumbered or closely trailed U.S. troop numbers' (Eichler 2015b: 1). This increased reliance on private security entities is bound up with the central tenets of neoliberal ideology and practice (Eichler 2015a; Singer 2003), and is linked to the weakening of 'transparency in states with high capacity' and an increase in 'vulnerability and conflict in states with weaker state capacity' (Eichler 2015b: 3; Singer 2003). Thus, they constitute a phenomenon bound up with a prioritisation of global markets and power dynamics over human needs and sustainable peace, and their use in some civilian peacebuilder security (discussed below) fuels this hierarchy.

The relationship between PMSCs and the humanitarian sector has developed over decades, and is tied into a desire to reduce risk and enhance security provision on the part of humanitarian organisations, not least for insurance reasons, on the one hand, and on the other a desire on the part of the PMSCs to improve their own reputations through humanitarian involvement. So, while some NGOs, donor organisations and so on seek out PMSCs to provide them with protection from violence, the security companies also 'increasingly look to humanitarianism as a future market opportunity' (Spearin 2008: 364), offering a seemingly mutually beneficial relationship. It is not always clear how many security contractors are in Afghanistan at any given time, how many of those are armed and who relies on them. In 2010, when President Karzai attempted to ban private security companies due to a series of scandals, the international community pushed back. At the time Nic Lee, director of the Afghanistan NGO Safety Office, claimed that only a handful of NGOs relied on PMSCs. *The New Humanitarian* (2010) reported, however, that 'private contractors and donor organisations warn they will be unable to work without private security arrangements – something that may indirectly affect the work of some civil society groups', highlighting the complex ways that civil society actors become entangled with PMSCs even if they do not choose to employ them. The report outlines that 'UN agencies have also hired private international guards at their offices in Kabul and elsewhere in the country' but that 'US government agencies and contractors are the biggest users of private security services in Afghanistan'. PMSCs employ both Afghans and those foreign to Afghanistan.

I suggest that PMSCs are a deeply performative phenomenon in global politics and the politics of war. The embodied performances of PMSCs (dress, demeanour, weapon use/placement) can have a relationship to the business model of a given company or the organisation that hires security contractors, and is linked to the requirements, resources and expectations of that particular entity (Higate 2012a; Eichler 2013), connecting into the broader neoliberal market configurations that arguably guide intervention to begin with (Pugh 2004) and the way that gendered and racialised (see Chisholm and Ketola 2020) ideas are implicated within them (Higate 2012c; Eichler 2015a). Bearing in mind what Amanda Chisholm and Hanna Ketola (2020: 2), drawing on Barkawi (2017), articulate as the 'profound degree of precarity' which marks those private military bodies shaped through 'imperial encounters' and 'the configuration of a corporeal global raciality apparatus' (Agathangelou 2019: 251), I do not conflate private militarism with power. Rather, I recognise the contribution that private security bodies make to logics of liberalism, security and gender in Afghanistan. My critique in this chapter focuses on the use of armed contractors and a heavy reliance on security routines within the international project, yet it must be noted too that many organisations avoid employing armed contractors out of adherence to 'humanitarian principles' (*The New Humanitarian* 2010) and that the implications of private militarism are always shaped by context and intersectionality.

Military–Peace Complex Entanglements

Liberal Logics
The Afghan example from a critical perspective is illustrative of an approach that seeks to equate counterinsurgency, development, market

Figure 2.1 A coffee shop entrance in Kabul. Author photograph.

liberalisation and democracy promotion with progress and recovery, and thus to 'converge on a notion of *peace-as-governance*' (Richmond 2009a: 561, original emphasis). Billaud, for example, points to the manner in which international activities in Afghanistan were (and are) wrapped up with a 'narrative of progress, rationality and freedom' which stems in practice from the jargonistic rational individualism of foreign experts and is often divorced from the needs and realities of those it claims to speak for or in aid of (2012: 19). Thus, taking into account the broader geopolitical implications of the civil society and military industries, especially with regards to democracy promotion and women's rights (Billaud 2012), and merging these with the elevation of technical skills and templates and the embodied security hierarchies that value foreign lives above Afghan lives (Fluri 2011a, 2009a), a very specifically gendered, neoliberal, racialised and militarised design emerges from critical scholarly evaluations of the Afghan peacebuilding project as a whole since 2001 (Duffield 2010; Fluri 2011a, 2011b, 2009a).

With this in mind and in practical terms, the liberal logics that marked the statebuilding project in Afghanistan seemed often to be counterproductive in terms of peace promotion and equality. Speaking of the liberal peace project, Claire Duncanson writes: '[p]ost-conflict interventions continue to share a set of common assumptions. They largely conform to a fairly standardised model of reconstruction based on the ideology of open markets' (Duncanson 2016: 12).

Duncanson goes on to explain that in the case of Afghanistan, '[t]he funding for the stabilization and state-building mission was dependent upon the usual mixture of neoliberal reforms, Afghanistan's economy was already very weak, but the reforms have consolidated an almost total dependency on aid or foreign investment' (Duncanson 2016: 84).

As part of the liberal peace project in Afghanistan state enterprises were rapidly privatised, diverting the plentiful natural resources of the country away from the population. At the same time, while 'Afghanistan [was] the world's greatest recipient of aid' by 2011, 'US$3 million a day was said to leave Kabul airport corruptly to buy property in Dubai' again, clearly not reaching those who were most in need of it (Duncanson 2016: 85) and the way that this aid was used when it was spent in Afghanistan was in some cases deeply wasteful. Indeed, in leaked documents from the Lessons Learned papers, high-level military and civilian policy makers in the US admit that enormous amounts of public money were squandered on the Afghan project (see Whitlock et al. 2019).

Conceptually, the overarching mandate of the liberal peace, as it manifests in both civilian and military (counterinsurgency) paradigms, is grounded in a 'legal-rational conception of legitimacy that permeates Western political thought' (Egnell 2010: 285). There is a very strong link within the counterinsurgency paradigm and wider statebuilding projects between the promotion of good governance, focusing on central government capacity, authority and popular approval, and the defeat of insurgent groups and restoration of peace. However, this particular understanding of the centrality of externally mandated good governance to the garnering of legitimacy is founded in the development of the Western state model, based in ideas of the democratic social contract and individualism in relation to citizenship rights and responsibilities (Egnell 2010: 283; see also Gani 2019).

In relation to Afghanistan, this kind of legitimacy paradigm is not necessarily convincing given the political importance of a more community-focused and regional understanding of citizenship and governance for some of the population and a history of violent external interference which undermines claims to good governance and the strengthening of a central state apparatus (see Dodge 2013; Kakar 2003; Heath and Zahedi 2011: 10). Echoing this disjuncture, some of my interviewees demonstrated a scepticism around the notion of central government in Afghanistan and the ability of foreign military intervention to successfully install and maintain one. Mike (a civilian liaison to the US military) and James (a former British soldier) articulated doubts about the applicability of this particular kind of governance paradigm. Mike was quite clear that he did not believe military-run development projects and government capacity-building would have a lasting impact at the local level. Lisa (an American NGO worker) argued that the Afghan central government had a poor track record of designating funds below the provincial level and she attributed the unsustainability of PRT projects to this issue. In her view, all their short-term projects would fall apart over a few years once the internationals left, as they would prove unsustainable in the longer term. For Lisa, as for others, the PRTs were operating within a misplaced governance rationale which failed to take into account the particularities of the Afghan context. Multiple Afghan women's rights activists/civil society worker participants also articulated concerns regarding the short-termism provoked by short-sighted donor mandates.

Bird and Marshall have argued that a central strand of Afghan identity (linked to a history of warfare with outside parties and suffering at the hands of imperial politics) is based on defining what is Afghan against what is foreign, and 'resistance to outsiders who seek to impose their will' (2011: 6). As Manchanda (2017) points out, this kind of argument can be dangerous, as it potentially reifies ideas about Afghanistan as lawless and Afghan people as warlike that in turn perpetuate racialised logics. Yet, as Dodge suggests, it would seem clear that a 'competitive state-building' which internationals of various kinds have pursued within Afghanistan 'poses historic and geographic problems' (Dodge 2011: 81–2) that are bound up with colonial violence and bordering praxis as well as other political and geopolitical dynamics. The idea that external actors should be instrumental in bolstering the legitimacy of the central government and unified state fails to take into account the importance of context, and the fact that outsiders, especially militarised ones, may simply not possess true legitimacy in Afghanistan, given the country's history of violent external interference.

Moreover, the focus on a strong state and central government within the liberal peace and evidenced by counterinsurgency and civilian statebuilding is also contradictory since the private sector is so significantly privileged within a neoliberal model (Duncanson 2016). Neoliberal economics in fact requires a reduction of the strength of the state, along with the privatisation of industry. The military–peace complex relies on private actors, such as PMSCs whose very existence in the contemporary context is inseparable from 'post-Fordism', the revolution in military affairs which relied on private (especially technology) companies, and the dominance of neoliberalism globally which paved the way for private-public partnerships in the defence sector (Abrahamsen and Leander 2016: 3). Within these neoliberal circulations, the private military industry carries its own racialised logics, whereby third-country nationals and non-Western contractors and recruits suffer greater precarity and financial insecurity, feeding into racialised hierarchies of labour and martial power operating globally (Chisholm and Ketola 2020; Chisholm 2015).

So, the military–peace complex is shaped on one hand by notions of legitimacy based on particular conceptions of the state and on the idea that peace/stability promotion (undertaken by military and civilian actors) is linked to building the capacities of a central state government. Yet, on the other hand, the military–peace complex itself relies on private contractors, facilitates the power of non-state actors such as so-called 'warlords' and promotes neoliberal reforms which reduce the financial capacities and fiscal authority of the state as well as its ability to deliver welfare provision for its own population and its control over natural resources within its borders.

As articulated by Duncanson (2016: 41), '[t]he intervention in Afghanistan … was committed to private sector growth with little attention paid to the way this approach favoured big business, military power-holders and the informal and illicit players of the war economies'. Recent documents released by *The Washington Post* (Whitlock et al. 2019) as part of the US Lessons Learned Project highlight the performative nature of these liberal logics, and the extent to which concepts of failure and mistakes in Afghanistan were papered over by the American political and military establishment at the time. They also highlight the opinion that, in some cases, key powerbrokers in Afghanistan, like Hamid Karzai, had very little interest in pursuing governance reform in any case (Hadley, Lessons Learned Interview, 2015).

Despite doubts, efficiency issues, failures and contradictions around any 'one size fits all' model of statebuilding, many military–peace complex practices pursued template application. These liberal templates can be seen operating in the counterinsurgency doctrine, security routines, project design and implementation, training, funding systems, donor and grant requirements, gender programming and more (Autesserre 2014: l. 259, l. 1473). Many of these approaches to peacebuilding that are template-oriented rely on pattern and repetition rather than emotion (like empathy) and perception (see Cohn 1987; Mac Ginty 2012; Orford 1999: 704; Sylvester 2012: 500). Arguably they are dehumanising on two levels – crafting particular expected performances in those who enact them (see Cohn 1987) and Othering those who do not (Mac Ginty 2012) – within a hierarchy of knowledge production that values external expertise over local understanding (see Autesserre 2014: l. 1078; Duffield 2010; Sabaratnam 2017). Moreover, those people or ideas that exist outwith the technocratic domain can be perceived as disruptive, ineffective or irrelevant (see Mac Ginty 2012), and this might impact, say, certain Afghan organisations seeking international funding: 'grassroots communities construct their appeals to reflect what they think the expatriates what to hear, as a way to ensure funding and help' (Autesserre 2014: l. 3652).

Additionally, this (neo)liberal logic tracked down from the general, macropolitical level to the particular, micropolitical level. For instance, James, a former military respondent, told me that his experience of COIN was centred on the premise that the army would 'give them [Afghans] stuff and they'll like us'. This speaks directly to the collapse between notions of individual consumption, security and democratic progress (Billaud 2012; Duncanson 2016; Fraser 2009). What starts in material terms as a relatively simple tactical decision to exchange money or goods for information or to garner popularity (or, on the civilian side, to implement economic initiatives conducive to the aims of donor-mandated programming) is arguably indicative of a much deeper structural push towards privileging economic values over human ones and embedding this privileging in a social fabric made weak by violence. In this way

> commercialization of aid policy and humanitarian assistance is also highly conditioned by the ideals of liberal peace, to stimulate outcomes congenial to a particular view of political economy. This includes the transmission of democratic/market values and ideas by peacekeepers and peacebuilders in war-torn societies. (Pugh 2004: 46)

Equally implicit in James's words here and an evident issue with the military–peace complex is the use of the army as a compliance tool for a supposedly freedom-based ideology of democracy, legitimacy and liberal rights (Mac Ginty 2010a: 398; Higate and Henry 2009). Essentially the use of military force to induce democratic engagement underwritten by free-market reforms that disempower populations long term (see Duncanson 2016) amounts to 'democracy at gunpoint' (MacGregor 2009) which is inherently contradictory but also central to the slippage and entanglements embedded within the military–peace complex.

As a soldier required to do counterinsurgency work, liberal logics targeted at racialised bodies are transmitted through James's embodied and performative everyday practices of giving out 'stuff' to try to persuade Afghans to 'like' his military. This is not separate from but entangled with the logics that shape the embodied labour of the third-country national employed by a PMSC to guard an international organisation compound in Kabul at a lower wage than their white counterpart. These embodied micro-battles and bordering practices, shaped by geopolitical encounters as well as by gendered and racialised performances of risk, 'peace' and the liberal state, do the work of reproducing material difference, value and ownership at sites of violence and crisis. Of course, the body of the martial envoy, delivering 'progress' and a 'civilising mission' to a racialised frontier space is nothing new, and evokes a long history of imperial praxis which consistently entangled logics of war with logics of 'progress', social change and the protection of women. I do not suggest that the military–peace complex signals any radical departure in this sense, but rather that it is an important re-enactment and invocation of the duality of violence and global order on both an ideational and an everyday scale.

Gendered Logics

Another facet that unites various elements of the military–peace complex is the predominance of gendered logics. They manifest through and between bodies, in the particularities of performative engagements with Afghanistan, in the approach to women (Afghan and international) and the perpetuation of martial politics (Howell 2018). While I discuss the logics that circulate around women and femininity in particular in Chapter 4, I turn here to look at masculinity and the role it plays across military and civilian spaces.

Counterinsurgency as a paradigm can be analysed through considering the role of masculinity in soldiering and the alleged 'feminisation' of the COIN paradigm, highlighting that 'gender is integral to understanding population-centric counterinsurgency' (Dyvik 2013: 411). In terms of the ideational component of the paradigm, the gendered story being told is based around the notion of a less combat-centric style of warfare (Welland 2015: 3). Counterinsurgency is framed as civilian-focused, softer, and more development-oriented and thus potentially depicted as 'feminised':[3] '[t]his coding of counterinsurgency as the civilianized option which aims at winning the hearts and minds of civilian populations and persuading them to support the counterinsurgents has a particular gendered character' (Khalili 2011: 1473).

It emerges clearly in my research materials that the COIN doctrine is often understood like this, as somehow feminised in relation to the more typically masculine framework of violent, enemy-focused war-fighting. This gendered dynamic also arguably had a wider political rationale: to make the ailing war in Afghanistan appear softer, less aggressive and more palatable to domestic populations (Gilmore 2011; Khalili 2011; McBride and Wibben 2012). In a COIN framework, soldiers are being asked to conduct social projects and development-style work, to build interpersonal skills and to play with children. This kind of social work style warfare promoted within a particular kind of intellectual framework by hybrid 'soldier-scholars' (Khalili 2011) is implicitly contrasted with the hypermasculine violence of the insurgents themselves (McBride and Wibben 2012). Thus, '[i]n the narrative promoting COIN, this new brand of soldier-scholar is directly contrasted with images of the misogynist warriors of the Taliban and Al Qaeda and more broadly with the barbaric, gender-segregated society of Afghanistan' (Khalili 2011; McBride and Wibben 2012: 204).

However, this perceived 'feminised' war did not always sit easily with expectations of soldiering. The idea that masculinity is important to soldiering was highlighted in the introduction to this book and is long recognised in feminist scholarship. Military respondent James suggested that 'soldiering was an existential test of manhood' for him when he first signed up and that 'many soldiers did understand it in those terms' (James, former British Army). Ben found the appeal of the military in its 'ultra-masculine' identity (Ben, former American Air Force). A Special Forces operator, interviewed in a *Rolling Stone* piece on General McChrystal, uses gendered imagery to criticise the COIN strategy: 'I would love to kick McChrystal in the nuts. His rules of engagement put soldiers' lives in even greater danger. Every *real soldier* will tell you the same thing' (Hastings 2010, emphasis added). In this account, which makes use of sexualised violence (kicking someone in 'the nuts'/attacking their manhood) the idea of real soldiering is pitted against the irrational and unmilitary COIN approach. Interestingly, danger/bravery/courage here is not the masculine centre of the argument, but 'real' soldiering versus irrational, unnecessary strategy.

In a different vein but with a similar result, Mike explained to me that the COIN approach, which required soldiers to wait for long periods in the base until their Afghan counterparts could be considered sufficiently trained up, exacerbated macho attitudes among soldiers:

> I think that created a lot of anger and fear and you know macho-ness if you want to call it macho-ness, whatever . . . that was a difficult thing being down there for that period and for those guys seeing everyone get killed and being, you know, told 'wait, wait'. (Mike, civilian liaison to the US military)

Implicit in his explanation is the idea that soldierly masculinities are not well suited to inaction and that this, more than anything, created tensions. His words illustrate a need to heighten performances of masculinity as compensation for the way that COIN is often linked to a kind of feminised inaction. Jack discussed an incident where soldiers in an armoured vehicle had taken fire from someone in a crowd using a pistol. The pistol would not be able to penetrate the vehicle and the soldiers returning fire into the crowd using their machine guns would cause civilian casualties. However, he explained that not returning fire, as stipulated by COIN and often rules of engagement, was a challenge to their masculinity: 'it takes a lot of pride swallowing, again from a macho guy to say "somebody is firing at me and I am going to choose not to return fire"' (Jack, former US Special Forces).

Sarah discussed the horror provoked among the infantry by General McChrystal's policy of 'courageous restraint': 'it was McChrystal and basically he was saying on no account can you shoot or return fire if you think that there is going to be a civilian injury'. She explained how this was anathema to the military mentality and the behavioural expectations of soldiers. She said that she remembered 'the lads saying, "we're almost fighting with our hands tied behind our backs, because we've got to be so sensitive to not have civilian casualties"'. Sarah suggested that, though she did not share it, she could understand their dismay: 'to a soldier, who is trained to return fire, to protect himself and the people in his patrol, I could see that it was just a big step to ask them not to return fire' (Sarah, Major, British Army). There were also concerns raised by military personnel that COIN's rules of engagement made soldiers more vulnerable, and Sarah's comments indicated this as well. So, there was a dualism between the COIN vision of feminised restraint, the unwillingness to return fire even when attacked and the resulting weakness or vulnerability, and the more traditional understanding of soldiers as masculine warriors who would automatically fight back and demonstrate strength. Tracing these ideas, a British soldier interviewed in a documentary focusing on the Royal Marines, spoke about how the Taliban 'saw our laws and our kind of behaviour as weakness, do we walk around being the weak security force, or do we have to project an air of Taliban masculinity?' (Terrill 2014). This quote highlights the gendered performativity involved in military perspectives and the impossibility of separating out ideas of masculinity (and the implicit association between weakness and femininity) from the military–peace complex in Afghanistan.

In keeping with gendered dichotomies, civilian liaison Mike made a distinction between development style work and more traditional war-fighting praxis, and he did so with implicit reference to masculinity and the expectations of true soldiering. He discussed how the various national contingents were perceived differently in different contexts and used the example of the Dutch. He suggested that their COIN-based population-engagement focus might resonate well in a more secure district, but in areas where the Taliban were a bigger problem, the population expected more traditional soldiers:

[Y]ou could go to one village and yeah the Dutch were really well received, you know, but because they had a nice light hand and they were doing development work and they built something for someone, they were less likely to fire back, you know, when being fired on, and so there was fewer civilian casualties. And then you go to the next village over and they would have a completely different perception because perhaps the insurgents had overrun their village two months ago and they had tried to call on the Dutch and say 'can you come in and get these guys out, we don't want them here, we need your help'. And the Dutch said 'no, we're standing back, we're dealing with development' and so their perception of them was – 'well, the Dutch are really weak, you know they don't fight, why would you have a soldier here if they are not going to fight right?' (Mike, civilian liaison to the US military)

His words are filled with implicit dichotomies indicative of gendered tensions within COIN, such as between 'light' and heavy handed, 'weak' and strong, and 'development' and fighting. For Sarah, there was a fundamental dissonance between the culture of British and American militaries, and the requirements of a COIN strategy. Interestingly, she suggested that other nationalities might find it easier to adjust to the population-centric expectations of the doctrine:

Because counterinsurgency doctrine is asking so much of a British or an American soldier. It might not be asking the same of perhaps a Norwegian or a Swede, but I think that the way British soldiers are trained and how we behave, I think that we are probably one of the best armies in the world. But I think that that comes at a cost in that we are possibly not as good at thinking about civilians, as we are at thinking about the opponent, the enemy. (Sarah, Major, British Army)

She framed this in terms of a dichotomy between 'soft' practices and 'hard' training and expectations of warfare: 'I think it is this soft effect, you know giving posters out to people and trying to win hearts and minds. I just think that for an infantry soldier it was too much for them to see how it linked to the training that they've undergone' (Sarah, Major, British Army). Clearly this has highly gendered undertones, and by way of unpacking her observations Sarah went on to talk about an interview with a marine that she herself had read. When asked about the difference between him as a soldier and as a civilian, he explained that 'basically I've got a set of bollocks and they haven't' (Sarah, Major, British Army). This is a deeply embodied kind of distinction, which speaks to the gendered identity frameworks of the military in interesting ways. The soldier is essentially a man, in comparison to the civilian (male or female) who is not, and this is framed as a tangible bodily distinction – hard and with a set of 'bollocks', as opposed to 'soft' and without – as well as a metaphorical one.

Sarah located some of the disconnect between COIN practice and military training in this distinction from civilian life that training fostered: 'I mean from the moment they joined the infantry, their training almost disconnects them from being a civilian' (Sarah, Major, British Army). An American ex-military contractor I met in Kabul supported this idea with a comment he made during a conversation about his background; he stated that his military training made him forget the sound and lyrics of civilian songs (Author notes, 5 May 2014) thus disconnecting him from his civilian self.

Sarah, who was well aware of the gender dynamics of military culture, explained to me that she was in a dilemma in relation to COIN, since she saw it as vital that soldiers learn to work with and respond properly to civilians in combat contexts, yet equally she worried that this could deplete their 'toughness': 'I don't want British soldiers to stop being tough, because that's what makes them an effective military' (Sarah, Major, British Army). Equally, when she made reference to civilians who might need protection or care from a more sensitive armed force, she referred to victims of sexual violence, suggesting soldiers should be 'better be prepared to respond to survivors of rape in conflict' (Sarah, Major, British Army). This is interesting in that it traces the rationale for COIN-style soldiering along quite stereotypical gendered lines, linking it into the idea of women as victims and soldiers as masculinised protectors, albeit sensitive ones (Elshtain 1987; Higate 2012b; Stiehm 1982; Young 2003b).

One last point of complexity and disjuncture to consider when looking at expectations around soldiering and masculinity in relation to COIN is the role of one of its major figureheads in Afghanistan, General Stanley McChrystal. McChrystal is depicted in the media, particularly in the 2010 *Rolling Stone* profile piece that garnered much political controversy, as someone who prides himself on a performative and stereotypical machismo (Hastings 2010). He is described as a maverick who did not perform well at West Point despite being from military pedigree. He was caught drinking and was frequently disciplined for pushing back against authority and bending the rules. Upon taking charge of military operations in Afghanistan, he gathered a set of motley individuals (men) around him, as advisors and aides, who allegedly referred to themselves collectively as 'Team America' and one of whom is on record in the article describing a diplomatic dinner in Paris as 'fucking gay'. The piece reflects the seemingly deeply deliberate performance on McChrystal's part of a cowboy-style, salt-of-the-earth all-American manhood. He allegedly prefers beer and Irish pubs to anything fancy: 'The general hates fancy restaurants, rejecting any place with candles on the tables as too "Gucci". He prefers Bud Light Lime (his favorite beer) to Bordeaux' and so on (Hastings 2010).

All of this is especially interesting because as a military figure he is associated with the implementation of COIN, its defence and, indeed, attempted rehabilitation. Michael Hastings notes an incident where McChrystal's reputation for toughness and bravery comes up against the frustration and anger of the infantry at the enforcement of a feminised and apparently failing COIN policy of restraint. The journalist describes how McChrystal received a letter of complaint from an infantry soldier, detailing the danger and suppression involved in going out on patrol in a highly kinetic area, without being allowed to fire as (apparently) needed. In response to a challenge offered by the soldier, and by way of showing that non-traditional soldiering requires masculine bravery of the highest order, McChrystal went to visit the infantry battalion in question, going out with them on patrol: '[t]hen he showed up at Arroyo's outpost and went on a foot patrol with the troops – not some bullshit photo-op stroll through a market, but a real live operation in a dangerous war zone' (Hastings 2010). McChrystal and this representation of him seem to seek to call upon ideas of machismo and bravery to focus on and justify COIN tactics.

This demonstrates the importance and centrality of masculine performance to the maintenance of war's reputational heart and highlights the complex interaction between different enactments of gendered expectations rather than any linear gendered order. What is clear in all of this is that there was a certain disconnect between how soldiers were trained and how they were expected, or at least officially expected, to conduct themselves in Afghanistan (see Welland 2013). That disconnect is a gendered phenomenon on multiple levels and highlights that 'the messages that a soldier receives about appropriately masculine soldierly behaviour are fundamentally at odds with what is then expected in a peace operation' or something that parallels one in some ways (Whitworth 2004: 9).

Moreover, the disjuncture inherent in soldiers' performative praxis manifests through emotional rupture. This was evident in discussion with James around his practices of internal and intellectual resistance to the logics of the war, even as he also desires to carry out its violence. He explained in relation to COIN work that:

> out there you're in a constant kind of threat, unless you're in the base, and also you don't get to hit back, there is no release, you're just like sucking in up, sucking it up, sucking it up, smiling, sucking it up, you're going [speaking of someone he suspected] 'I'd really like to just fucking blow your brains out, you know, because you're Taliban'. (James, former British Army)

While feeling this way he explains he was required to act as peacemaker and diplomat. He suggested that 'you end up like a sponge, and this is why the rates of PTSD are so high' (James, former British Army). His allegory of the sponge was designed to illustrate the notion that the soldiers absorbed threat, danger and attack and should not react, a notion heavy with gendered affective meaning and symbolism around weakness and pacificity when contrasted with a 'natural' sense of enmity and desire for violence in war. According to James, COIN required him to be friendly and diplomatic, even towards individuals he suspected of being Taliban operatives, and he told of an incident where he handed over money to a community leader for a refurbishment, while being sure this man had known about or even orchestrated an improvised explosive device (IED) attack on his own battalion that had come close to claiming lives (James, former British Army). At the heart of this discussion, again, is the complex, gendered 'performative infrastructure' involved in COIN war in Afghanistan and the gendered emotional sensations that it provokes. Ideas of masculinity both facilitate and fuel gendered conduct and frameworks but also point to moments of tension and trauma and to the contradictions inherent in the military–peace complex.

Equally, gendered logics help to make sense of the phenomenon of PMSCs in Afghanistan and this draws the 'peace' side of the military–peace complex into the equation more directly by implicating civilian organisations. Security routines for large international organisations involving PMSCs were performative and relied on the iconography and symbolism of hypermasculinity as a physical stabiliser and point of reference. As Higate elucidates, armed security personnel operate through performances of masculinity in various ways and with varying degrees of theatricality and visibility (Higate 2012b). Yet most centre on weapons, masculine physicality and a stoic, tough demeanour; often sunglasses and military-style clothing feature strongly and the notion that these indicators will be perceived as threatening and dominating by others is vital for their success (Connell and Messerschmidt 2005; Higate 2012a, 2012c). Additionally, however, this performative masculinity is shaped by racialised hierarchies and the layers of insecurity faced by contractors from the Global South which diffract and complicate gendered logics (Chisholm and Ketola 2020; Chisholm 2014).

Private security is largely, though not exclusively, centred on the male bodies of security guards, and the 'field of private military security is intensely gendered' so that it is the 'image of burly, masculine private contractors' which in some cases comes to signal a safe and secure space in an insecure environment (Eichler 2015b: 1). These performances of masculinity were evident in Afghanistan and were, in fact, integral to the way that security operated and particular spaces were delineated. They were also racialised. Many of the most visible contractors guarding businesses and international spaces in Kabul were Afghan or third-country nationals. Chisholm (2014: 13) describes how 'racialized contractors within the security industry must accommodate more hardship than others' and articulates how third- country nationals in sites like Afghanistan receive lower wages and are given more dangerous tasks than their white counterparts, as well as being bound up with complex racialised global labour supply chains (see Abrahamsen and Leander 2016; Chisholm 2015; Eichler 2015a).

I will explore here two dimensions to this gendered performativity which comes with some civilian security routines in the peacebuilding paradigm. The first is the physical reliance on the male body and symbols of hypermasculinity within wider racialised configurations of security and profit; the second is the linked structural issue of the martial politics of bodies and everyday interactions, and the connection between gender hierarchy and militarisation in society (Eichler 2015a, 2013). These two aspects feed into and rely upon each other in a fluid and symbiotic interplay and relate back to neoliberal economic praxis (Eichler 2015a; Singer 2003).

At the level of individual bodies, the threat of violence required for security in the liberal peace paradigm is condensed and refined into the countenance of singular persons and embodied identities (Fluri 2009a). Security guards are performing a particular type of embodied masculinity which they project through their posture, facial expression, body type, fitness level, and choice of clothing, weapons and other props (Higate 2012c). One of my civilian respondents spoke about the PMSCs in her workplace as follows: 'it is this macho culture, very like good guys versus bad guys, fully tattooed and all muscles ... it was very much like "I've got a gun, I've got a machine gun" full display of masculinity or sort of the militarised version of it'. This does not represent all PMSCs, but it does strongly reflect a particular trope associated with private military security, and that is significant. In many ways the PMSC performativity is similar to that of the soldier – weapons, military fatigues and physical prowess might all play a role (though there are, of course, variations and complexities in both identities). The parallels are important – there is a masculinised rationale here that validates the militarism of soldiers' performances and emulates it, albeit with contextual adjustments (Higate 2012a). This signals the fact that, on an individual and visceral level, the theatre of the liberal peace calls for hypermasculine and militarised performance, props and costumes, even in spaces that first appear to be devoid of war, if not of violence.

Research in psychology is illustrative of the problematic impact of symbols of violence in a peace promotion context. It has demonstrated the so-called 'weapons effect' whereby the presence of weapons increases the likelihood of violent behaviour by those who carry the weapon and by those who see it (Yuhas 2015). Anderson et al. attribute this to a 'priming process' whereby '"[w]eapon" concepts (e.g. gun, sword, club) are linked closely to aggression – and hostility – related concepts in semantic memory because of their similarity in meaning and their close association in common experience' (Anderson et al. 1998: 308). Psychology professor Brad Bushman, speaking to *The Guardian*, stated that '[w]eapons increase all of those thoughts, feelings, hostile appraisals and the type of thinking that somebody's out to get you or wants to hurt you' (Yuhas 2015). He suggests that the power of the weapons effect lies in the fact that 'people don't think about it much. The effects are very automatic' (Yuhas 2015).

Moreover, psychological research has linked the weapons effect to gender performance, connecting the handling of weaponry by men to increased testosterone levels, and thus increased willingness to do bodily harm to another (Klinesmith et al. 2006), which can be tied into hypermasculine frameworks (though these, of course, are not 'naturally' male). Equally, similar research has demonstrated the link between the adoption of security-based roles, the wearing of certain militaristic uniforms and the possession of certain props (like sunglasses), and the willingness of individuals to commit acts of cruelty or dishonesty, as well as the willingness of others to react with hostility towards them (Yuhas 2015). This research is not all-encompassing and does not offer absolute principles, but it is suggestive of important dynamics.

Additionally, the visuality of the many racialised bodies of contractors from the Global South and Afghan nationals guarding spaces oriented towards often (though not exclusively) white internationals feeds into logics of risk and violence (re)producing bodily hierarchies and conceptions of vulnerability. Racial politics of risk and precarity disaggregate the effects of masculine performances, so that there are layers of inequality and gendered stratification at work in PMSC and security guard performances in Afghanistan. This is well illustrated by Chisholm (2014: 36) who discusses the experiences of Gurkhas (Nepalese soldiers or contractors):

Because of their cultural hybridity in their ability to relate to both locals and internationals, Gurkhas were positioned higher in the hierarchy of security contractors than Afghans – yet not on the same level as white contractors. The almost but not white status of Gurkhas was further observed during informal conversations with three white security managers where they revealed their belief that Gurkhas lack the specialist skills and cultural competencies held by white contractors that allow them to assume higher-paying roles in the industry.

Her analysis demonstrates that masculine performances within the domain of private militarism, attuned to modes of security and logics of risk and violence, are also mapped onto racialised inequalities that further stratify bodies according to modes of gendered protection and value.

Young writes that in any social world 'collective actions have produced determinate effects on the physical and cultural environment which condition future action in specific ways' (2006: 113) that 'may even be counter to the best intentions of the actors' (2006: 114) Masculinised, racially stratified symbols of violence in Afghanistan that include a range of actors can arguably reify violence and make it more possible even as these symbolically laden practices seek to protect people. Taking the analysis beyond the individual body, it is important to consider the potential impact of this gendered security framework on the social or collective body. Fluri (2011b: 282) suggests that '[b]odies represent the most immediate and delicate scale of politics and markers of gender and national identity' (see also Hyndman and De Alwis 2004; Parashar 2013) and this delicate scale is thus indicative of broader dynamics. Eichler points out that on a big-picture level, 'the privatization of military security is a deeply gendered process, with gendered underpinnings and effects' (Eichler 2015b: 2). A signifier like a private security body can become a part of the foundations upon which civilian peacebuilder security routines and rituals are built. Thus there might be a gradual and implicit acceptance of martial bodies and militarised private, racially disaggregated entities as being linked to peace and development (Billaud 2012; Duffield 2012, 2010). One of my civilian respondents also spoke to me about how, in the aftermath of an attack, she noticed that her ostensibly civilian workplace shifted: 'the celebration of guns . . . we literally turned into a base'. From a feminist perspective, gendered militarisation, violence and war are inextricably linked (Cockburn 2012) and the structures that entangle certain ideational modes of masculinity with military practices also produce violence and strive to ensure the primacy of logics of violence. This complex, self-perpetuating dynamic of gendered militarism and violence is illustrated by the concern that the increased use of security contractors raises questions about immunity within Afghanistan and the perpetuation of modes of violence-as-norm. As articulated by Mariam Amini (2018):

> Afghanistan already has a poor track record prosecuting members of its security forces implicated in serious human rights abuses, including killing civilians. Given the impunity already enjoyed by the security forces, placing them under the command of private security contractors could further undermine accountability.

Thus, the martial performances of individual bodies contribute to the martial, racialised and gendered logics of space and society even though they emerge (in the case of private security protecting civilian peacebuilders) as a response to violence. I continue to consider this issue and the question of security logics further in the section below.

Security Logics

> Tens of thousands of diplomats, soldiers and contractors remain in Afghanistan, but most live like people who have overstayed their welcome, behind blast walls and layers of security.
>
> – Sune Engel Rasmussen (2016a) writing in *The Guardian*.

Security within the military–peace complex in Afghanistan is an embodied practice, one that arguably generates distinctions between valuable and marginalised or threatening bodies (Fluri 2011a, 2009a). It centres on 'spaces of privilege and power' in Afghanistan in which inequalities are racial, economic, physical and security-based (Fluri 2009a: 986). Despite often genuinely valuable work and intentions, international actors, taken as a whole, formed a group of prioritised individuals, whose community was separated from and appeared in hierarchical relation to local populations. I have engaged with these categories in the introduction and made it clear that they are not totalising, nor do they always map onto actual persons in the full sense; however, they are social categories with meaning and power, and they are partially produced by security logics, even though it is easy to recognise why the need for such logics arose.

Many (though certainly not all) peacebuilding personnel in Afghanistan, especially those who worked with the UN or a few tightly regulated NGOs or government-linked bodies, lived in conditions that were privileged, but heavily restricted and remote from the particulars of their context. Security procedures were a central component of peacebuilder ideologies, mandated by donors and institutional rules. Civilian and military persons occupied different spaces and had different approaches to security, though, as I outline, there were parallels. Looking to the civilian side, security processes were extremely tight for many individuals, especially as the Taliban became more active over time, and included guards at their residences (armed in some cases), cars and drivers (and sometimes bomb-proof vehicles), fortified workplace compounds and a small network of foreigner-friendly cafés, restaurants and bars with rigid security measures. Some of these required you to give your identification over to a guard at the entrance to hold while you were on the premises. They were often surrounded by razor wire, patrolled by armed guards and required complex networks of checks in order to get inside. Thus, in Kabul, it was possible to observe the extent to which the category of the 'international' was patterned around a repetition of danger-prevention measures and safe zones.

Civilian peacebuilder residences had safe rooms, personnel were provided with flak jackets, weapons to use in self-defence and (sometimes armoured) organisation cars to drive them around. Many had night-time curfews imposed by their employers, and they were banned from frequenting establishments perceived as lacking appropriate security measures, as well as homes that did not have guards at the door. One story recounted to me by a friend and colleague about the repercussions of violating these stipulations involved immediate job loss for a foreign worker who had visited an unguarded residence in his private time. These measures did not seem designed for stunning effectiveness; I met one individual whose safe room was also his bathroom, and his given weapon was essentially a large kitchen knife. Yet equally they were a vital component of the everyday lives of many civilian peacebuilding personnel and part of the wider ideology of how peace/statebuilding functioned. My respondents consistently made reference to these measures while also resisting them, through their everyday choices or their opinions, and thus, again, though these security logics were dominant they were in no way complete or uncontested. This resistance, in fact, highlights once again the disjuncture and contradiction within the military–peace framework.

One of my civilian respondents explained that she found the security procedures in place in her work damaging and oppressive:

> It is the reason for why I'm not going to prolong my contract any more. I mean I love my job here and I am a little bit tired but when I joined the

> UN I had been in Afghanistan for three years already and I can say with
> some confidence that I do understand the city and the security circumstances
> involved better than most of the people that work in the security department.
> And it just really frustrates me that they basically feel like they need to restrain
> us, and like hold us back, and it's the main reason for me not actually staying
> in this job. (Luise, German UN worker)

Given that Afghanistan has been impacted by extensive violence it is hard
to imagine removing security thinking from the picture, and yet the ways
it manifested across the military–peace complex seemed counterproductive at times, as the above extract from my interview demonstrates.

Another respondent described her complex feelings about security
logics and highlighted the fact that security practice disaggregated
between the categories and associated bodies of the international and
the local:

> There was a big disconnect between the internationals and the locals. The
> resentment was growing. And even where I work right now that resentment
> really is becoming more obvious. And the reason for that is that now we have
> much stricter security measures. After the attack . . . we had a number of ex-
> pats that lived here, they all were pulled out. [Names organisation] has much
> stricter policies, so ex-pats are under very, very strict conditions.
>
> And as part of that of course there are certain privileges, you can leave
> the country in case something happens, we have security, when we walk we
> have a tracker with us that notifies security if something happens. In terms of
> security, you get more privileges but then you are also the main target too.
>
> I think they [the Afghan population] forget that part. That, you know, we
> are targeted much more than if you are a local and kind of living here.
>
> So, I feel in this area where I am, that tension is much more, and it is
> directly related to I think the security deterioration but also the measures that
> we're taking, that different organisations are taking in protecting the ex-pats
> versus protecting locals.

This reflection very clearly indicates the respondent's discomfort with
the security logics that protected international bodies as somehow
innately more valuable, but she also points to a genuine fear of violence
and indicates a sense of constant threat. This respondent is of Afghan-
Canadian nationality, and thus positioned in a space of complex liminality between the 'local' and the 'international'. Her words illustrate
the disjuncture at work within the military–peace complex whereby disaggregation between bodies is felt viscerally by the subjects of security

logics in different ways and produces modes of insecurity and difference while also appearing innately justified by the continual backdrop of threat through which the international project itself is actualised.

Emotionality played an important role in the unease and discomfort felt by internationals around security logics. This is clear in the words of humanitarian and academic Henri Myrttinen (2019, 96). When a car bomb explodes in Kabul, he is offered the option of leaving Afghanistan and states:

> I knew I would not leave. What kept me was not a sense of adventure, but rather a mixture of emotions. There was a sense of shame attached to the fact that I had the possibility of leaving at the drop of a hat, knowing that some of the Afghans I was working with were at that very moment desperately seeking a way out of the country, and that card was not one I wanted to play. There was undoubtedly also an element of pride, or perhaps cowardice – part of me was likely afraid of being seen as a coward, someone who is frightened by a minor attack on the other side of town that did not even directly endanger me.

Affective sensations of shame, privilege and solidarity underwrite Myrttinen's decision and frame his experience as an international and his complex contestation and refusal of security logics that seek to distinguish his implicit embodied value and experience of risk from the Afghan persons he works with. Paying attention to these affective sensations and discomforts frames the international project in Afghanistan differently and problematises the foundations of the security logics that constitute it by elucidating the instability of its conception of security and the complicity of the international project as a structure and practice in the production of modes of insecurity also.

Afghanistan differs from other peacebuilding contexts because it still manifests aspects of an active conflict and has done since 2001, and the security practices I discuss in this chapter are directly linked to a high level of threat perception (Duffield 2012: 477). Security practices also shift and respond to security events, like attacks on civilian spaces and spaces known to be frequented by internationals, so there is a clear evidence base to support the need for caution and protection. Yet this does not detract from the importance of examining these practices and protection logics, especially since the increased threat levels render them commonsensical and difficult to question (Enloe 2004: 3). Of course, I understand that security measures are seen as necessary in a working environment like Afghanistan where there is ongoing conflict; however, taken as a whole, the most intensive security practices and logics within the military–peace complex have gendered, racialised and disaggregating implications and can be seen as reifying militarised violence.

I suggest that a certain kind of approach to security governance is characteristic of the military–peace complex as a paradigm. It centres on the attempt to streamline and homogenise through the application of security routines and the use of repeated, ritualistic behaviours. This is part of an underlying ideological framework: the 'endeavour to tame unpredictability' (Zanotti 2006: 152), to impose order on that which is perceived to be without it. Some of the damaging aspects of the intervention stem from a desire to simplify the narrative (historical, con-textual, ethnic, gendered and so on) in order to facilitate adherence to a template-based, rather than a context-dependent, institutional approach to programming, security and governance (see Kothari 2006a).

Security thinking in particular requires a particular understanding of the world in which some people constitute the objects of protection and others the potential for threat (see Kothari 2006c; Shilliam 2008). The assumption seemingly implicit in dominant modes of security within the military–peace complex, such as rituals and training, is that the host people and country present a continuum of threat, not overcome by any particular action but secured against through generic, habitual, militarised patterns of behaviour (see Duffield 2010). From a feminist and postcolonial perspective, attuned to 'race thinking' (Basham and Vaughan-Williams 2013: 515) this is deeply troubling. This thinking is part of a way of looking at the world, of profiling and categoris-ing people, based on simplified gendered, racialised and bio-political markers of value and expected behaviours in which the pacifistic is largely devalued, and the racial (often gendered) Other is cast out or feared (Fanon 1986; Orford 1999; Razack 2008).

Security routines are a prime example of an assemblage between particular bodies, objects and spaces. They are based around innocuous processes such as getting to work and back in organisation cars, and more obviously violence-oriented processes such as security training, safe rooms and the prevalence of armed guards. They are thus very much everyday practices, but are also institutionally mandated in spe-cific ways, forming a clear component of the overarching ideology of the liberal peace as practised by key institutions such as the UN and large NGOs (Duffield 2010). The vectors of these practices, such as organisa-tion cars (Smirl 2009) or checkpoints that are suspicious of all Afghans but not of internationals (Fluri 2009a), function as 'mobile sites of pre-emptive risk assessment and identity management that facilitate the faster mobility of the trusted few at the expense of an array of suspicious Others' (Basham and Vaughan-Williams 2013: 512).

Dominant security practices can be understood as 'ritualized patterns' (Autesserre 2014: l. 208) through which 'interveners' can establish a distinctive 'system of meaning' (Autesserre 2014: l. 209) particular to them and their context. Ritualistic behaviour in peacebuilding is most in evidence around these security practices designed to keep foreign personnel safe which constitute a security ideology (Smirl 2015; Duffield 2010; Kothari 2006a).

These measures are arguably as much about performing a militarised vision of security as they are about providing it and rely on violence-oriented material objects. Duffield argues that such security procedures tap into cognitive processes based on fear and de-emphasise personal awareness in favour of a reliance on proscribed routine (Duffield 2010, 2012), though, as outlined above, I suggest they are also resisted and questioned by those asked to enact them. They are performances in which gender and race 'interlock' (Basham and Vaughan-Williams 2013: 515), and in which the commonsensical value of treating the orientalised Afghan space as a constant potential threat is reified in the name of peace (Autesserre 2014: l. 5774; Kothari 2006a; Said 1979). This set of processes based around aid compounds, institution cars and expatriate establishments arguably comes to offer some level of comfort and control over daily existence, providing 'consistency' through which to impose a sense of 'predictability' on an uncertain and (understandably) anxiety-creating lifeworld (Autesserre 2014: l. 1301). The problem with this consistency, and with security performances, is that they rest upon the creation of an unequal, racialised and gendered bio-political order, which at its heart carries deep assumptions about which gendered and racialised bodies count and in what ways (Basham and Vaughan-Williams 2013; Fluri 2011a, 2011b; Razack 2008).

These assumptions slip through in contrasting fragments. Security routines, for instance, have differentially gendered implications for civilian peacebuilders. My respondents noted the distinctions between the security-based requirements and expectations placed upon male or female bodies. Referencing her own experiences as a civilian peacebuilder in Afghanistan, Autesserre states '[w]hen I worked in Afghanistan . . . my NGO's internal rules forbade foreign female staff members from leaving our compound, whether on foot or by car, unless accompanied by a male colleague' (Autesserre 2014: l. 7205). It is worth asking about the elements that led to this decision and what gendered or racialised ideas are cutting through these practices, often unknowingly and perhaps with the best of intentions in some cases (see Rutazibwa 2019). It is also worth noting that gendered and racialised security performances are marked by practical contradictions as well as the disjuncture of internal resistance. These contradictions are illustrated by the argument that this approach to security can have negative consequences in the form of host population resentment and an association between international civilians and foreign military objectives, the latter potentially increasing the chances of targeted attacks on civilian foreigners (Duffield 2010: 459).

So, my point is not to suggest that international staff in Afghanistan should not have tried to avoid attack, but rather to highlight that on the one hand COIN strategies and linked approaches perform two-dimensional and unconvincing development and humanitarian projects as military strategy (as discussed above), and, on the other, certain international organisations, private contractors, the UN and so on employed ever stricter militarised security regimes, hired military contractors and consultants, and used militarised technologies (Duffield 2010: 463; 2012: 25–9; Goodhand 2013). Security routines thus fed into the martial practices of civilian peacebuilders. On the one hand these martial practices could be explicit, such as in joint programming or boundary negotiations over humanitarian tasks, or in the activities of civilian liaisons to military units (Shannon 2009: 25). This explicit collapse is arguably detrimental; entities like the PRTs and programmes like the USAID Quick Impact Projects present as development work but have a clear military rationale. They therefore 'blur the lines between civilian and military action and in so doing, compromise NGO neutrality and thus, their ability to access communities in need of aid' (Shannon 2009: 18).

On the other hand, security routines elucidate the more implicit and unacknowledged entanglement between military logics and peace work. Some civilian personnel are trained, in an increasingly militarised security training paradigm, to distance themselves cognitively from their context and from local specifics (Duffield 2012; Kothari 2006a, 2006b, 2006c), people and dynamics (Duffield 2010). This training becomes ingrained in the way those civilian peacebuilders operate and understand their role. While '[i]t is absolutely understandable that the NGOs must protect their staff, their beneficiaries and their assets . . . at the same time having to do so creates a sense of unease and has affected costs and turnover with associated capacity implications' (Shannon 2009: 24).

Moreover 'insecurity and the measures adopted to deal with it drives aid workers out of communities, reducing contact, at best, and preventing aid reaching many, at worst' (Shannon 2009: 24), meaning that the martial logics of peace and development work chip away at the ostensible aims of that work. Additionally, and relatedly, the use of private security contractors has complicated implications, as discussed above, but those include perpetuating war-like environments and disaggregating between differently racialised and differently valued bodies. A UN working group on the use of mercenaries (Shameem 2010) reported on its country visit to Afghanistan that, having spoken with many local and international organisations, they had found:

> The vast majority of these stressed that the high presence of armed private guards did not generate a feeling of increased security among the Afghan population and that, to the contrary, the large number of armed individuals, vehicles and weapons created a feeling of fear and insecurity.

Additionally, they reported that '[m]ost NGOs pointed to the difficulty for Afghan citizens of distinguishing between international troops and international or local security contractors. This, they said, complicated the process of accurately reporting incidents and human rights violations.'

Among the complaints registered by members of the population, the report included 'the intimidation suffered by local Afghans from PMSCs' as well as other issues regarding, for instance, transparency and accountability (Shameem 2010). This illustrates some of the challenges and difficulties of relying on corporate security entities and most especially the way that PMSCs can help to perpetuate a structurally violent environment.

Overall, in the case of Afghanistan, the transformational macro-ideologies of the liberal peace paradigm are belied by routine realities such as security practices, social practices and architecture (discussed in the next chapter) which create hierarchical distance between internationals and Afghans and entangle peace and war work. As Goodhand and Sedra suggest, '[t]he transformational hubris of the liberal peace doctrine disappeared on . . . the streets of Kabul as the international community retreated into their diplomatic enclaves and high-security compounds' (Goodhand and Sedra 2013: 242).

Echoes of colonialism within the liberal peace paradigm entail a juxtaposition between the idea of an enlightened, democratic West, providing rational masculine governance (Cohn 1987; Kothari 2006a, 2006b, 2006c; Said 1979), and the 'failed state' of the barbaric hinterland – where the latter are 'spaces of moral "bankruptcy" and threat that require the transformative influence . . . of the *mission civilisatrice*' (Higate and

Henry 2009: 45; see also Hudson 2014; Shilliam 2008). Feeding into this framework, the 'Othering' that takes place on an everyday level in the Afghan context is 'motivated by the construction of geographical and social distance through processes of differentiation and demarcation' (Hudson 2014: 106). The most intensive security logics rely upon the idea of 'an endlessly shifting and unreadable threat environment that demands constant vigilance' (Duffield 2012: 486). Through this paradigm of Othering, locating fear in the inability of the Other to self-govern while equally distancing from that Other through a mode of militarised and routinised remoteness, the daily praxis of internationals can re-inscribe global hierarchies and inequalities onto conflict-affected contexts, bypassing any complicity in that conflict to begin with. Thus, instead of addressing and reducing structural violence, these practices arguably legitimate it.

The military in Afghanistan also follow principles of security thinking, though of course this approach is more highly suited to a war-fighting institution. Mike, who had been embedded with the military, drew the distinction between the bunker-based lifestyle on a military base in Kandahar and the bunker-based lifestyle of internationals in Kabul, with the implicit assumption in his sentiment that the military needed their bunker, while the internationals in Kabul did not need theirs:

> It was probably less difficult than say living in the American Embassy here [Kabul] and having to be literally behind all these walls inside Kabul city . . . there we were in a base and there was a good reason for you to be in that base . . . it wasn't like oh man I wish I could go out and go to L'Atmosphere [a rooftop pool bar] and have a drink, you know, or you know go see somebody you know, it's like nah nah that isn't even a question, it's good that we're inside this base. (Mike, civilian liaison to the US military)

The counterinsurgency doctrine was in some ways designed to reduce this remoteness. The increased focus on development, discussed above, was supposed to soften the appearance of heavily militarised distance from Afghan communities. Yet, as the counterinsurgency doctrine ostensibly sought to remedy a remoteness in one aspect of the military–peace complex, the increased targeting of international civilians led to greater levels of distancing in another. At the same time, COIN logics, as articulated above, were belied by an underlying 'hard' security logic which manifested as night raids and collateral damage (see Kakar 2011; McBride and Wibben 2012).

The cumulative impact of military–peace complex security logics is to reiterate ideas of violence and distrust (Duffield 2012, 2010; Smirl 2009, 2008; Fluri 2011b, 2009a). The assumption is that liberal peace work acts in a state of Hobbsian anarchy and must secure against the inevitable threat of the surroundings (Young 2003b).[4] Moreover, this particular securitised approach to international living and mandate may end up a self-perpetuating phenomenon, since the more expatriate civil society in Afghanistan is associated with military objectives, the more it will be perceived and quite possibly violently targeted as such (Duffield 2010: 458). The more foreign civil society workers are violently targeted, the further the process of martial entanglement will continue. Thus, the militarising liberal peace promotion paradigm self-sustains within the everyday mentalities, practices and interactions of foreign interveners in this context, many of whom may as individuals genuinely intend to alleviate suffering and be of use to the Afghan population (Autesserre 2014: l. 6902; Rutazibwa 2019).

Conclusions

In this chapter I have developed upon the previous one, exploring further the contextual dynamics of Afghanistan but this time within a very specific military–peace complex engagement. I have outlined what I understand to be three of the dominant logics which define the military–peace complex as an idea, and which shape the entanglements between different actors within Afghanistan's international project. I have argued that these logics map the production of modes of difference while, perhaps unintentionally, reifying violence. I have been interested in performances in this chapter, as they constitute the micropolitical embodiments of these logics, which continue to track between the geo-political and the everyday. I have sought to give the reader an under-standing of how such logics are self-sustaining and bound up with racialised forms of lived knowledge and encounter. What we gain from exploring these three groups of actors and three logics that cut through them is a vision of an international project beset with performative entanglements. This chapter helps to form one aspect of the lens I wish to apply to the international project, a lens that casts a different light on how interventions manifest in praxis.

I am not trying to suggest in this chapter that private security entities, humanitarian actors and counterinsurgency militaries are all the same or operate with the same mandates. What I aim to get at is thematic and less tangible linkages which make for a collective endeavour. As counterinsurgency, rendered partially through gendered logics, drew closer to humanitarian praxis and development work, some humanitarian praxis relied upon a martial approach to security thinking, also rendered intelligible via gendered ideas. At the heart of my explorations in this chapter and the wider book is the point outlined by Olivia Umurerwa Rutazibwa (2019: 66) that we must work harder to understand 'how good intentions coexist with a system of international aid and intervention that seems harmful not for the few but for the many'. What I argue, then, is that we must look to logics beyond intentionality and recognise how the disaggregation of bodies, the reification of modes and performances of violence, the frameworks of neoliberal governance and the gendered expectations of war tangle together to produce particular political effects, exclusions and erasures. In the next chapter I continue this line of argument but move to explore the objects and spaces of the military–peace complex in more detail.

Notes

1. I do not go into differences in conceptualisation between performance and performativity in this context but draw on conceptions of performances salient to my analysis while keeping Butler's formulation in view.
2. These authors suggest that norms come to prominence in international affairs due to promotion from key players such as powerful actors or states whom they call 'norm entrepreneurs'.
3. Importantly, I am not suggesting that COIN is in fact a feminised warfare strategy, but rather that gendered ideational frameworks can be mobilised to better understand its logics.
4. For a discussion of anarchy as a concept structured by racist frameworks within international relations theory see Henderson (2013).

CHAPTER 3

The Martial Politics of Things and Spaces

In this chapter I explore the dynamics of the military–peace complex in spatial and material terms. I demonstrate some of the thematic dynamics of this paradigm, as I understand it, and some of the ways that everyday or unnoticed spatial practices and objects are significant in contributing to the assemblages that bind the international project in Afghanistan together. I want to highlight the complexity within this context and recognise that academic analysis by nature tends towards simplification for analytic purposes and thus there are always multiple exceptions to the trends I discuss. Yet, I suggest, they are still trends.

Thinking through the Martial Politics of Things

Before discussing the material dynamics of the military–peace complex in detail, I will explore and outline what it means to consider materiality a political and social force in conflict-affected spaces. My approach in this chapter is not exactly a part of but draws loosely on the wider 'New Materialisms turn' in the discipline of international relations. As outlined by Tom Lundborg and Nick Vaughan-Williams (2015: 5) 'the New Materialisms turn encourages a more direct engagement with the political force of materiality'. Broadly, this 'turn provides intellectual resources for investigating the material realm independently of the means by which language and nonlinguistic signs such as images come to construct the "meaning" of this realm' (2015: 5). Lundborg and Vaughan-Williams (2015: 11) suggest that 'the New Materialisms literature has recently found considerable traction in IR as an antidote to the perceived excesses of a focus on discourse as language and the twinned emphasis on the politics of representation and meaning-making practices'. Yet, they argue, materiality and discourse are not in fact separate domains, and the insights of New Materialism thread through and are compatible with poststructuralism. In line with their insights, in this chapter I do not mean to suggest that a focus on the material is somehow an alternative to or a separate domain from the discursive or the social. Indeed, I consider material things to be so significant in this context because of their complex intra-action with social worlds and meanings, including the realm of the discursive (see Aradau 2010; Connolly 2013; Davis 2009; Lemke 2015; van der Tuin 2011).

Concerned with the artificial separation of the material and the social, Sara Ahmed (2008: 24) has criticised New Materialism as negating a 'history of feminist engagement with biology, science and materialism' by routinely asserting the anti-biological and social-constructivist nature of feminist thinking. Ahmed reminds us that '[y]ou can only argue for a return to biology by forgetting the feminist work on the biological, including the work of feminists trained in the biological sciences'. She critiques new materialist perspectives for active forgetting in service of particular intellectual framings. Though I signal the importance of the material world in this chapter and in the wider book, I do not infer that feminist work has not incorporated this focus before or that it is somehow incompatible. I draw on the insights of feminist materialist Karen Barad (2003; see also Hudson 2018), who, as outlined by Claudia Aradau, argues not only that 'matter is agential as it enters into a permanent and historical reconfiguration of the world' but also that performativity can speak to the 'dynamic entanglements of humans and non-humans, through which these acquire their specific boundaries and properties' (Aradau 2010: 498, drawing upon Barad 2007). I am thus interested in the importance of material things and spatial sites in their own right, but also how they intra-act with the performative engagements of the military–peace complex and its actors.

In her pivotal book *Vibrant Matter: A Political Ecology of Things*, Jane Bennett (2010: vi) writes about the centring of the material facets of our lifeworld(s) as a political project. She suggests that the 'quarantines of matter and life encourage us to ignore the vitality *of* matter and the lively powers *of* material formations' and thus she focuses attention on the vitality of material objects:

> By 'vitality' I mean the capacity of things – edibles, commodities, storms, metals – not only to impede or block the will and designs of humans but also to act as quasi agents or forces with trajectories, propensities, or tendencies of their own. (2010: vii).

What influences me in this chapter and in the book more generally is that for the study of peace and conflict

> the New Materialisms turn prompts a reconsideration of matter and its political status: not as something intrinsically inert, nothing 'in and of itself', and without any function or implication; and neither as something whose political significance can only come about through linguistic forms of identity construction; but rather as an active, affective, and politically significant set of forces in its own right. (Lundborg and Vaughan-Williams 2015: 12)

Thus, in the sections below I look at how '"things" condition the possibility of human interactions, shape political communities, and influence behaviours and outcomes – indeed, matter cannot be divorced from the "we" it in part constitutes' (Lundborg and Vaughan-Williams 2015: 12). As such I seek to explore military–peace complex assemblages which may 'include material circuits, flows of matter, and nonhuman assemblages without losing sight of the impacts of human agency' (Lundborg and Vaughan-Williams 2015: 14). Moreover, and centrally, I suggest that recognising these assemblages is crucial to understanding the existence of the military–peace complex as a paradigm. I follow Mac Ginty (2017: 856) who recognises 'interstices, hybridities, and assemblages comprised of the complex interactions between humans and non-human objects' as well as 'the vibrancy of matter or that things have power and energy in themselves independent of interpretations and representations imposed by humans' but is cautious 'of the tendencies towards neophilia, dematerialisation, and posthumanism found in some debate on new materialism' (2017: 857). Moreover, though influenced by a consideration of the vibrancy of matter in this chapter, I am equally and relatedly (if not perhaps more substantially) concerned with space and spatial practices, and with the social constructions attached to them. Mostly, I am interested in materiality as manifested through spatial practices and in performative interaction with social and discursively rendered imaginaries.

Space and (Post-)Conflict Sites

Lisa Smirl is one of the main scholars of conflict-affected and humanitarian spaces. She 'develops a model through which scholars, practitioners and policy-makers can understand the impact of spatial considerations and material culture on aid work' (Smirl 2015: l. 135). She highlights how 'built forms' have 'played a key role in the evolution of development practice' (l. 139). Space is agential and powerfully so, but it is also in symbiotic partnership with human performance. In a conflict-affected context especially, which draws together a range of actors, the way people act and embody a given role has an impact on the landscape: a formative relationship with the way a space comes into lived iteration so that 'bodily performances themselves constitute or (re) produce space' (Higate and Henry 2009: 99).

Spatial practice is central to conflict, occupation, intervention and peacebuilding. Historically, colonial practices, foundational to the construction of the contemporary world of states, centred on space. Edward Said argued that 'we would not have had empire itself ... without important philosophical and imaginative processes at work in the production as well as the acquisition, subordination, and settlement of space', and something similar can be understood for liberal peacebuilding projects and military interventions (Said 1979: 218; Kothari 2006c). Historical struggles of power, violence, oppression and conquest are layered upon particular material spaces, shaping them, reimagining them and saturating them with significance. Smirl outlines the various ways that space can be understood to operate within humanitarian praxis and imaginary. She draws on Lefebvre to distinguish between the 'space of everydayness' called perceived space, and the notion of 'conceptualized space' which is a product of the imaginary and of design (Smirl 2009). She builds on Ed Soja's work to suggest a First Space 'which is real and mappable', a Second Space which is imagined and a Third Space which is both, pointing to 'the role that a hybrid space between so called reality and imagination plays in interrogating, building and contesting conceived as well as perceived spaces' (Smirl 2009; see also Bhabha 1994).

This spatial framework is, as outlined by Smirl, useful in understanding liberal logics and humanitarian spatial practice (Smirl 2009). Thus, she argues that the 'abstract spatial constructions of humanitarian assistance', while created within the macro-level parameters of liberal ideology, are salient also at the micro-level, since: '[w]ithin international organisations, the established mode of service delivery is through technocratic tools and approaches which rely upon the conceptual belief that the spaces of assistance are as they are constructed within the humanitarian imaginary' (Smirl 2009).

Unquestionably military practice is also about space. Military logics imagine space in particular ways that are linked to the gaining of advantage and the protection of personnel. James, one of my military respondents, described the Afghan context, explaining: 'So it is all basically based around terrain and space, as you'd imagine, it's a military kind of ... it is a military conflict'.

Derek Gregory (2016: 4) has written that:

The spoils of war include the short-term bludgeoning of landscapes and the long-term toxicity of contamination (what Rob Nixon [2011] calls 'slow violence'), but it is also important to trace the bio-physical formations – the conditions, provided the term is understood in the most active of senses – that are centrally involved in the militarisation of 'nature'.

Military practice leaves a distinct mark on the spaces it encounters. Photographer Simon Norfolk (n.d.) writes about Afghanistan that:

The land has a different appearance where there was fighting in the early 90s. In this instance the tidy, picked-clean skeletons of buildings are separated by smooth, hard earth where de-mining teams have 'swept' the area. In places destroyed in the recent US and British aerial bombardment, the buildings are twisted metal and charred roof timbers (the presence of unexploded bombs deters all but the most destitute scavengers), giving the place a raw, chewed-up appearance.

Thus, the landscape is 'a medium through which military and paramilitary violence is conducted' and parts of Afghanistan can be understood as sites where 'terrain and life-forms were saturated with the debris of violent conflict' (Gregory 2016: 4).

Moreover, from 2005 the American military implemented the Human Terrain System (HTS) in counterinsurgency conflicts, namely Iraq and Afghanistan. The idea behind this was the inclusion of social scientists, as part of military operations, in order to produce 'cultural knowledge' for military purposes (Zehfuss 2012). This system, I suggest, echoes the use of cartographic praxis and anthropological knowledge by colonial powers, as it is driven by a desire to control, and render governable. It also highlights a performative encounter with bodies as spatial signifiers, thus 'human terrain', whereby racialised bodies are considered symptomatic of their spatial praxis and also mappable (Zehfuss 2012: 177).

Thus, both spatial imaginaries and attention to objects and concepts of mapping are at the heart of how power and relationality can be understood in all their fullness:

Crucial to understanding the workings of power is an understanding of the nature of power in the fullness of its materiality. To restrict power's productivity to the limited domain of the 'social,' for example, or to figure matter as

> merely an end product rather than an active factor in further materializations, is to cheat matter out of the fullness of its capacity. (Barad 2003: 810)

Moreover, I suggest that it is useful to consider the role of a kind of spatial intertextuality in this context, whereby fragments of the past layer through and are referenced within the landscape and material/spatial echoes consistently and powerfully recall other moments of violence and power. Intertextuality, as understood by poststructuralist thinkers, refers to the referential capacities of texts (where texts constitute multiple discursive materials) and the implications of such cross-context referencing (Hodges 2011). What Derrida (1977) called 'citationality' refers to a process whereby the samples of 'prior text' are quoted and 'draw attention to the previous context in which those words were spoken while reinterpreting them in the current interactional setting' (Hodges 2011: 10). Norfolk (n.d.) refers to the Afghan landscape as a 'Chronotopia'. He explains his inspiration for this term: 'Mikhail Bakhtin might have called this kind of landscape a "chronotope": a place that allows movement through space and time simultaneously, a place that displays the "layeredness" of time' (see Bakhtin 2002). In a similar vein, forensic architecture (see Weizman 2010) searches for echoes and remains of the past, or of previous political moments or intentionalities across multiple contexts, and though Afghanistan is of course not unique in this sense, paying attention to its spatial citationality helps to unpack meaningful spatial and material hauntings. Hauntings as outlined by Welland (drawing on Gordon (2008: 8)) 'refer to the "*un*-visible" and unspoken – but vibrantly "real" and present – socialities that fall outside mapped and fixed social forms' (Welland 2013: 886). Thus, the ideas of hauntings/intertextual spatiality and a chronotope together converge on the idea that space and materiality are referential meaning-scapes laden with affect and significance drawn, at least in part, from events and enactments unbound to their current temporality.

I move now to consider the idea of materiality in general within the overarching framework of the military–peace complex and the liberal peace in which it is situated before exploring different material and spatial dynamics that offer insight into the everyday and performative working of the paradigm.

The Materiality of the Liberal Peace

While scholars have outlined, discussed and critiqued the liberal peace from various perspectives, few have explicitly centred the specifically material and spatial nature of it as a paradigm (important exceptions include Higate and Henry (2009); Fluri (2009a, 2011), Duffield (2012), Kothari (2006), Mac Ginty (2017), Shepherd (2017) and Smirl (2015, 2012, 2009, 2008), and multiple authors in a volume edited by Annika Björkdahl and Susanne Buckley-Zistel (2016)). In spatial terms, liberal peace locations map onto the framework of post-crisis sites described by Smirl and discussed above. As referenced in the previous chapter, the liberal peace is also a concept often fundamentally concerned with the material world in the Marxist sense: money, markets, labour and economic structures.

Moreover, at the more everyday level, the activities within the military–peace complex often focus on 'stuff' – things that capture the ideology of the liberal peace in particular ways. These things include, for example, buildings that are built or repaired as part of a plan to develop and invest in infrastructure, such as speaker systems, schools, roads, wells and so forth. In a blog, the aid organisation Oxfam (2011) criticised the short-term material logic of counterinsurgency, describing the activities of an American marine called Lavoie:

> One ten-minute conversation with some vegetable-sellers ends with Mr Lavoie agreeing to give them over $8,000 to fix up their stalls. 'I'm like Santa Claus!' he says . . . Just how does this have anything to do with long term development, rather than just buying some short-term acceptance of the US military (a clue: it doesn't)?

As referenced in the previous chapter, one of my former military respondents summed up the counterinsurgency paradigm like this:

> the fundamental thing about COIN though in the Afghan context, is it was essentially based on, like to my mind at a very basic level, *give them stuff and they'll like us*. It is based on this . . . it is basically saying – the fundamental thing on COIN is everybody wants a better life, everyone wants a better stand-ard of living, and that may or may not be true I think in the Afghan context. It depends on who is giving it to them, very much like the Afghan mindset, is well like why would I take this from you, you bastards, you know it is quite a liberal view of the world, and even accepting it from foreigners you'd have to be quite moderate, quite liberal perhaps.

In his comments it is easy to see that the counterinsurgency project, fitting into the liberal peace project more generally, is also a material project, bound to material objects and material logics. But the material products themselves do not necessarily translate well; or they potentially produce divergent performances that are not quite what were intended. My respondent critically highlights the assumption that those at the receiving end of the 'stuff' of liberal war will perform good liberal subjectivity but, in reality, both those subjectivities and materialities are potentially unruly, without necessarily having or creating 'a liberal view of the world'.

Another respondent, a civilian liaison to the US military, also emphasised the role of the material:

> [W]hen you're a company commander and you're in central Kandahar and you're in a district that is very much a Taliban stronghold and you're in a small outpost, your main goal is to get the community members to get the Taliban to stop firing at you. Right? And to stop killing your soldiers, right? OK it's such an asymmetrical type warfare and even if you try to do very surgical style missions, you're never going to get at that problem, and so they were interested in using those *things* at their disposal, whether it's *cash for food* programs to employ the locals or you know *building that school* or doing those things, they were interested in doing whatever was going to be, whatever means available to reduce casualties amongst the men under their command. (Mike, civilian liaison to the US military)

Thomas Gregory (2020) writes about the use of condolence payments by militaries as another illustration of using material things and trade-offs within the overarching remit of military strategy. Gregory argues that the material logic of these payments, which offer cash to offset the death of a family member, injury or damage to property, centres strategic goals, primarily the negation of any negative fallout from collateral damage. There are clear uses for monetary allocations in cases of injury (medical costs) and infrastructural damage (repairs), and maybe even deaths (funeral costs), and yet the insidious dynamics of these schemes are unavoidable. Gregory (2020: 161) offers a telling sample of racist discourse around these payment programmes, citing the context of Australia where: '[t]he debate prompted one parliamentarian to suggest that "in a place like Afghanistan, losing an animal may, in fact, be more devastating than losing a relative" on the grounds that camels can have a higher value than a human'. In some ways this is pure neoliberal praxis whereby racialised lives have a militarised cash value, but it is also bound up with what Judith Butler (2010) sees as the politics of differential 'grievability' and the idea that money has an innate strategic value within martial frameworks.

Some of my respondents recognised the failings of the material logic of counterinsurgency and liberal peace approaches. For instance, this respondent explained his increasing doubts:

> [P]eople like myself who started to realise that OK wait a sec, these cash for work initiatives, or canal cleaning, or even building a school, were at odds with, were essentially not meeting the classic do no harm tests, and were creating false economies and were replacing duties and social structures that should have been there and taken care of by the communities, without anyone else coming in and having to offer incentives for them. Or the building of a school was essentially putting the cart before the horse, in that we didn't have teachers for the schools so there was really no reason to build it, but those are usually the hard things, is to find the teachers that want to teach, not to build the school. (Mike, civilian liaison to the US military)

The detritus of liberal militarism in this context is very telling: the physical shells of public investment in an unsustainable imaginary. These material fragments fit with a wider trend whereby the detritus of war's legacy marks the country. For instance, on a visit to Swimming Pool Hill in Kabul in 2014 with friends (Figure 3.1), I came across an abandoned tank. It is notable that the swimming pool was built by the Soviets and used for executions by the Taliban (Rashid (2006) comments that the blood stains remained visible for many years). Visits to Chicken Street Market in Kabul showed extensive collections of old guns for sale and military symbols – drones, military planes, tanks – woven into rugs on display in shops (Fig. 3.2). Around the time of the First Anglo-Afghan War in the 1800s, the British military were housed in a 'cantonment' just outside Kabul: '[l]ocated some 2 kilometres (1.2 mi.) north of the Bala Hisar, the cantonment *was built on land that today includes the site of the U.S. embassy*' (Lee 2018: 245, emphasis added). Capturing this sense of echo, Norfolk (n.d.) draws on his own experiences to articulate the view that in Afghanistan:

> ruins have a bizarre layering; different moments of destruction lying like sedimentary strata on top of each other. There are places near Bagram Air Base or on The Shomali Plain where the front line has passed back and forth eight or nine times – each leaving a deadly flotsam of destroyed homes and fields seeded with landmines.

Though aspects of Norfolk's depiction falsely reify the idea of a landscape inescapably bound to war-making, his words offer insight into

Figure 3.1 Swimming Pool Hill, Kabul. Author photograph.

Figure 3.2 Rugs in a shop in Kabul. Author photograph.

the affective significance of material and spatial practices and depth of entanglements between war and the everyday that leave traces across time and space and forms of violence.

Space and Material Things in the Military–Peace Complex

The Field

The spatio-material domain of the 'field' is an important paradigm in the military–peace complex. In humanitarian aid praxis the field refers to the locus of the beneficiaries of a given project or programme. In military terminology, the battlefield is the space of actual (direct, interpersonal) violence. Field manuals refer to military praxis in sites of war. Academic terminology refers to fieldwork to signal research that takes place at the site of study. I regularly used the term to refer to my visit to Afghanistan and consider myself bound up with the spatial imaginary it evokes too (see Richmond et al. 2015). Jeremy Fox, a professor of ecology and evolutionary biology, undertook informal research into the origins of the concept of 'field' to refer to fieldwork in the academic sense and found that early uses (though unlikely to be the first) can be found in nineteenth-century British cartography reports (Fox 2016). In one example from 1818, William Lambton, a British cartographer mapping

India, uses the term 'field work' to refer to his activities (Lampton 1818: 515). Thus, for the sake of argument, let us say that, intertextually, the term fieldwork as referencing the material spaces of research is linked to cartographic praxis.

Cartographic practices have their own martial politics (see Howell 2018). As Edney (1997) argues, '[i]mperialism and mapmaking intersect in the most basic manner. Both are fundamentally concerned with territory and knowledge'.[1] William Lambton, this mapper of India, was a soldier, and one who fought wars in India before undertaking a cartographic survey of the country (Edney 1997: 155). Imperial praxis is rooted in violence and conquest, the fundamental principles are militant and oppressive, and mapping forms part of the knowledge structure that makes possible ideational conceptions of empire as geographic reality (see Manchanda 2017). A map makes material dominant geographical knowledge bound by the ideological commitments of powerful knowledge producers in a given context, thus in many cases materialising imperial power over colonised lands, gained by war-making. The idea of the field is thus arguably bound into physical objects like maps, which make spatial designation more possible. It is also a material location itself in which and on which forms of knowledge are created.

In the context of Afghanistan, the idea of the 'field' signals both Afghanistan and something beyond or, rather, deeper within, Afghanistan. As Smirl (2015: 8) notes: '[t]here was an impression among fellow aid workers that it was impossible to ever reach "the field" as it truly was. Instead that experience was always mediated through the process, rituals, practices and built environments of the international aid community'. This idea offers a sense of continual mediation, so that the field appears as a material space but also at the end of an assemblage of meaning-making that is not actually physically accessed in some cases.

For one of my international humanitarian worker respondents who was based in Kabul, the field meant working outside the urban hub and came with further performative expectations:

> the way that I dress in Kabul is obviously not the same as the way that I dress in the US or when I'm somewhere else . . . but then the way that I dress when I go to *the field* is even more so. Being extremely covered, I wear my scarf much tighter, I try to be way more conservative.

The field is thus in some cases a space of intra-action with objects like clothing that signal conservative and respectful performances. It is agential, in that it imposes restrictions on human conduct. The field might be understood as far outside of the 'norm' for internationals and lends itself to ideologically weighted spatial separations. An anonymous aid worker writing in *The Guardian* (Anonymous 2016) argues:

> The field does not necessarily mean the frontline of aid work anymore, but instead has come to mean any location in a (already problematically labelled) developing country. It is a fabrication, a social construct to separate us (those writing policies in comfortable offices in supposedly superior, civilised western capitals) from them (our more virtuous colleagues testing our policies out in some dark, underdeveloped expanse).

The field is arguably always already a site of Otherness, a conceptual and spatial remove from normality, and it is thus always at least partially co-created by the imaginaries of those who frame it as such. It is, then, a tangible but also fluid site that can be entered and left, a site of possible risk, discomfort and violence. One of my former military interview respondents used the term to make reference to a space of life and death: '[i]n the paras [a military regiment] of course there is a saying, like – who aims better and shoots quicker will leave the field victorious'. Another referred to a 'training programme for Afghan soldiers who were going to be in the field', as in the space most proximal to direct violence, while another referred to a military exercise as a 'field mock' – something that could simulate the space of the field. The Afghanistan War Logs, archives of leaked documents hosted on WikiLeaks, reveal forty-three uses of the term 'field' in a randomly selected three-month period at the start of 2009. Salient terms (selected via an unsystematic review of the documents) include 'field questioning' to refer to questions asked while on patrol, for example the questioning of a farmer near Bibi Haagera village in the Alingar District who had discovered an IED[2] and 'Resident Field Squadron' to describe a military unit.[3]

The guidance document which explains how to read the war logs refers to 'field units who have been under fire or under other stressful conditions all day'. The spatial imaginary of the 'field' in military parlance, then, is as space marked by being physically closer to where fighting and violence might occur than other spaces are. The field spreads to the actors and activities within it, units become 'field units', questioning becomes 'field questioning'. Like the term 'battlefield', it perhaps indicates a terrain where battle takes place, and yet in Afghanistan 'field questioning' can take place on a farm, and violence is possible in everyday spaces not designated for war, so the 'field' is a strangely slippery spatial signifier. The farm in this context is evoked in the context of 'field questioning' because the farmer discovered an IED. This material object, signalling war, violence, threat and potential death, has the agential capacity to link up with particular spatial imaginaries and is implicated in turning a farm into the 'field'. So, in certain contexts, material objects produce the field or call a particular spatial imaginary of the field to action. An IED can arguably turn any space into 'the field', significant not simply as a word, but as a symbol of 'perceived space' and material practice.

The field is also a space of containment and distancing. Richmond et al. (2015) argue that:

> The field serves as a tool to create security and maintain the *status quo*. It becomes an entity in which danger can be contained, and in which conflict is seen to be located in a contained setting rather than affecting wider global networks of power.

Additionally, I suggest it draws military and peace work/humanitarian praxis together into an assemblage of spatial, material and discursive meaning intimately connected to violence-oriented governance. Of course, it is important to stress that I am not arguing that the use of the same word makes military and civilian practice the same, but rather that within the domain of the military–peace complex each is drawn into intertextual connection with the other through particular conceptual framings of the space and semiotic exchange of the field. Since this notion of bounded space signified by the 'field' via intertextual and interspatial linkages to cartographic practice, and the making mappable of empire (Manchanda 2017; Said 1979) is entwined with racialised knowledge-making around the territories and lifeworlds of a colonised Other, it is affectively stuck to modes of distancing and dominance. The field as a fluid material space is an example of what Bennett calls 'vivid entities' that are 'not entirely reducible to the contexts in which (human) subjects set them, never entirely exhausted by their semiotics' (2010: 5). Both the civilian actors of the liberal peace project and the soldiers from the military intervention into Afghanistan interact in the 'field' and imagine the field as a space where violence is more possible, Afghans are likely to be located, norms are different from those in other locations, and where one must be prepared, perform specific practices, engage in certain risk-oriented behaviours and be more proximal to the authenticity of whatever Afghanistan might be in the imaginary of the international project.

Alcohol, Restaurants, Social Gatherings

There were few chances to go off base, and when we did the places we visited were equally surreal. The Nato base at Kandahar airfield was particularly memorable. You could go for tango and belly dancing lessons or to a massage and nail studio run by Kyrgyz migrants. There was all-night American Idol-style karaoke, a Pizza Hut and Burger King. All this was designed to provide a sort of relief from more dangerous places just beyond the fortified walls, but instead it was both a drastic contrast to life at home and detached from the rest of Afghanistan . . .

Going to Kabul for meetings was like going to New York – suddenly there was a nightlife for foreigners, an abundance of alcohol, a variety of good restaurants and even some short shopping expeditions. Our Afghan colleagues witnessed this as a temporary western parallel world to their own and it was hard to shake the sense we weren't living most people's reality – we were heavily guarded even in the popular evening party spots that were considered safe and there was no link between the expat and Afghan lifestyles outside of work or business.

Extract from 'Secret Aid Worker', *The Guardian*, 31 May 2016

Another material object and related spatial domain I want to consider is alcohol and the spaces in which it is served – especially restaurants oriented towards internationals. Alcohol is a 'special form of embodied material culture' and has 'increasingly has come to be recognized as an important component of the political economy and as a commodity centrally implicated in strategies of colonialism and postcolonial economic and political struggles over state power' (Dietler 2006: 229). Distilling practices for example, were spread around the world by European colonialism. In anthropological traditions, alcohol holds meaning which reflects and transcends the experience, social norms or pathology of the individual, and

> drinking patterns are not viewed simply as reflections of social organization, manifestations of deep cognitive structure (in the structuralist mode), nor as simple expressions of cultural identity, but rather as practices through which personal and group identity are actively constructed, embodied, performed, and transformed. (Dietler 2006: 235)

Though usually devoid of nutritional value, alcohol is technically a food, and as such is a

> self-altering, dissipative materiality . . . It enters into what we become. It is one of the many agencies operative in the moods, cognitive dispositions, and moral sensibilities that we bring to bear as we engage the questions of what to eat [or drink], how to get it, and when to stop. (Bennett 2010: 51)

Alcohol has a capacity to influence human conduct; it interacts with bodily processes to create particular behavioural effects (see Bennett 2010). As a material substance with associated cultural and normative attachments, it also carries social and contextual weight. Though it is a vastly understudied substance in the literatures around conflict and statebuilding, I suggest that in the context of Afghanistan it highlights some key entanglements and themes. Firstly, it demonstrates the messy entanglements between bodies and material products in the military–peace complex; secondly, it shows how this entanglement manifests in ways that draw civilian and military dimensions of praxis into one spectrum of performative encounter with Afghanistan. Thirdly, it highlights the role of the material and its intra-actions with the international in producing modes of separation from the population of Afghanistan.

With this in mind it is worth recognising that though alcohol is effectively banned by the state for Afghans in Afghanistan it seemed relatively accessible for internationals (this changed for military personnel, as I highlight below). For example, a large government-linked organisation delivered specialised parcels to their 'field' staff a few times a month; these parcels contained food, alcohol and other items requested. Substances like alcohol arguably distinguished internationals from the majority of the Afghan population (though not necessarily from the elite or all sections of society). Alcohol in particular seemed to have both a kind of 'vitality' in Afghanistan in terms of a capacity to distinguish between spaces and a kind of symbolism (Bennett 2010).

For instance, the following examples are arguably indicative. Fluri, who conducted field research in Kabul, writes that: '[i]nternational restaurants that serve alcohol post signs that read either "Foreign Passports Only" or "We regret we cannot serve alcohol to Afghan Nationals"' (Fluri 2009a: 991). She suggests that even when Afghans are theoretically allowed in these establishments, the high prices prohibit access for much of the population. Alcohol-serving space is also disaggregating space, setting some bodies apart from others in this context. When upon entering Kabul airport my bags were searched and the bottles of alcohol I had brought with me as gifts were found, an urgent, tense moment with security personnel ensued, where they immediately sought to verify my nationality. On being reassured that I was an international and permitted to bring alcohol into the country on that basis, the tension subsided. Tim Mcgirk (2010), writing for *Time* magazine and discussing a number of restaurants in Kabul writes: 'The trouble with most of these places is that, because they serve liquor, which is illegal, the armed Afghan guards at the gate won't allow the patrons' Afghan compatriots to come inside, since good Muslims aren't supposed to drink.'

In addition to this disaggregating element, Smirl (2015: 32, 90) writes that alcohol functions as a core component of humanitarian experience, perhaps as a coping mechanism for some. Health-focused studies have identified high alcohol consumption amongst aid workers and military veterans as population categories (see Jachens et al. 2016). Interestingly, female aid workers were found to be particularly susceptible to the use of alcohol as a mechanism for dealing with stress (Jachens et al. 2016). Though not the focus here, this potentially indicates additional stress levels associated with gendered identities in humanitarian work. Moreover, alcohol is also regularly linked to military experience too, and most especially to the experience of military-related psychological trauma (Bulmer and Eichler 2017: 168; Kelsall et al. 2015). Thus, in addition to disaggregating bodies in Afghanistan, modes of alcohol consumption potentially help to mark out some bodies as having participated in an encounter with war-making.

I am not suggesting that individual internationals in Afghanistan do anything wrong by consuming alcohol, and I should note here that I drank alcohol while I was there too (so, again, I am not apart from the argument I am making). However, in the context of Afghanistan, it seems important to recognise that consumption of alcohol is also layered over and interacts with the politics of cultural praxis and feeds into the military–peace complex in particular ways. Largely, as stated, alcohol consumption is illegal for Afghans. Internationals, on the other hand, especially in the years during which security practices were less rigid, were marked as a population of excess (again, this signals collectives rather than individuals), which contributes to a culture of separation as well as feeding into a wider, politically salient conceptual binary between conservative Islam and the liberal West.

Writing in 2010, one journalist and medical doctor who worked in Afghanistan sardonically described the centrality of alcohol to modes of distancing from the population:

> Kabul has finally left the dark ages and now offers expat bars for journalists and diplomats alike, where alcohol serves as the lubricant for self-congratulatory war stories and chest-beating. And how convenient: you don't have to deal with any pesky local Afghans either. With the exception of Afghanistan's upper echelon, Afghans aren't allowed in. Under Afghan law, the sale of alcohol to Muslims is prohibited. (Jilani 2010)

She goes on to say:

> It doesn't get more colonialist than invading a country, setting up shop, selling a prohibited, culturally and religiously forbidden product like alcohol, and throwing centuries of tradition out the window. But of course there is a good reason. For who can go without a beer for six weeks anyway?

The use of alcohol fits with the idea of a space of exception (Autesserre 2014; Fluri 2009a; Smirl 2015: 90) whereby the international as a social category was constructed against or in relation to the local. Fluri (2009: 992) cites one of her interview respondents as saying the following, illustrating lifestyle dynamics that signal this idea of a space of exception among peacebuilders in Afghanistan:

> You know what we say here? 'What happens in Kabul, stays in Kabul.' You can drink, smoke, do drugs and of course sleep around. Stuff that you wouldn't do at home, it's okay here because the [international] community here is always on their way elsewhere.

Journalist Matthieu Aikins (2014), writing in *Rolling Stone*, also paints a very particular picture of expatriate social life in Kabul at a certain point:

> Every Thursday night – Friday is the traditional day of rest in the Muslim world – there would be a slew of parties hosted by the NGOs and embassies that served free booze and went very late, the most desirable – the ones with all the pretty interns and A-listers – always the subject of frantic guest-list negotiations.

The following report in *The New York Times* (Ahmed and Rossenburg 2014) conveys a similar narrative as well: 'foreigners have enjoyed relatively unrestricted activity in the capital, including access to a handful of Western-style restaurants and weekly parties brimming with music and alcohol. Though attacks were common enough, they rarely targeted Western civilians'.

I suggest that this 'booze' and brimming alcohol meant something, that it captured a sense of alternative space, outside of the domain of Afghanistan while still being in the country, evoking fun, normality, transience and a kind of abandon. This affective link to alcohol draws military and civilian actors into one assemblage bound up with the category of the international. Alcohol and related objects of enjoyment or release and the perception and social norms surrounding those things produced a space that, at its height, included all foreign persons who wished to be a part of it, civilian and military.

As the *New York Times* article goes on to report:

> [T]roops based at Bagram Air Base north of Kabul, for instance, used to drive to the city for a break from military life. As recently as 2010, top generals with the NATO-led coalition would sometimes swap their uniforms for khakis and button-down shirts and head to dinner at restaurants in Kabul. (Ahmed and Rossenburg 2014).

On the military side counterinsurgency praxis included a recognition that alcohol and certain restaurants played a role in perceptions of remoteness from the Afghan population. Hastings (2010) writes that when charged with shifting the war towards a counterinsurgency mandate, 'McChrystal *banned alcohol on base*, kicked out Burger King and other symbols of American excess' (emphasis added). Alcohol as a material product symbolised excess in this context (McChrystal believed) and excess separated the troops out and gave off a particular impression of remoteness and elitism. In his memoir, McChrystal (2013: 295) writes about the importance of alcohol within the wider spatial framework of the war. He articulates how seeing a landscaped garden within the ISAF compound 'seemed blatantly inappropriate given the austere and dangerous conditions our troops faced only a few miles away. *So too did the fourteen bars inside the compound that served alcohol*'. He goes on to articulate that 'given my intent to reenergize and refocus our war coalition, the garden and bars were relevant pieces of terrain'.

Private security actors – martial bodies, not exactly military not exactly civilian, that facilitate the weaving of civilian and military together – also had an interesting reputational relationship with alcohol in Afghanistan, as demonstrated by the Kabul hazing scandal.[4] This was the revelation that ArmorGroup guards, private security employed to secure the US embassy in Kabul, were engaged in hazing and other practices deemed inappropriate and problematic, especially in a war-affected environment (Higate 2012b). An organisation called Project on Government Oversight wrote a letter (Brian 2009) to then Secretary of State Hillary Clinton which included a reference to images of the contractors and noted that the PMSCs had committed 'countless infractions involving alcohol'. In the context of this consumption of alcohol, the letter also points very explicitly to concerns about potentially racially loaded and inappropriate engagements between foreign guards and Afghan nationals. In one section it states:

There is also evidence that members of the guard force and their supervisors have drawn Afghan nationals into behaviour forbidden for Muslims. For example, photographs show guards posing with Afghan nationals at the U.S. facility at Camp Sullivan as both the guards and nationals consume alcoholic beverages in scenes that suggest drunkenness, and one photo shows a near-naked U.S. guard who appears to have urinated on himself and splashed an Afghan national. Afghanistan is a conservative Muslim country where alcohol consumption and public nudity are considered offensive and, in some instances, prohibited by law.

Higate (2012: 456) writes that 'drinking vodka from "butt cracks"' formed part of the homoerotic and carnivalesque praxis the PMSCs were pictured engaging in. He points to the role that alcohol played in shaping the complex power dynamics of the norm-bound 'fratriarchial' rituals captured by the images of the PMSCs: 'infused by the celebration of an unfettered, western authentic manhood and lubricated by alcohol, it could be that these ritualised activities were used – quite literally – to lay bare the emasculated and marginal status of racialised men's gender orders' (2012: 459).

What can be seen here is that the complex social value of alcohol is infused with modes of disaggregation and hierarchy in the context of Afghanistan, even as it, as a substance, enters an agential dance with human will and intention. Alcohol participates in the material politics of the military–peace complex, capturing a performativity that transcends the discursive.

Restaurants as both spatial and material sites play a role in the military–peace complex in Afghanistan. Paying attention to the assemblages around and material/affective significance of restaurants oriented towards internationals, and operational at various points since 2001, can elucidate interesting stories. For example, one restaurant called Gandamack Lodge in Kabul (shut down in 2014 by Afghan police due to safety concerns (Nordland 2014)) took its name from what Mcgirk (2010) in *Time* magazine calls 'a hilltop where Afghans massacred retreating British soldiers in 1842'. It was opened by a former BBC journalist who had travelled with Mujahideen fighters en route to battle the Soviets in the 1980s and is described by Mcgirk as a 'military buff'. The article notes that the Lodge is 'decorated with 19th century maps and prints as well as rows of antique muskets'. It claims that '[t]he grub is decent, but you're really paying for its British Raj ambience'. Along these lines one reviewer of the Lodge on TripAdvisor ('Gandamack Lodge' 2014) states that it constitutes a 'very "British colonial" experience'.

Many material and spatial signifiers are scattered across even this minimal account. There is the hilltop evoked by the name of the premises upon which a massacre (of British forces) took place, a large-scale act of killing that is bound to the colonial practices of war and governance. Gandamak, according to historian William Dalrymple (2013), was 'the site of the British last stand' at the end of the First Anglo-Afghan War. As articulated in Chapter 1, this war was essentially an invasion by the British in service of their wider geopolitical interests in the region. At the battlespace in question, the hilltop at Gandamak signals a history of violence, misguided intervention, sacrifice, the intense defence of Afghanistan from outside invaders. There is also something about the idea of a 'last stand' that glorifies British militarism. Moreover, as outlined by historian Jonathan Lee, depictions of this very battle were at the heart of a rehabilitation of the First Anglo-Afghan War, a process of national forgetting (of the true circumstances and motivations) and a glorification of sacrifice in service of imperial power as well as a valiant quest to bring an 'ungrateful' people (Afghans) into the civilising light (Lee 2018: 304–5). As well as evoking this history (probably humorously), and the idea of the unsuccessful 'last stand', the Gandamack Lodge also seems to have reified the material and affective signals of British colonial practices and other practices of violence – the maps, the muskets and the Raj-evoking 'ambience'.

This space, with its particular material and discursive signifiers and affective colonial stickiness (see Ahmed 2015), drew civilian internationals like journalists, private security contractors and the military – past and present – into its orbit of meaning. A journalist who blogged about staying at the Lodge in 2004 highlighted the proximity of violences of different kinds and the entanglements between alcohol consumption and war experience. He writes:

> On my first night there, the Taliban blew up a school just down the street and the explosion woke me up. After that, I slept fitfully for the rest of the night, and was anxious to get breakfast and meet some of the guys who I had heard drinking and partying well into the night. It turned out that they were two British ex-SIS guys (Secret Intelligence Service) and a retired Navy Seal from Iowa. They were all doing private security in Kabul. (Grobl 2009)

These intersecting modes of engagement, the violences of war, the relationship between state military experience and private security, the consumption of alcohol which I have suggested could often delineate foreign bodies as set apart from Afghan ones, the spatial and material practices that evoke imperialism while also participating in the contemporary separating out of international, heavily securitised sites as well as the drawing together of different modes of civilian and military encounter, all help to constitute a distinctive military–peace complex.

There were, as I have outlined, changes within international approaches over time, and increased moves towards the securitisation of international-oriented space. It was common for those internationals I spoke with in 2014 to suggest that their lifestyles had changed over the years, and that the situation in Kabul was currently the least conducive to 'normal' social engagement it had been in recent post-intervention times. One event that seemed to mark the transition in a lot of people's minds was the Taliban attack on the La Taverna restaurant (Aikins 2014). Since many internationals had been killed in this attack in early 2014, it held a particular significance for many individuals and organisations and heralded a transition to greater levels of anxiety and increased security measures. One international respondent stated, 'the attack on Taverna in Jan 2014. That is the watershed, that changed everything after that'. I myself remember the feeling of witnessing something momentous and sad as I drove past it in May 2014, when by that point it was a bombed-out site. The attack also had a big impact on businesses that catered to internationals, and many in the popular Wazir Akbar area had been closed (at least temporarily) due to their inability to provide security for their expatriate clients according to the newly rigorous standards.

One of my interview respondents, Mina, an Afghan-Canadian, told me in 2017 that the Taliban's increased targeting of public, ostensibly civilian spaces like restaurants as the war wore on impacted Afghans and internationals alike: 'it is everyone's security that is being affected, like Afghan families and internationals and kind of everybody avoids restaurants now when they can. None of them are doing well'. In general, then as now, Afghans were more likely to be targeted, injured, killed and impacted by violence in Afghanistan but the markedly increased targeting of spaces associated with the international, such as restaurants and hotels, provoked heightened caution and additional layers of security routines for international personnel. One civilian respondent described this kind of security process to me as follows:

A friend of mind was working for [names organisation] and when we met it was basically not a kind of normal hey let's meet at L'Atmosphere [a rooftop bar with a pool] or something like that, it was really that she had to ask her security if she could, if the restaurant was cleared for this specific evening and when she came, she kind of had a lot of security personnel around her. You would think this was for a diplomat, but she was just a normal project manager.

The journalist Matthieu Aikins, writing in *Rolling Stone*, outlines how the restaurant scene and business success were linked to security practices and conceptualisations of risk and allowable behaviours:

> [B]ecause it [a particular restaurant] was in the heavily guarded Wazir Akbar Khan neighbourhood, it usually kept its place on the constantly changing 'green' lists of sites that those who worked for embassies and NGOs were allowed to visit. And that meant business, especially on a Friday night. (Aikins 2014)

He states: '[r]estaurants like this, along with private homes and guest-houses, comprised the hidden archipelago of expatriate social life in the capital' (Aikins 2014), and also touches on the racial and risk management profiling which took place upon entry to these spaces, designed to attract a primarily expatriate clientele: '[t]he door would swing open and you'd be admitted into the vestibule for a body and bag search; if you were a young Afghan male – or looked and spoke like one, like I do – you might face some questions about your business there' (Aikins 2014). Linking to the previous chapter of this book and the idea of security logics, the modes of security that circulate around restaurants as material spaces rely on particular conceptions of Afghans as Other and a possible risk.

There is also an aspect of economic governance at work in these architectural designs, specifically in the relationship between the constraints imposed on international life, especially as attacks became more common, and the mechanisms restaurants and businesses have to put in place to be designated secure and safe for foreigners (Autesserre 2014; Aikins 2014; Duffield 2010). The limited number of 'safe' locations limited the daily lives and freedoms of personnel, and the institutionally defined and template-based parameters of what constituted a safe location affected the urban landscape and business model in Kabul, feeding into the very structure of the city. Aikins illustrates this dynamic when discussing restaurants in Kabul and the relationship between being found on the 'green list' – marked as safe for internationals – and having a viable business (Aikins 2014).

In Kabul, parties and ex-pat focused bars, hotels and restaurants arguably functioned 'as "spatial escapes" from Afghan culture, particularly for women who are bound by greater restrictions regarding their mobility, dress, and behavioral expectations' (Fluri 2009a: 992). These spaces were thus infused with gendered and racialised assumptions and expectations. As material practices, though understandable and seemingly innocent of politics, they also helped to foster a liberal space of exception, in which certain bodies (internationals) and objects were commonplace and welcome, and Others (arguably many Afghans) would be out of place, even threatening. These parameters certainly do not apply to everyone, but they signal modes of performance and ritual that help to delineate the bounds of the 'international' and the 'local' as social categories within the military–peace complex.

Based on the spatial theorising outlined above, the First Space (tangible, mappable) is Afghanistan, the Second Space (imaginary) is the liberal domain in which the restrictions of a socially conservative conflict-affected context do not apply. The Third Space, then (a combination of the two), is the liberal haven, the 'spatial escape' hybridised by context but still liminal, exceptional and separated out (Smirl 2009). The prevalence of spatial escapes marked by the availability of certain material products – such as alcohol – contributes to a distancing of internationals from much of the host populations and points to a kind of elitism (Fluri 2009a). Again, it is easy to recognise that these small comforts might be desirable; I am not critiquing people for their individual choices here and must acknowledge enormous variety within international lifestyles in Afghanistan.

Analytically speaking, however, it is worth recognising that, seen collectively, these distinctions had various implications including artificially inflated rents and prices of goods, the generation of resentment among the less well-off majority Afghan population and potentially an inability among internationals to relate properly to many Afghans (Autesserre 2014: l. 4160; Fluri 2009a), all of which have negative effects on peace promotion. On the other hand, escapism points to the consequences of fear-reification and compound-living. As Matthieu Aikins notes of international weekend life: '[e]scapism was the objective, with people cooped up all week in their compounds now blowing off steam' (Aikins 2014). Arguably, the constant affective sensation of risk and potential violence, real experiences and accounts intersecting with the dominance of a logic of security, could lead to a surplus of anxiety, which might then be channelled into social outlets for some people (Autesserre 2014; Duffield 2010; Fluri 2009a).

Ostensibly ordinary and undernoticed aspects of daily life in Afghanistan for internationals take on an added geopolitical and economic significance, given elements such as massive wage differentials and the manner in which these everyday elements take place and rely upon modes of risk management and security governance (Autesserre 2014: l. 5837; Duffield 2012; Goetze 2016). Materially oriented security performances which mark out particular spaces as international spaces, such as guards outside restaurants, international residences or compounds, take place within a domain of exception. These are part of a liberal peacebuilder spatial practice which is coded and infused with gendered and racialised hierarchies (Fluri 2009a: 987). I unpacked some of the gendered and security logics of these spaces in the previous chapter and I continue to consider these practices by moving to discuss the spatial and material signifiers of compounds, checkpoints and vehicles below.

Compounds, Checkpoints and Vehicles
Compounds
Afghanistan's humanitarian space presented in 2014 largely (though not exclusively) an example of what Duffield calls 'bunkerisation'. The concept of bunkerisation highlights the importance of the physical

Figure 3.3 International organisation compound. Author photograph.

structures that represent and contain foreign presence in peacebuilding interventions, evaluating their symbolic and tangible implications
(Duffield 2010). The concept refers to the buildings in which many
international workers (and often local elites (Autesserre 2014: l. 5899))
work and live, noting that they are frequently designed like fortresses,
built in preparation for attack and to ward off 'enemy' activity.

The buildings that housed international organisations, especially
the UN, as well as restaurants and homes, exemplified various levels
of fortress design. On one occasion, I visited a prominent UN compound at the invitation of a senior employee and the sensation I felt was
one of heightened anxiety, suspicion and nervousness. The following
extract from my notes illustrates the level of security present in this
context:

> The compound was a fortress, armed guards everywhere, set back from the
> road, sniper towers, concrete blocks for stopping cars all along the approach,
> razor wire of course. They took my passport, scanned my person and my
> bag, issued me with an ID card, and finally, when N picked me up, let me in.
> (Author notes, 18 May 2014)

Conflict architecture was ubiquitous. As recorded in my notes, at this
particular compound, there were concrete barricades designed to stop
moving vehicles, high, looming watchtowers looking over the yard
which one needed to walk through between the external and the internal entrance to the compound, razor wire on the walls, which were
made of thick, blast-resistant concrete, and many unsmiling men with
large guns in a state of relative alert. Your possessions are searched
and scanned, and your passport is taken from you before you can pass
through the final metal detector and enter the building proper. It is hard
to imagine how intimidating and alienating these fortresses must be
if encountered on a daily basis as part of your city's landscape (Aikins
2014; Fluri 2009a).

Since the start of this research I have been curious about the relationship between the security architecture (material, human and mental) in
Afghanistan and the threats it protects against. On one hand, there are
examples of lives being saved by safe rooms and private security as well
as constant examples of violence against humanitarian actors. On the
other hand, the relationship is arguably not clear cut. For instance, one
respondent, Lisa, illustrated the complex structure–agent relationship
between peacebuilder bodies and behaviour and the violence-oriented
environment in which they operate:

> [T]he securitization of space matters so much, I don't know that I'm nearly as unsafe as I feel, I used to walk a lot, when I first came I walked all the time, I don't know that my decision to not walk is really based on anything rational or on the fact that nobody else that I know walks, everywhere you go there is razor-wire. I really think that the psychology of conflict architecture, of having blast-walls everywhere, police checkpoints every twenty feet, guys with AK47s everywhere makes you feel deeply unsafe, if you were in a safe place why would it look like it does? (Lisa, American NGO worker)

The extent of this bunkerisation in Afghanistan fluctuated over time and shifted in response to violent attacks, as I have outlined above. As one civilian international respondent told me, 'especially after 2009 and the attack on the UN guesthouse, the rules became a lot stricter, for UN personnel and for NGOs'. Organisations varied, and individuals could seek out work and lifestyles that were less restrictive – some of my respondents explicitly avoided adhering to strict security routines. One respondent described her approach like this:

> I really think this going there, it probably depends on the kind of person you are and again, I wanted to experience and see Afghanistan. If you want to do that, you need to put the idea that you can be in an explosion in a minute, you have to put that really very much out of your head. Otherwise you are just staying in [names organisation] HQ and never move. And of course you can do that, it is perfectly fine. It is just that it is not what I wanted to do.

This respondent seemed to be more in the minority (though her approach was not exceptional). For many internationals, compound living in Afghanistan was likely.

Duffield argues that fortified aid compounds create visceral binaries between the foreign interveners and the host population whereby the razor wire, watchtowers and fortress design imposes inequality and insecurity upon the landscape (Duffield 2010) perpetuating Us/Them dynamics between protected and threatening persons (Fluri 2011b). Smirl (2015: l. 143) writes about how 'the highly guarded humanitarian compound has drawn upon colonial architecture to maintain hierarchical spatial divisions between the aid workers and local residents'.

These architectural designs have thus arguably created modes of remoteness and distance. As Richmond et al. suggest:

> [t]his growing security practice of cloistering offices in walled compounds with armed checkpoints, using armoured cars and armed guards for transfor-

mation and protection, is used to impose a material and immaterial border and to increase distance between the international and the local. (2015: 10)

Smirl (2015: l. 150) argues that this mode of encounter which is spatially bounded has policy implications since the exposure of high-level individuals to the context that they are devising policy for can be highly constrained: 'policy made at headquarters is therefore also spatially constrained by an overly narrow understanding of the place that is being assisted'. In one example, I was told that the lead gender advisor in Afghanistan for a large donor entity, responsible for highly influential policy and funding designations impacting Afghan women in particular, had never been outside her organisation compound.

Compounds are common to both military and civilian praxis and the martial, war-like nature of the compound space signals militancy even in ostensibly civilian contexts. They also signal spatial histories and affective connections that feed into and help to shape the overarching framework of the military–peace complex. Speaking about military space and the changing geographies of the military compound, one of my former military respondents, James, told me:

> [T]he investment that was going into the base increased incrementally but noticeably the longer the troops were there, of course, and so what happened was within the base you would have had the build-up of internet facilities and then the changing of geographies into, you know, tents, and then a gym put in and so . . . but in terms of the space and the people, it's *a fort*. (James, former British Army, emphasis added)

He articulated that 'locals' had 'controlled access in and out' and went on to explain more about the space:

> [A]ll you have to do is think of a *crusaders' fort* really, like it even had the tower in the middle, just randomly, the way the compound had been built, it was actually an old Afghan narco lord's compound. It was very interesting, like you're doing your briefing, like your operations briefing room was an old harem, you know, so it had all the mirrors. And that's actually, you know the outhouse where I was, where they kept all the donkeys was actually where they kept their wives slash slaves or whatever, you know. (James, former British Army, emphasis added)

This highlights again the way that the built landscape in Afghanistan functions like what photographer Simon Norfolk (n.d.) has called a chronotope, with layers of previous architectural imaginaries haunting the present moment. Spatial and material sites are thus layered over each other, and over histories and ideas of violence that seem, in a ghostly way, to repeat.

Just as with the civilian compounds, there is a sense of remoteness associated with military compounds, though arguably this kind of securitisation is fully expected in a military context. James stated: 'you're separated from the population in terms of your location and your daily business but then you venture out', while another military respondent explained:

> I was completely isolated from the local population, and when I went out of the base I would either go by helicopter or I would go in an armoured vehicle and except on the very occasional times when I would go on patrol with someone else, I would just be holed up in another camp. (Frank, British Army)

James explained how, in some cases, spatial separation was maintained when soldiers left the base, since they might go out in giant armoured vehicles. James argued that these huge, visually intimidating vehicles were too heavy and clumsy for the landscape and that they were counterproductive for any population engagement strategy: 'you're meant to be getting out and amongst, winning the people, and how can you do that in that vehicle' (James, former British Army). Fundamentally, Frank suggested, 'you're cut off from the reality of what is happening in a village day to day' (Frank, British Army).

In the military context, however, there were also frequent ventures 'beyond the wire' for some soldiers, on patrol and time spent in small bases that were less remote and protected. This spatial conception more proximal to the 'field' was linked to danger, excitement and masculinity. Ben, for instance, noted that getting out of the safety of the big bases, going on missions, being stationed closer to danger 'beyond the wire' and experiencing that danger were all linked to proving one's masculinity in the minds of soldiers:

> The only reason that I came down to a FOB was to be in the heat of it, that's the truth of it. I met grown men who cried because they would go out on a mission time after time and never got shot at. (Ben, former US Air Force)

Ben explained that it was deeply disappointing for many soldiers to be stationed in the spatial safety of Bagram Air Base because it did not allow them to get in the thick of it and experience real war:

[B]eing at Bagram is like a nightmare for most guys in my career field, you don't do the job, you're not out there, in the troops in contact, you know, calling in the airstrikes, you're sitting at a desk em, watching everybody else have fun, kind of thing. And so Bagram is like the nightmare for a lot of guys. (Ben, former US Air Force)

For Ben, the very rationale of soldiering was violence and killing, rather than COIN or development praxis and this killing had a spatial logic: '[a]ll of us are trained to kill, as corny as that sounds, that's the only reason that we're out there' (Ben, former US Air Force).

This illustrates some of the ways that '[t]he distance-intimacy axis orders the . . . experience of killing' (Daggett 2015: 365). Moreover, it highlights the fact that

proximity to killing appears to be a powerful indicator of gender status, such that those who kill are elevated above those who do not, and those who kill at the closest range often achieve the most secure, and hegemonic, militarised masculinity. (Daggett 2015: 365)

For James the Afghan landscape itself was key to life and death and deeply entwined with his understanding of the Taliban as an enemy force:

So where there is IED laid by the Taliban, what they wanted to do usually was mark it, so that the locals didn't get blown up and so there became this little hidden language on the landscape, which you needed to be able to read, which was there to warn the locals about the IEDs, and so it could be scratches on a wall, the most obvious was like a small pile of stones, or we had one which saved us, which was like a plastic bag . . . it looked like it was caught in a tree, but it had been tied, you know, plastic bag in the tree just to say . . . these signs the Taliban were leaving for the locals and if you could read them, if you could see stuff, you'd be like there's an IED there, look, the sign. So it became something that was etched onto the landscape, this kind of secret landscape.

In his account, the 'dance of human and inhuman agency' (Bennett 2010: 31; Grove 2016: 348) is paramount and a matter of life and death, and this material understanding of battle spaces recognises them as being 'composed of "vibrant matter" . . . often also deadly matter' (Bennett 2010; Gregory 2016: 5).

Taken together it is possible to read a complex spatial imaginary within the military lifeworld in Afghanistan whereby the Afghan landscape is both alluring and dangerous, where much of the everyday life of the military for some may in fact exist at a remove from this landscape in spaces marked by greater levels of protection and security, while for others everyday encounters with the landscape are bound up with risk and the banal vitality of deadly matter. As a whole the Afghan landscape is orientalised as always already a space of violence and enmity in both the civilian and the military spatial imaginaries. At the same time echoes and hauntings of old invasions, incursions, dominations and brutalities layer through the landscape and conjure up the ghosts of a 'crusaders' fort', an imperial cantonment, discarded weapons or old blood stains.

Checkpoints

I discuss checkpoints and vehicles side by side because I am also interested in their interaction, notably the anxiety surrounding vehicles at checkpoints and their different objectives as material elements – vehicles explicitly seek to enable mobility, while checkpoints reduce it. Vehicles and checkpoints function as spaces and objects of transition. Vehicles carry bodies between sites, checkpoints function as small-scale militarised zones that serve to enhance the overall security sense of various spaces. In Afghanistan they are run by Afghan security forces and/or foreign ones and have also been set up by the Taliban. Checkpoints are dangerous places; Thomas Gregory, looking at the killing of civilians by US forces checkpoints, notes '388 deaths and injuries between 2008 and 2010' in Afghanistan (Gregory 2019: 132; ISAF 2011). Looking at news reports and the WikiLeaks Afghan War Logs,[5] it is also clear that checkpoints are targets for violence such as Taliban attacks.

Gregory (2019: 132) argues that when a tense situation emerges at a checkpoint and soldiers are faced with 'incredibly frenetic and confusing situations' they 'often rely on gut feelings and muscle memory when determining whether someone is a threat'. He further argues that 'these instincts are not neutral but are shaped by their pre-deployment training, their past encounters with civilians and their perception of the local population'. Checkpoints function as liminal spatial sites – people transition through them – and can be understood as border spaces on a micro scale (Basham and Vaughan-Williams 2013). As examples of materially constituted bordering practices they are marked by hierarchies of value and threat attributed to different bodies, and are impacted by particular affective atmospheres of tension and enmity.

One interesting comment from one of my civilian interviewees illustrates the privileged spatial practice of foreign bodies over Afghan ones in relation to security at checkpoints: 'sometimes people think I'm

Afghan, when I'm dressed in a particular way, especially when I'm not wearing my glasses, and I get harassed at checkpoints a lot and as soon as they discover that I'm a foreigner, that's, that's fine' (Kate, Australian research consultant).

This small example points to the wider mobility of international bodies, which can pass through militarised and securitised spaces with greater ease, since Afghanistan's security environment is built on racialised notions of threat. I only experienced a checkpoint once myself, and so have little right to comment on the experience from my own perspective, but the uneventful character of my experience supports the idea that international bodies might often pass smoothly though these spaces. I was in rural Afghanistan, in Bamiyan Province, on route to Band-e-Amir National Park with some friends – another international person and two Afghans, all NGO workers – as well as a young Afghan man driving the car who had been hired by the Afghan NGO that the trip to Bamiyan was on behalf of. On a rural road we were stopped by Afghan security personnel. They appeared to ask to take a look at us, and then, once the windows had been wound down and they had had a chat to the driver, we were waved on.

Ideas of racialised risk perception are not limited to ease of mobility but can feed into matters of life and death. An incident report from December 2009, available via the Afghanistan War Logs on WikiLeaks, describes the proximity of death at checkpoints, indicating the level of tension and the possibility of lethal action in this space.[6] Though the account is matter of fact and lacking any indication of emotion or stress, the rapid escalation depicted makes it easy to imagine the strain, fear and violence of this scenario.

> A car approached the checkpoint, was halted and the occupants (two males) were ordered out of the vehicle. The occupant on the passenger side reluctantly exited but then ran off toward the rear of the vehicle. Soldiers from the combined unit fired warning shots.
>
> The passenger continued to run and the driver made a threatening move. The ATF[7] element then engaged both males with lethal shots. One of the individuals was killed, the other seriously wounded and evacuated to Bastion treatment facility.
>
> The unit searched the vehicle and found 50kg of wet opium in the trunk.

The checkpoint here acts as a material impediment to potential and perceived enemies, and a site of spatial encounter between Afghans flagged as possible risks and coalition military forces. The space of the checkpoint itself arguably exercises a kind of agency or has its own vitality, since the material construction of a checkpoint shapes and delineates the behaviours of those who encounter it and who are located at it. In the scenario above, it seems likely that the erratic behaviour of the individuals in the car was a result of being stopped and fearing the discovery of their opium. The decision of the military forces involved to fire warning and then lethal shots is bound up with the fact that they are at a checkpoint, and thus the behaviour of the people in the car takes on a particularly threatening and highly risk-oriented frame. The material construction of the checkpoint itself is thus the locus of affective and practical signals of security performance and reaction that can result in death for someone who, in a different space, might not have been killed.

Vehicles
Vehicles play different roles in liberal peace and conflict-affected sites like Afghanistan. White UN vehicles with their blue logo offer the symbol of the international brand. Armoured vehicles and cars with drivers likely indicate the security and remove of internationals or

Figure 3.4 Vehicle in Kabul. Author photograph.

Figure 3.5 UN-marked helicopter. Author photograph.

national elites. Heavily weaponised vehicles signal the hypervigilant security climate of Afghan space. Yet, equally, as Mac Ginty (2017: 856) points out, 'the 4×4 is not simply a vehicle (pun intended) of intervention. It is also an object of resistance, mimicry, production, consumption, and war-making'. For me, taking taxis in Kabul, which I did a few times, was a way to avoid awkwardly burdening others (people would give me lifts in organisation cars sometimes), and, in certain instances, dictated by my language limitations, it offered the opportunity for an interesting conversation with the taxi driver about life in Kabul. In a different vein, Billaud (2015: 153) recounts her experience of being attacked in a taxi and needing to exit the moving car to escape. For one of my civilian respondents, driving a motorbike, especially as a woman, signalled the increased sense of freedom and personal strength she related feeling in Afghanistan. So, vehicles certainly carry different sets of meaning in Afghanistan as elsewhere. However, two dominant implications of vehicles as material signifiers include standing in for and augmenting the meaning of international space, and, in the case of Afghan vehicles, indicating unknowability and threat heighted by mobility.

In regard to the first implication, a female Afghan spokesperson for UNAMA told me she could go without a headscarf when she was inside a UN vehicle since she was linked to the power and symbolism of international status when she travelled that way. Yet if she did the same on the street, she would face condemnation, aggression and bodily insecurity (Author notes, 18 May 2014). This signals the idea that the space of a vehicle marked as international is almost international space – a socially exceptional domain of praxis – and is associated with high status. Of course, as Mac Ginty (2017: 874) points out:

> in order for a government, UN, INGO or rebel 4×4 to operate on a dirt road in Darfur [or Afghanistan] there needs to be set of economies and enabling conditions in place, many of which are far removed from the physicality of the object

and thus the vehicle itself is only one component in a chain of simultaneously highly globalised and localised meaning.

This notion of international space marked by the material signifier of the vehicle is not exclusive to Afghanistan. Smirl articulates how, in humanitarian aid memoirs discussing multiple 'post-crisis' sites, '[t]he space of the SUV or iconic Land Rover is prominent . . . There is a feeling of impenetrability within the vehicle, and of being above the land through which they travel'. Moreover, in late 2019 an attack took place on a UN vehicle in Kabul, killing one UN staffer. In their public statement, the UN noted that the attack targeted a 'UN-marked vehicle'. I suggest that this is especially significant since the branding of the UN is closely bound up with the signalling of mobile international space and an attempt to secure that space via branding. The attack on a branded vehicle (such as that depicted in Figure 3.4) is thus an attack on UN and international presence in Afghanistan as a whole and indicates a crisis of exceptionalism for internationally marked spaces.

The second dimension was highlighted in the discussion of checkpoints above. A former military respondent articulated to me how vehicles at checkpoints could bring civilian lives and military 'feelings' together with disastrous consequences:

> [I]n Kundus we had experience that a civilian car at nighttime came under fire at a German checkpoint, because the German soldiers were very nervous because the day before in a suicide attack two German soldiers had died. Of course, the soldiers who were standing on guard by this time were more nervous, more concerned and a car was very quickly approaching them and they are not reacting to all their signals to slow down at nighttime and one guy then opened fire. That was because he was very nervous.

This story illustrates 'dangerous feelings' (Gregory 2019) and highlights the sense of unknowability and threat that can circulate around vehicles as objects. While checkpoints can be targets for attack, they are also spaces where violence is constantly pre-empted. Gregory (2019: 132) cites General McChrystal stating in 2010 'in the nine-plus months I've been here, not a single case where we have engaged in an escalation of force incident and hurt someone has it turned out that the vehicle had a suicide bomb or weapons in it'. The emphasis my respondent puts on the nervousness of the soldiers is significant. It highlights the emotional and affective sentiments generated by the car, which at this point is a material object approaching without a clear and known human entity in control (of course there is a driver, but they and their intentions are unknowable).

Another incident relayed via the public release of military reports and by the American Civil Liberties Union (ACLU) highlights something significant about the material entity of the vehicle in Afghanistan. The incident happened in 2006 in Kabul, and the *Los Angeles Times* reported that it began when 'a U.S. convoy apparently rammed into a traffic jam' (Zaman 2006). Three people were killed in this initial collision. According to the ACLU report, 'a US Forces HEMMT vehicle lost control and crashed into several cars'.[8] The *Los Angeles Times* report continued: 'Witnesses said Afghans began throwing stones at the U.S. vehicles, and the troops responded by opening fire to disperse the crowd. When the convoy reached Kabul, it was met by more demonstrators and gunfire erupted again' (Zaman 2006).

The ACLU database details the deaths of civilians, including a 13-year-old boy, as a result of this incident, and the decision of the Americans (and Afghan personnel) to fire into the crowd.[9] Two things are worth noting: the first is the sense of vehicle agency conveyed in the ACLU-released incident reports. The vehicle, in this account, was outside the control of the driver, crashing almost of its own accord. This hints at the unruly capacity of the vehicle as an artefact, especially in sites of political tension. The second is that for the members of the public throwing stones, these US vehicles must surely have had a wider symbolism. It is notable that in the Palestinian context the act of stone throwing is a means of resisting Israeli and military authority often used by children targeting vehicles. The apparent futility of this act carries political capital as a form of self-actualisation through the performance of resistance in the face of military power (see Habashi 2013; Macfarlane 2018). Though this meaning may or may not hold parallels in the Afghan context, the power dynamics are not dissimilar, and indeed the excessive reaction of the troops signals the political weight of this act of stone throwing too. Vehicles then have complex agential implications and martial politics that span across civilian and military international domains. A focus on the vehicle tells us something about the ways that the 'global' manifests in context-specific terms, the ways the agency of the material contributes to acts of violence in warfare and the material entanglements of the military–peace complex as well as the extent to which the very idea of the international as impartial is in flux.

The Built Landscape

Taken as a whole, the built landscape of the military–peace complex can be understood as structural in a dual sense. Firstly, the fortified aid and military compounds constitute literal, visceral and visible structures. Secondly, these buildings are structural in terms of their vital capacities – offering a 'set of relatively unchangeable constraints' on conduct, shaping 'beliefs and behaviours' (Duffield 2010; Weizman 2011) and entering into a symbiotic relationship with embodied practices, constraining them but shaped by them as well. Thus the fortified compounds are much more than buildings – they are symbols of threat, of violence and of inequality (Duffield 2010; Weizman 2011) and they curtail and control behaviours and relations.

The manner in which these tangible structures are engaged in practices of exclusion and the reduction of physical permeability within the landscape perpetuates remoteness and signifies a counterweight to peace promotion by supporting inequality (Atkinson and Flint 2007) and reifying violence. Physical structures, and the spatial construction they are part of, have an agency and a political dimension, especially within a conflict-affected setting. They correspond with particular ideologies and relations of power: 'political forces, cultural habits, forms of knowledge, skills and expertise' are 'folded into' and inscribed upon 'physical structures and spatial techniques' (Weizman 2011: 4). Thus it is possible to argue that structures are visceral markers of the conflicts or spaces in which they are situated, political and fluid to the extent that they are constructed by the ideas and pre-knowledge of those who inhabit or build them (Omidi 2014).

As Omidi suggests, writing about anti-homeless urban designs: '[o]ne of the problems with architectures of control is that they don't discriminate' so that the measures end up impacting all those who use the space, rather than just those who are targeted (Omidi 2014). Applying these insights to the Afghan context, it is clear that violent architecture can perpetuate structural violence. In theory these measures are targeting the Taliban/violent attackers, but in practice those Afghans who experience them most are the general population: passers-by, those who pass through checkpoints or those Afghans employed to work in the compounds (Fluri 2009a: 989). The ACLU database of incident reports shows that in 2005, a man who had business dealings with the US military was fatally shot by the US military as he was approaching Bagram Tower 14 to conduct those dealings.[10] Though this relates to human behaviour and not architecture, it indicates the siege mentality likely to have played a role in perceiving those (especially Afghans) approaching the space of the compound tower as a likely threat.

These structures also echo racialised lineages of colonial architectures and, in fact, Kothari argues that the spatial practices of development personnel are more exclusive and remote than those of colonial officers: '[c]olonial enclaves certainly existed and most officers "in the field" did live within compounds, but these were more integrated with surrounding space than the more tightly bounded enclavic spaces in which development professionals tend to base themselves' (Kothari 2006c: 248–9). As my respondent illustrated above, military compounds echo the formula of the 'crusaders' fort'. The compound, in which biopolitical decisions about whose bodies are valued become tangible, 'performatively produces and secures the borders of political community' (Basham and Vaughan-Williams 2013: 513) in which liberal citizens are defined against illiberal and warring Others coded through racial and gendered markers (Howell and Richter-Montpetit 2019; Hudson 2014; Mohanty 1984; Said 1979).

It is easy to understand how, in an environment of deep insecurity, these buildings and compounds, and the security measures that come with them, are understood as necessary (Duffield 2012, 2010; Shannon 2009). My aim here is not to refute that understanding or even to consider alternatives. However, there is equally no doubt that these architectures contribute to a landscape of violence in which peace becomes less possible (Shannon 2009). They rely on inequality between foreigners and the host population (Smirl 2015; Fluri 2009a) and thus contribute to structural violence by cementing and furthering these inequalities over time (Galtung 1969). Smirl (2009) has pointed to research on gated communities which suggests that architectures of security increase inhabitants' fear of what may be outside. These structures reify and validate direct violence and its mechanisms as legitimate and necessary parts of the post-conflict domain, by being physical and obvious emblems of violence and insecurity and employing militaristic modes of defence

(Fluri 2009a). They have negative implications for positive peace, and curtail the ability and intentions of peacebuilders, shaping ideologies of peacebuilding in a mode of violence and remoteness (Autesserre 2014; Duffield 2012).

Conclusion

As Smirl points out: 'if the physical circumstances, or habitus, of the international community in a country is circumscribed, then this will have an effect on how they interact with their intended beneficiaries' (Smirl 2008: 239). There are clear differences between the military and civilian sides of the intervention practices in Afghanistan since 2001, as I repeatedly recognise. Yet, looking to the material and spatial dimensions of the liberal peace, certain kinds of connections, echoes and assemblages between military and civilian spaces come into view.

In this chapter I have highlighted examples of material and spatial performance and dynamics that frame and delineate the military–peace complex and help to constitute the 'international' and the 'local' as separate categories. I have illustrated the ways that material and spatial dynamics produce and reproduce forms of martial politics in agential interaction with human lifeworlds and have shown the significance of inhuman agency from the everyday to wider geopolitical levels in shaping intervention praxis. In looking to seemingly banal or ordinary, unnoticed components of spatial and material imaginaries such as alcohol, restaurants and 'the field', I have shown the reader new ways in which statebuilding/intervention encounters can be understood and have also framed more traditional martial concerns such as checkpoints, vehicles and architecture through a different lens. I suggest that looking at these modes of encounter shows us a different angle of a by-now familiar picture of international engagement with Afghanistan and offers up new considerations and new questions. Keeping in mind calls within international relations scholarship for modes of theorising around intervention in Afghanistan that are conducive to holism (see Friis 2012) I suggest that this chapter offers crucial innovation in terms of conceptualising the interconnection dynamics of what is arguably a fundamentally material and spatial encounter. My exploration of this facet of the military–peace complex is helpful for thinking about other intervention and statebuilding contexts as well and pushes the boundaries of critical peace studies in terms of considering the significance of objects and spatial environments as key to the meaning of conflict and post-conflict sites. I return in the next and final chapter to focus explicitly on a feminist analysis and explore the centrality of gender to understanding both the paradoxes and performances of the context under study.

Notes

1. For more on postcolonial geographies and critical cartography see Blunt and McEwan (2002) and Mahmud (2010).
2. Available at https://wikileaks.org/afg/event/2009/03/AFG20090303n1673.html
3. Available at https://wikileaks.org/afg/event/2009/02/AFG20090228n1727.html
4. Higate (2012b: 452) makes an important point about focusing on misconduct which is worth noting here: 'While there exists intimidation of local families on the roads by some PMSC convoys, occasional random shootings by contractors and SEA perpetrated against women by a small number of those in the industry (Eley 2010), it is also important to note that the majority of employees in the industry uphold high professional standards, a point that can be missed through an exclusive focus on problems'.
5. Available at https://wardiaries.wikileaks.org/
6. Available at https://wikileaks.org/afg/event/2009/12/AFG20091222n2404.html
7. Listed as coalition forces.
8. Available at https://www.aclu.org/sites/default/files/webroot/natsec/foia/log.html
9. Available at https://www.aclu.org/sites/default/files/webroot/natsec/foia/pdf/Army0030_0034.pdf
10. Available at https://www.aclu.org/sites/default/files/webroot/natsec/foia/pdf/Army0023_0029.pdf

Liberal Feminism, the Third World Woman and the Third Gender

All my research for this book has been situated within feminist international relations, broadly defined, and I have previously pointed to gendered ideas, constructs and bodies, especially in Chapter 2, where I considered the role of masculinity as a concept and set of performative expectations in shaping counterinsurgency and the protection logics (and protective bodies) of humanitarian spaces. In this chapter I look further at the operation of gender and the complex place of different female bodies within the military–peace paradigm in Afghanistan. I consider how the use of gender, women's rights, gender mainstreaming and so on operates as justificatory, fuelling the liberal rationale by providing a subject (similar in nature to the 'average third world woman' (Mohanty 1984)) in need of rescuing and narrating a 'broken' society in need of externally mandated social engineering (Billaud 2012). I also look to the liminal figure of the international woman, sometimes framed as a 'third gender' and the unease that surrounds this figure. Within my exploration I am alert to resistance and critique; for instance I reference the 'politics of clothing'[1] circulating around female performance in Afghanistan, and the ways it was navigated and resisted. At various points in the chapter I draw on Annick Wibben's and Akanksha Mehta's work (Wibben 2011; Mehta and Wibben 2018) on a feminist security studies narrative framework, which allows me to pay attention to the multiplicities of this subject. Wibben (2011: 86) articulates that:

> A key component of the narrative approach . . . is that the differences among stories and storytellers, which characterize personal narratives, are explicitly acknowledged, rather than ironed out as they are in traditional social science approaches . . . What is more, they are interrogated for what they can

tell us about the storytellers' conflicts, the multiple strategies that might be employed to address them, and the multiplicity of perspectives that exist in relation to them.

Drawing on these ideas at points, I am interested in navigation as a mode of political expression that complicates the gendered politics of the military–peace complex.

While feminist and gender-focused scholars have recognised the centrality of ideas about women to the war in Afghanistan from the outset (see Abu-Lughod 2002; Abirafeh 2009; Azarbaijani-Moghaddam 2014; Hanifi 2018), especially in terms of justifying military action, less work has been done on tracing those ideas over time and in practice. Moreover, and importantly, it has not been well recognised that ideas about women and female bodies, Afghan and international, circulate around and entangle together military and civilian modes of work in important ways within the wider international project in Afghanistan, while also exposing the complexity and disjuncture within it.

This chapter proceeds in five parts. It engages with the role of gender in general terms within the military–peace paradigm before moving to consider the question of instrumentalisation and the deep trope of an 'average' Afghan woman which acts as a foil but is also complex and contested. It then looks to the notion of the third gender as a liminal gendered experience and to gendered negotiations within the context of the military–peace complex.

The Role of Gender in the Military–Peace Complex

As articulated by Billaud (2015: 5), '[w]hen the United States began bombing Afghanistan on October 7, 2001, the oppression of Afghan women was the moral grammar mobilized to rally popular support for the military invasion of the country'. This moral grammar was nothing new, and in fact had been mobilised in different ways before in relation to Afghanistan, as articulated in Chapter 1 (see Zulfacar 2006).

While it is important to recognise patriarchy where it appears, it is also important to be careful in unproblematically assigning the label of fixed patriarchal society to Afghanistan. Billaud's (2015: 11) arguments in this respect are worth quoting in full here:

In the Afghan postcolony, women are obliged to subscribe to norms and ideologies whose social effects further diminish their dignity and exacerbate their inequality. Women cannot make choices that do not show – at least partly – their adhesion to these norms without fearing the social sanction reserved for those who are considered as traitors. These norms take a variety of forms: some have to do with family honour and feminine modesty; others have to do with the glorification of motherhood and feminine virtue indexed on women's capacity to endure. Reading in these norms the expression of a fixed 'Afghan culture' is misleading simply because the terms of participation are constantly negotiated in everyday practice.

This quote from Billaud's work demonstrates the complexity in play in the experience of patriarchy faced by Afghan women. It is an experience that is not possible to separate out from its history and from the extent to which women's rights and freedoms have repeatedly been politicised (see Auchter 2012; Burki 2011; Chishti 2010; Cloud 2004; Zulfacar 2006).

So it is especially crucial to note that, as has been clearly articulated by feminist scholars, in the most recent phase of international involvement in Afghanistan, both military and civilian peace and statebuilding approaches were built on gendered foundations and used gendered ideas as justificatory, and to fuel daily practices (Abu-Lughod 2002; McBride and Wibben 2012; Welland 2013; Wright 2019). Gendered performances also masked certain disjunctures in these paradigms, such as the gap between the expectations held and realities faced by soldiers in counterinsurgency-style warfare discussed in Chapter 2 (Khalili 2011; McBride and Wibben 2012; Welland 2013). On the other hand, it is through a gender analytic engagement that the practices and performances of power and inequality within the military–peace paradigm become most visible. By examining military and civilian praxis through a feminist lens, the unintended consequences, slippages and cracks in the liberal peace framework in Afghanistan are highlighted, such as the unsustainability of certain donor-driven gender mainstreaming projects (Ferguson 2014: 390–1), the essentialising strategies that mark narratives of liberation (Hanifi 2018; Wright 2019) or the gendered unease around female soldiers in violent contexts (Dyvik 2013; Millar 2015).

As I have outlined, there are particular norms of good governance relied upon within the foundational conception of the liberal peace, and both military and civilian development, peacebuilding and statebuilding praxis within it. These norms have deeply masculinist and racialised roots (Howell and Richter-Montpetit 2019; Shilliam 2008; Young 2003a) and are gendered in both ideational and practical terms (Duncanson 2016: 13). Neoliberal peacebuilding involves a set of economic and political reforms and restructuring which rely on a con-

ceptualisation of the state that marginalises women: '[n]eoliberal economic models, for example, tend to involve cuts to the very services that
women are particularly reliant upon because of their designated caring
role in society' (Duncanson 2016: 13). Moreover, the military–peace
complex is structurally masculinist in its approach to national actors
and profits those who benefit from a war economy marked by violence
and corruption (Duncanson 2016; Joya 2009; Mac Ginty 2010b). In an
overarching sense, '[n]eoliberal policies offer incentives to the mostly
male agents of the combat economy to keep fighting because they rarely
offer the alternative livelihoods necessary to persuade them otherwise'
(Duncanson 2016: 74).

In particular, military actors seeking tactical victories work alongside
and financially reward so-called 'warlords' and militias who likely have
no interest in human rights, democracy or gender equality, and actively
counteract these things (see Kakar 2011; Joya 2009; Mac Ginty 2010b:
583). While commitments to gender equality abound, 'warlords',
militias, provincial councils and certain social structures are actively
but selectively supported by the intervening forces and foreign money
(Chishti 2010: 261; Joya 2009). These actors form a kind of 'indigenous
brotherhood' which functions in a 'neo-patrimonial relationship with
male dominated governments' in Afghanistan and globally excluding
women *a priori*, even as the rhetoric of liberalism invites them to the
governance table (Hudson 2012: 452).

There are exceptions, and Afghan women's rights activists have
achieved additional space and voice over the last two decades, linked
to international support in some instances. There have unquestionably
been positive achievements in this regard, such as the facilitation of
women's civic participation and ability to vote in national elections
and the increase in female students at all educational levels. There is no
doubt that many international actors have had good intentions in terms
of improving women's livelihoods, rights and freedoms in many cases
as well as equitable social relations within the 'gender order' (Abirafeh
2009: 26) and Afghan women's and Afghan male allies' labour and
sacrifices in terms of working towards these aims have been monumen-
tal. However, even these successes have been plagued by politicisation,
short-termism and misunderstandings and have been damaged and
limited by violence and so-called backlash.

With all this in mind, one of the core feminist concerns that emerges
in relation to gender in the military–peace complex is its instrumentalisation in service of wider liberal peace or overtly military objectives.
Lucy Ferguson suggests that tick-the-box policies for gender inclusion

at the UN lead 'to gender being a "component" of policy and activities, but not an on-going structural consideration in terms of the procedures and approaches of an institution – an integrationist rather than transformative approach' (Ferguson 2014: 392), and something similar can be said about many of the programming strategies evident within the military–peace complex. Beyond this, in some cases gendered ideas directly facilitated war-making practices.

Nancy Fraser has articulated in broad and mainly materialist/economic terms the manner in which feminism became complicit with the neoliberal paradigm. For Fraser, feminism's success in the cultural domain, and the symbolic equalities achieved by second wave feminism in particular, have helped to facilitate other kinds of structural injustice (Fraser 2009: 99). She notes that what was once a holistic feminist critique of an androcentric and statist paradigm became fragmented, resulting in the 'selective incorporation and partial recuperation of some of its strands' into a neoliberal mode of practice (Fraser 2009: 99). Fraser argues that the correlation between a certain branch of feminism and neoliberalism served to 'resignify feminist ideals', diluting and hybridising any 'clear emancipatory thrust' (2009: 108). These ideas of fragmentation and partial inclusion are evident throughout the military–peace complex. They are most obvious at the very beginning of the Afghan intervention in the discursive collapse performed by Laura Bush in 2001, and others subsequently, between the war on terror and the defence of women's rights (Bush 2001). To suggest that the 'fight against terrorism is also a fight for the rights and dignity of women' is to fuse together the war-fighting intentions of the American military and political establishment, with a certain kind of white, liberal and racialising feminism premised on women's rights as civil participants and equal consumers and 'saving brown women' from their context (see Khalid 2011). The images Laura Bush invoked in her radio address, of Afghan women wanting to paint their nails and listen to music, and her implicit linking to symbols of American freedom and consumption, such as through the mention of Thanksgiving, evoke a particularly neoliberal mode, where rights and happiness are conflated with consumption and Western conceptions of the good life. As with the incorporation suggested by Fraser, this discursive political move splits apart and reconstitutes certain feminist ideas within (neo)liberal modes while neglecting any structural complicity in gender inequalities and injustices to begin with.

The selective incorporation of gender and a kind of neoliberal feminism layered through the engagement with Afghanistan as a whole and led to a pervasive tick-the-box logic, which, while perhaps more consistently pronounced in the military context (see Wright 2019: 98), was evident in civilian programming as well and is a core commonality that spanned the military–peace context and highlighted the parallel logics of military and civilian actors in relation to gender. I explore this idea of instrumentalising gender and women's rights/freedoms in particular in the next section.

Instrumentalising Women and Gender

The notion of instrumentalisation indicates the selective mobilisation of ideas around gender equality and women's rights to serve particular political, reputational, strategic, intelligence-based or short-term objectives without a desire or capacity to fit these ideas to the context or conceptualise modes of holism needed to truly protect people from violence and injustice and reflect on what brings them about.

On the military side instrumentalisation manifested in two main ways: the first was in terms of the approach to female soldiers, the second in terms of the approach to Afghan women (see Dyvik 2013), while gendered ideologies cut through the COIN framework in different ways. I discussed in a previous chapter that COIN was seen in some ways as sitting at odds with the more traditionally, perhaps more 'macho' behaviours of regular war-fighting. Part of this supposed 'feminisation' of COIN was generated through the focus on accessing women, and the creation of the Female Engagement Teams (FETs – for a detailed report on the FETs and their work see Azarbaijani-Moghaddam 2014). These units were all-female and often attached to male units. The members of these units were technically not combat soldiers, since the combat ban on women was still in place in the UK and the US at the time when they first became operational. Their purpose was to conduct hearts-and-minds work, often specifically targeted at women. This work was designed within the overarching COIN logic to allow access to female members of the population in order to gather previously untapped intelligence as well as to address the needs of the female population more directly (since it was seen as culturally inappropriate for male soldiers to interact with Afghan women). As articulated by the US military, access to the female population, and thus the reliance on female soldiers, had strategic benefits: 'Co-opting neutral or friendly women through targeted social and economic programs builds networks of enlightened self-interest that eventually undermine insurgents. Female counterinsurgents, including interagency people, are required to do this effectively (US Army et al. 2007: 296, cited in Dyvik 2013: 415)'.

However, these soldiers had a tough job trying to pursue anything like their given objective: '[t]hey were often confronted with problems they had no capability to address and repeatedly failed to deliver on promises made to residents, as their mission was not the primary concern of military commanders' (McBride and Wibben 2012: 199). The dual use of women – as soldiers and sources of military intelligence – co-opts and is facilitated by certain kinds of liberal feminist and gendered ideas (see Dyvik 2013; Khalili 2011; McBride and Wibben 2012; Welland 2013). Women soldiers can offer good news stories, tapping into stereotypical gender categories to indicate a more humane and peace-oriented style of warfare (McBride and Wibben 2012; Wright 2019). The presence of women as part of the FETs links back to the idea that COIN is framed as a 'feminised' from of warfare at times and in certain ways, and this has political meaning. The use of these units can be understood partially as 'an attempt to reframe the U.S. military intervention in Afghanistan as a humanitarian, even progressive, mission' (McBride and Wibben 2012: 200) and partially as a strategic asset. The trajectory of the war/peacebuilding project in Afghanistan was thus wrapped up with and dependent upon certain discourses, images and frames of women, either as victims or soldiers, calling upon feminist narratives and partial inclusions to legitimise a masculinist neoliberal pursuit: 'the war has become framed as a feminist war' (McBride and Wibben 2012: 202). As McBride and Wibben suggest, 'paying attention to gender reveals much more than just where the women are; it provides insight into the assumptions, means, and goals of the [international] involvement in the war in Afghanistan' (McBride and Wibben 2012: 211).

There were some important arguments in favour of the FETs. For example, Sarah, one of my military respondents, who was a vocal and active advocate of the FETs, linked the inclusion of women in the military to the military necessity that came with a COIN approach: 'definitely from a counterinsurgency perspective, it is ludicrous to be in an environment where you are with male and female civilians, and yet you don't have females in your patrol' (Sarah, Major, British Army). The FETs mark a distinctive shift to incorporate women into combat proximity and into the central strategic logic of military operations in Afghanistan (Dyvik 2013; McBride and Wibben 2012). The combat ban for American female soldiers remained in place in practical terms for the duration of official and full military engagement in Afghanistan (Millar 2015: 2), so the FETs are the most significant symbolic female military presence in that war. They could arguably be seen as a force for equality and inclusion as well as a necessary way to access the needs and experiences of Afghan women.

And yet, even if one were to accept this ostensibly inclusive (of Afghan women and female military actors) logic and purpose in theory, in practice the FETs, under-resourced and ill-equipped, faced a massive task. Mike argued, 'it is difficult to judge the efficacy of a FET team because you're going out into an environment in which there is no social structures in place for you to really empower those [Afghan] women' (Mike, civilian liaison to the US military).

Moreover, the use of female soldiers, rapidly reassigned from their original roles to the FETs for the simple reason that they were female, reified and reinforced gendered ideas within the military and demonstrated an instrumental use of female soldiers for their female bodies. One of my civilian respondents, Lisa, who was specifically critical of the work the military did in Afghanistan relating to gender, had conducted research for a report on military press releases that promoted gender-related programmes and was very sceptical of their content. She expressed criticism of the use of military women in international military press releases, suggesting that far from depicting female soldiers in ways that spoke to their professional qualities (see Pin-Fat and Stern 2005; Millar 2015; Wright 2019), there was a sense that these women were being deliberately and firmly located within the feminine sphere:

[A]ll the photos that were accompanying those press releases were of women in military uniforms holding babies or you know, teaching little girls hygiene skills or sewing classes for women, these sort of motherly archetypes that they were putting even the foreign women soldiers in. (Lisa, American NGO worker)

Lisa further suggested that ISAF were guilty of tokenism in relation to their gender advisor, and, speaking of a person who had held this post in the past, stated:

She just happened to be a person with a vagina in the right rank, needed to be reassigned, there was an opening. Literally they just take women and put them in these positions assuming that that means that you'll have an effective gender policy. And I think it is also just – to use the phrase 'to tick a box' – just to say 'we have a gender advisor', but I don't really know what it amounts to in practice. (Lisa, American NGO worker)

Additionally, despite the inclusion of Afghan women's voices in consultations with civilians, it is unclear how seriously this was taken in reality. Kate, a civilian research consultant, framed COIN approaches as being in fact very male-oriented, suggesting that the military looked to deal with male civilians primarily, neglecting female members of the population:

> When you look at activities, like the PRT and other activities that the military has been involved in. And I'm not sure how successful they have been at reaching women in particular.
>
> . . .
>
> They are interested in who makes the decision about who joins the Taliban, I mean they are interested in – there is a whole branch of the military that is sort of human terrain and it is all about understanding sort of culturally what is happening out in Afghanistan around the provinces and how that impacts on security, and if you look at that research, they are interested in understanding things that they don't necessarily connect to women or gender so, you know, how do people get drafted into insurgent groups and you know, what do people think of the military, how do people see the military, do they support them? There is a whole range of things that they are interested in understanding and I don't think they see women as key decision makers in the sorts of processes that they are interested. But they are, of course they are. (Kate, Australian research consultant).

Sarah also commented that for the most part, COIN 'key leader engagements' and general work with communities was male focused: 'all the time they were only talking to the men' (Sarah, Major, British Army).

Lisa deemed the military's engagement with gender in Afghanistan to be counterproductive and limited. She was dismissive of the manner in which military promotional materials depicted the Afghan women they claimed to be assisting, which Lisa felt reinforced traditional gender ideologies in harmful ways:

> [T]he way that the military likes to present their work on gender, which I found completely ridiculous and comical. A lot of it – just the way they talk about women in the first place is this complete sense of helplessness, Afghan women as these complete victims, talking about child mothers wanting to give their children a better life, and the poverty – it's just like dripping with imagery – you know, a mother swaddling her child in the freezing cold as she tried to adjust her headscarf and ensure that her burka is on properly and blah blah blah. So like it's just, and especially if you've been here you know that these people have never actually talked to an Afghan woman. (Lisa, American NGO worker)

Thus, although there was a clear association between the ideational part of the COIN doctrine and how it sought to reorient warfare praxis, and ideas of a kind of softening, 'feminising' and increasing gentleness in my interview materials and in wider research (Duncanson 2013; Gentry and Sjoberg 2007, 2015; Khalili 2011; Pin-Fat and Stern 2005; McBride and Wibben 2012), equally there were contradictions at work and other views particularly coming from those outside the military but working in Afghanistan, which undercut even this approach to gender inclusivity and viewed it as disingenuous, shallow and unsuccessful. The question of Othering and a racialised victimhood trope is also relevant here, and is something I will come back to below to discuss the idea of the 'average third world woman' (Mohanty 1984).

On the non-military side, and similarly, one of the key points that emerged was the extent to which ideas around gender and gender mainstreaming were often externally driven and deployed as a tool to satisfy donor requirements, rather than to address structural conditions.

Lisa spoke about it in these terms:

> Yes, practically every donor template has a section that requires you to address 'gender' [the transcript is not reflecting my air quotes, but I would like it noted that there are air quotes around the word gender]. Because what they are actually asking is how many female beneficiaries you're going to have, and how are you going to ensure that women are included in your project, which is considered gender here I guess (Lisa, American NGO worker).

She then went on to explain how the requirement to include women in programming activities often did not coincide with any deeper understanding of the social structures that allowed gendered relations to be hierarchical or with any attempt to engage through a more nuanced gender lens. For her, this meant that gender programming could be conducive to 'backlash' against women, in the form of increased violence (Abirafeh 2009) and resistance to changes in the gender order as well as to unforeseen risks and failures (discussed further below). Rebecca, an environmental NGO worker, explained to me that a consultancy in the area had been criticised by donors for having no gender programming so had added a women's beekeeping project to their remit as 'a tick-the-box thing' (Rebecca, NGO worker).

There was a sense of disconnect from the meaning of gender, while at the same time a ubiquity of its inclusion. In an informal conversation, one male foreign civil society worker told me that he had attended a meeting on gender at his well-known organisation, in which there were exclusively male staff (Author notes, 2 May 2014); while, as mentioned in the previous chapter, another male foreign civil society worker told me at a social gathering that the person at one of the biggest donor institutions in charge of allocating funding for gender programming had never worn a headscarf because she had never been outside the compound in Kabul (Author notes, 15 May 2014). My respondent Asal suggested that there was a utilitarianism in the use of gender: 'by international donors it has been used as a sort of scapegoat, to say that "oh we are doing gender mainstreaming" but no specific programming to support women' (Asal, Afghan activist). Part of the problem, as she understood it, had to do with the allocation of international resources:

> [T]his sudden, I think, flow of money and attention, and at the same time because aid and suddenly so much money and so much resources came to the country, where people just started finding ways to just earn that money, to be able to get an amount of that money without understanding that – would it really have any place in this society? How much of a meaning it will have on our lives? Nobody thought about it. And a lot of organisations were made just to be able to get resources from contractors, from donors, and it is funny that now, so many man organisation they suddenly turn to gender programmes and they talk about 'Oh we have a lot of gender programmes and different meetings here', while these are the men that have no idea about gender. (Asal, Afghan activist)

Kate outlined the pervasive tendency of donors to understand gender in narrow terms as linked directly to the inclusion of women in particular ways, and suggested that this could have unintended consequences: 'My impression of donors is despite all the evidence, globally and here, there is still this really narrow conception of what gender means, and that can have quite serious ramifications for women' (Kate, Australian research consultant).

Moreover, it was articulated by Rebecca that the obsession with having a 'women's section' to satisfy donor gender-mainstreaming requirements could be damaging to the original aims of programming:

> We have this small grants programme, and the same thing, like [donors say] 'We really want you to do something with gender, what do you do with women, what do you do with women?' Well this project is about environmental sustainability and doing environmental projects, and it is not always very easy to incorporate women there, and if you need to do it because your donor

wants you to write a little paragraph about what you do for women, yeah it is not very useful. (Rebecca, NGO worker).

During my research it was noted that, in many cases, the various categories of peacebuilding actors had genuine (though sometimes misguided) intentions behind their mandates and that the drive to improve the lives of Afghans generally, and Afghan women in particular, came from a well-meaning worldview. Lisa commented:

> I think the intentions are good, especially donors and NGOs – there is a genuine wanting to improve the situation of women in Afghanistan. The way that it was presented was wrong but there were a lot of challenges for women after the Taliban, that was by no means, it wasn't like they created something where there was nothing, women's rights were subject to extreme violation. (Lisa, American NGO worker).

Yet despite this, gender was a tokenistic tool in the eyes of many peacebuilding actors. The following extract from an interview with Graham, a British UN worker, illustrates a simultaneous expression of impatience and frustration when talking about gender programming. He had forgotten something he was about to say earlier in the conversation, and when I asked him if he had remembered he said:

> I think I was trying to justify our own approach to trying to bring gender issues in a UN kind of sphere where we have to keep so many different donors and their different objectives happy, and this gender thing is always the thing that is just kicked in as a side, and to be completely honest it is, and any donor would be lying if they said otherwise. (Graham, British UN worker)

Overall, there was a sense of tension at play between, on the one hand, understanding that equitable social change and the inclusion of women were often positive and well-intentioned goals to aspire to, and, on the other hand, an unease with the process of inclusion and the requirements of donor-driven peacebuilding and its templates. The following extract from my interview with Rebecca illustrates this well. She was referring to being given control of a beekeeping project by an agricultural consultant who needed to be linked to something gender-related:

> Donors want you to do something with women . . . the way it comes about is not very pretty because you just, well this is my honest opinion to you, I could say like, you know, pretty stories about it, but it is just [names consultant]

wants to tick the gender box and that's how we [pause], but it worked out well.
(Rebecca, NGO worker)

The trope of donor-driven projects and their potentially short-sighted implications for women and gender in Afghanistan was one that came up again and again during my interviews and spoke to the contradictions inherent in the way that gender operated within the liberal military–peace complex. Arguably, then, there was a shared mode of instrumentalism at work in terms of gender and women's rights and freedoms in both military and civilian work and approaches to peace and statebuilding practices in Afghanistan.

One very serious implication of this mode of instrumentalism and short-termism was the increased possibility of what is referred to as 'backlash'. When it came to discussing gender and activities around women's rights in Afghanistan, there were repeated references to the idea of backlash. There was an understanding that with the enormous focus on women that had come about as a result of international intervention since 2001, there was a huge risk of backsliding and of ideas around gender equality imported from outside being disconnected from, and rejected by, Afghan society.

One respondent explained the dangers of short-term programmes:

So some NGOs they highlighted women in the rural areas, women who said 'OK wow'. During these very enthusiastic beginning years. 'We would like to live like the women in the West'. Those NGOs are long gone from these villages or areas. They are doing other projects now, they left Afghanistan. And they are working meanwhile in Pakistan or in Uganda or wherever. The women are still there. And people blame them and say you, was it couple of years ago? You want to live like the European women?

. . .

That is a big problem, some were isolated because of this. In the rural areas we can't protect people. You have to do things that, where it is possible to reach the goals without causing damage. And there are some things in Afghanistan that work, and others that don't work.

In his example these NGO mandates were short-term and the women they worked with were interested but isolated; it speaks to some of the major challenges of this kind of project and highlights the pitting of 'European/Western' lifestyles and rights against 'traditional' Afghan lifeworlds. Another respondent asked: 'If [the] donor goes, then what will happen with that, what will be the future of those women?' She pointed out that 'in Afghanistan, NGOs have very short-term projects' (Damsa, Afghan civil society worker).

These challenges and failings were articulated in different ways alongside stories of navigation and success (in the sense of supporting people in need of support). Speaking about what she considered to be the Afghan women's movement, Asal told me:

> We did a lot of mistakes I believe, many of us . . . maybe because we didn't have a lot of experience, suddenly the global attention also came and poured into us and we were overwhelmed and we tried to kind of actually run faster than our society. (Asal, Afghan activist)

This idea of running faster than Afghan society is interesting and highlights the question of navigation again, and how Afghan women's rights activists in particular needed to contemplate the political and social ramifications of their work since (unlike sections of the international project) they were active in the long term. Asal also pointed to the acute awareness of history among Afghan politicians in relation to the politicisation of women's status, and the cycles of change and repression. She stated that 'the misery or the difficult situation of Afghan women is not only the result of the Taliban', pointing out that these patterns had very deep historical roots (Asal, Afghan activist; see also Joya 2009).

Kate suggested that 'backlash' can be linked to the exclusionary approach of gender programming which separates the sexes and focuses only on women (see also Abirafeh 2009):

> [W]hen you are working in a really sensitive environment in some contexts where there is very conservative norms about what women can and can't do, excluding men is actually really detrimental to your programming, and it doesn't make sense. And there have been quite a few projects that there has been backlash. (Kate, Australian research consultant)

Damsa, another high-level Afghan civil society worker, agreed that the neglect of men within the implementation of gender programming had damaging effects: '[W]hen we enter and we provide skills for women, and suddenly the woman start generating income and the male doesn't have anything, then there is a conflict among that family' (Damsa, Afghan civil society worker).

In part as a way to avoid 'backlash' and unintended consequences, the idea of needing to fit gender programming to social and cultural contexts was echoed by many respondents, highlighting the extent to which the perceived Westernisation of women's rights frameworks could be damaging and thus reiterating the dangers of instrumentalisation on all sides. For instance, speaking about a lack of contextual understanding within the international community, Afghan NGO worker Nahal emphasised the importance of Islam:

> But in the first place when they [the international community] came here they didn't take it into consideration that it is a very strict Islamic country, they thought maybe like other countries, African countries or some European countries, we can fight for women's rights, but it isn't possible since it is Afghan society, it is a very strict Muslim society.
>
> They should develop their ways according to the Sharia law and Islam in order to make the male gender to accept that this is the right of women. (Nahal, Afghan NGO worker).

As with many cases where 'equality' is externally imposed (Abirafeh 2009; Fluri 2009b), there was a disjuncture between the aspirations and rhetoric and the actual reality, especially given that the presence of female bodies does not necessarily equate to any kind of structural change and when the threat of a full Taliban return to power hangs over the country. Kate explained the findings of her research into women's political representation:

> [W]hat we found was that the national level – even though women are being included on committees, on the High Peace Council – they are not necessarily having their voices heard, and they are not necessarily having their voices heard at the negotiating table, so when there is meetings with the Taliban for instance in different countries or wherever, women aren't being represented and I think one of the greatest concerns is that women's rights will suffer as a result of a power-sharing agreement, because something will have to give. (Kate, Australian research consultant)

Kate's point speaks to the issue of sustainability and the contradictions inherent in pushing measures for gender equality on the one hand and negotiating with the Taliban – who are historically strongly anti-gender equality, though not opposed by all Afghan women – on the other (Abirafeh 2009: 35). Similarly, Asal told me with reference to the Peace Jirga in 2010: 'I realised that we women have only like, we are just used for slogans, for political purposes, but when there is real discussion on politics and how for example power is shared, we are not there' (Asal,

Afghan activist). Thus, the politicisation and instrumentalisation of Afghan women's rights and freedoms emerged across the military–peace complex (Abirafeh 2009; Fluri 2009b; Zulfacar 2006).

Moreover, the notion of backlash, though salient in articulating the range of ways in which changes to what Abirafeh calls the 'gender order' (be they big or small) were resisted, can also fail to capture some of the dynamics of that resistance. Namely, the fact that change and backlash in relation to women's rights and freedoms in Afghanistan have often been two sides of the same coin. What I mean by this is that change in terms of women's status and livelihoods were sought by internationals and Afghan civil society on the one hand, while the same international apparatus (particularly the US) overlooked past human rights violations and pervasive 'anti-genderism' (Ackerly et al. 2019) in its Afghan allies (Joya 2009). At the same time, the Ministry of Women's Affairs was underfunded (Abirafeh 2009: 17), national assets were privatised (a move that is bad for women; see Duncanson 2016) and in some parts of the country a discussion with Afghan women about their needs could be held within the parameters of military strategy rather than as a goal in and of itself. In these circumstances, backlash is almost innate in the frameworks for change that were pushed in the first place and links back to the false but fundamental structuring dichotomy between 'tradition' and 'modernity' that, as outlined in Chapter 1, so often shapes international engagement with Afghanistan.

As the intervention in Afghanistan progressed and changed and any notion of military 'success', as it had originally been framed, receded, talks with the Taliban were increasingly on the agenda. This can be seen as further evidence of the destabilisation of the work of feminist activists within Afghanistan and any commitment to gender equality espoused by the drivers of the military–peace complex. As previously referenced, however, the idea of Taliban reintegration is not a clear-cut option for Afghan feminists because the Taliban is a complex entity and the prospect of peace is of course hugely appealing (see Coomaraswamy 2015), something I expand on in more detail below.

Additionally, at times, projects that stemmed from a desire to protect women from gender-based violence could also be read as having shallower undertones or neoliberal logics, especially when 'race thinking' (Basham 2016: 890) and postcolonial critiques are taken seriously. An interesting example of this came up in a conversation with Sally, who worked for a media consultancy and was doing feminist work linked to the shifting of discriminatory language within the Afghan media, an important aspect of the women, peace and security agenda.

Sally told me about a project designed to map women's rights violations using crowd-mapping technologies. As she put it:

> [T]he aim of this project was to enhance the use of innovative tools in report-
> ing about violations of women's rights . . . in the form of a map . . . You
> can basically record it by type of the case: rape, kidnapping, stuff like that.
> Everything what you need, and then you can have access to this data in the
> visual way, so you can use it for better mediation, or approaching donors, or
> media. (Sally, media consultant)

This project used the same technology as that used in India, Kenya,
Egypt and elsewhere (Grove 2015: 350–1). While this is clearly an
interesting and well-meaning initiative, there is an element of coding
violence across non-Western contexts which is somewhat insidious, and
the subsequent use of this visually represented information about the
abuse of women to secure donor funding can be seen in a negative light,
whereby the suffering of particular individuals can be slotted within a
neoliberal paradigm of efficiency and information technology in order
to generate finances. This bypasses both the intersectional structural
foundations that contribute to the abuse of women in the first place
and the complicity of global powers in maintaining the conditions in
which these abuses can take place. It also feeds into a certain recognition
of what is expected in a non-Western context (see Khalid 2011; Hanifi
2018; Tuastad 2003), recording abuse in a potentially dehumanised way
that services an ideology of confirmation around non-Western society
(Grove 2015: 347).

Nicole Sunday Grove, writing about HarassMap, a similar initiative
using the same Ushahidi software to crowdmap gender-based harassment in Egypt, points out that this approach constitutes a 'specific configuration of data collection, processing, and representation' in order to
'produce a particular knowledge of targeting that resonates with other
projects of securitization' (Grove 2015: 346). This rendering of the gendered and orientalised spatial imaginary in Afghanistan depicted in this
seemingly well-meaning project potentially allows certain actions to be
visualised and converted into funding while contributing to the belief
that the country is 'in need of intervention' from outside (Grove 2015:
346; Said 1979). Grove points to the gendered neoliberal implications
of such mapping. She raises questions about the technological power
and liberal drive of mapping projects focused on gender-based harassment, touching on issues linked to spatial practice and performance
to ask 'to what extent can attempts to "empower" women be pursued

at the microlevel without amplifying the similarly imperial techniques of objectifying them as resources used to justify other forms of state violence?' (Grove 2015: 345).

Linked to this concern and to modes of instrumentalisation discussed here is that, as Jennifer Hyndman and Malathi De Alwis argue in relation to development practitioners, gender has become a 'buzzword in agencies and staff providing humanitarian assistance to people affected by conflict, but its integration into everyday operations is less apparent' (Hyndman and De Alwis 2003: 212). Thus, while it has 'become part of the development and humanitarian lexicon to be employed when preparing proposals and evaluating programs' as well as seeking funding, gender equality as a concept is often devoid of contextual grounding or consistent intent (Hyndman and De Alwis 2003: 212). Added to this, the use of FETs to soften the image and palatability of the military presence in Afghanistan and to utilise potential intelligence provided by women for strategic purposes exacerbated a sense of short-termism attached to gender within the military–peace complex as a whole. All of this took place in a context written into the Western imaginary through orientalist narratives of 'saving brown women from brown men' (Abu-Lughod 2002; Manchanda 2014: 132), a racialising logic which negates the historical and structural complicity in violence on the part of multiple actors, such as the US, Afghan political elites and white liberal feminists (see Manchanda 2014: 132; Thobani 2007).

Gender issues were framed in such a way as to suit the objectives of various actors (Autesserre 2014: l. 4236). They were often understood as a means to an end and could thus be sacrificed when required. When international players or Afghan political elites cut deals with the Taliban or other conservative elements, they could offer concessions on women's rights (Duncanson 2016: 85). Hamid Karzai was repeatedly criticised for his tendency to backslide when it was politically expedient to do so (Burki 2011; Dodge 2011: 86–7; Joya 2009). This is linked into the fact that, as elucidated by my research, gender issues are tied in perception, and in practice, to influence from outside. The understanding of gender issues as foreign, transient and a by-product of donor requirements or military strategy meant that there could be a lack of Afghan ownership of changes that took place (Abirafeh 2009; Billaud 2012) and thus it was much easier for global political elites to renege on them. Moreover, gender served, as it had done before, as a symbol of the foreign Other, and could be manipulated by conservative forces in domestic power struggles. Equally, the regular reliance of gender-based programming on donor-driven criteria or military doctrine, rather than grassroots engagement, meant that when international interest dwindled, as it has done in the wake of the troop withdrawal, the removal of financial support may mean additional financial strain on large numbers of women-focused projects and gender-based programming.

Before moving on from this discussion of instrumentalisation it is worth highlighting a few points that complicate these arguments. First, I wish to return to the idea of negotiations with the Taliban and the possible reintegration of its fighters. During research in 2014 analysing interviews collected by EQUALITY for Peace and Democracy, Marie Huber and I found that some women across Afghanistan did not oppose Taliban reintegration (though many did), so it is not a clear-cut argument to suggest that negotiations with the Taliban necessarily undermine Afghan women's political and peace-oriented desires going forward (Partis-Jennings and Huber 2014). For instance, a respondent from the north of the country explained:

> Our community has no choice but to accept them [the Taliban], and maybe this way we can stop them from doing violence. At first they must include women in the peace process for planning, to raise the awareness of all women and society, to encourage them to welcome Taliban fighters to join and also invite other men to join the peace process. (Partis-Jennings and Huber 2014: 8)

Indeed, Radhika Coomaraswamy (2015), in a UN report, made the point that women have complicated relationships to insurgent groups like the Taliban in Afghanistan and to counterinsurgency and reintegration processes too. Perspectives are influenced by family ties, regional experiences and political persuasion, as with many issues in different contexts. So, while it is arguably fair to state that the Taliban do not seem likely to be champions of gender-equitable social arrangements, it is not accurate to say that Afghan women in general oppose their engagement with peace and security in Afghanistan.

Moreover, and secondly, as stated above, international support and resources did help to carve out space for Afghan women's rights activists and organisations to operate. Significant work was done to improve access to education, healthcare, political enfranchisement and political representation (Coomaraswamy 2015). For example, Coomaraswamy's UN Women report (2015: 175) highlighted that 'gender quotas have seen an increase not only in the election of women to parliament, but in the registration of women voters, women participants in rallies and public demonstrations, and as candidates'. At the same time, activists in

Afghanistan continue to highlight concerns around the sustainability of this shift in light of talks between the government and the Taliban and the US–Taliban agreement in early 2020 (Council on Foreign Relations 2019).

It is also worth highlighting that organisations and individuals did learn from past mistakes and sought out more context-specific programming and approaches as time went on, attempting to minimise the impression of external interference. This is something I will return to below, when I come to discuss navigation.

The 'Average Third World Woman'

It's always been said Afghanistan is so patriarchal and traditional, and women can't have rights. But all that has actually been a myth.

– Wazhma Frogh, Afghan activist
(Council on Foreign Relations 2019)

I discussed different modes of instrumentalisation above, as manifesting within the military–peace complex, and here I continue the thread of that analysis, exploring one ideational construction of the Afghan woman as a trope, in fact, what I term a 'deep trope'. I use the term deep trope to refer to the way that certain tropes become so deeply entrenched, as stereotypes, through intertextual circulation, repetition and even contestation, that they structure meaning even when critiqued, or not adhered to. As such, the abstracted figure of Afghanistan's 'average third world woman' facilitated different elements of the liberal project and highlights the entanglement between the military and civilian sides of the military–peace complex. It is important to acknowledge, as I have made reference to elsewhere in the book, the fact that there were significant patriarchal restrictions placed on Afghan women, especially under the Taliban, but also before the Taliban came to power and since 2001, sometimes leading to terrible suffering as well as societal marginalisation and enforced relegation to the private sphere. Yet (and unsurprisingly), as indicated in the Introduction to this book, these patriarchal constraints were not total, nor, of course, indicative of a lack of agency. I argue here that the international engagement with the figure of the Afghan woman subject to patriarchal codes often relied on an abstracted idea of the 'average third world woman', usually burka-clad and in need of saving, that fixed down and reified a lack of agency (see Dogra 2011; Shephard 2006:25). This functioned as an aesthetically driven imaginary, as a justificatory framework and as a foil for military–peace complex logics and acted as a structuring force, delineating the boundaries of gendered knowledge production, even when resisted by individuals or institutions.

According to Mohanty (1984: 337) the 'average third world woman'

> leads an essentially truncated life based on her feminine gender (read: sexually constrained) and being 'third world' (read: ignorant, poor, uneducated, tradition-bound, domestic, family-oriented, victimized, etc.). This, I suggest, is in contrast to the (implicit) self-representation of Western women as educated, modern, as having control over their own bodies and sexualities, and the freedom to make their own decisions.

As articulated by feminist scholars, the notion of the veiled and victimised Afghan woman acted as a justificatory force from the start of the American-led war in Afghanistan and folded into the whole military–peace complex over the years of international engagement. A generic trope of the Afghan woman as victim which seemed to sit beneath the self-definition of internationals helped to make sense of the concept of the 'third gender' which I unpack below. Yet, equally, the idea of the Afghan woman as a homogeneous cultural Other was not simplistically articulated by my respondents; in fact Afghan and international respondents alike critiqued this idea. Drawing on Wibben's (2011) framework of feminist security studies and the deployment of narrative which can highlight contradictions and dissonance, I articulate some of the complexity around and framing of the idea of Afghan women as victims of a patriarchal code in this section as well.

Recognising the centrality of the trope of an abstracted Afghan woman as veiled and victimised requires us to look briefly at the visual mode. The visual politics of Afghan women is complicated and has historically been significant, domestically and globally (Abu-Lughod 2002; Cloud 2004; Edwards 2006; Khalid 2011; Heck and Schlag 2013; Shepherd 2008). Feminist and postcolonial scholars have pointed out that the imaginary of the Afghan women, crafted through aesthetic mediums and in particular the visual, is one centred on victimhood and oppression and, symbolic of these, the veil (Abu-Lughod 2002; Cloud 2004; Kearns 2017; Khalid 2011; Heck and Schlag 2013; Shepherd 2008).

The visual mode used in this way allows for the fact that 'concerns for the very real abuses of women's rights in Afghanistan and Iraq become co-opted into a discourse that is deployed to justify military violence' (Khalid 2011: 19). In the early stage of the Afghan intervention in particular, visuals of Afghan women in veils were equated with 'tradition', and repression and liberation was signified by the removal of the veil: 'military intervention had freed Afghan women, with the removal of the burqa providing evidence of this liberation' (Khalid 2011: 22). As such, debates on gender relations within Islam (see Ahmed 1992), historical context and the complicity of various nations and actors in the position of the Taliban government to begin with are bypassed through the reification of a two-dimensional cultural iconography of the burka (Abu-Lughod 2002), so prevalent as to constitute a highly powerful, almost automatic signification, a deep trope.

An abstracted notion of the Afghan woman also played a role in forging the self-definitional boundaries of the international, especially international womanhood, which was often framed in my research materials in terms of liminality, negotiation and/or the concept of the 'third gender' (I explore this concept further below). In defining how they were situated as international, and in a liminal position between masculine and feminine public performances in Afghanistan, respondents and others in my research materials implied or referred to the backdrop of an abstract imaginary of the Afghan woman that appeared fixed in a place devoid of agency.

Speaking about needing to get a tyre fixed on her motorbike, for instance, Eva said: 'an Afghan female could never do that, and you had a huge amount of freedoms and you became kind of more conscious about this freedom, because you had a direct comparison so to speak' (Eva, international personnel). An FET soldier cited in Dyvik (2013: 421) states: 'I think that women in the United States have a lot of freedom and Afghan women don't. And I want to help in some way.'

In these depictions, foreign womanhood is tied to freedom/doing/ agency, which is contrasted against a passive Afghan femininity. This is a distinct conceptualisation of agency and freedom as against a 'direct comparison' with non-agency and un-freedom. In the military context, Synne Dyvik (2013: 420) points out that the military understanding of women soldiers as liminal gender actors (not fully performing either male or female roles) in the Afghan context was rendered intelligible via a 'cultural essentialism' which functions by 'grouping numerous women under the rubric "traditional"' whereby the 'traditional' is a foil against which the 'liberal' international woman becomes definitionally possible.

Importantly, the backdrop of the 'average third world woman' was something that respondents were aware of and, in some cases, highly critical of, and even less critical respondents rarely presented a simplistic perspective. When discussing concepts of protection, gender and victimhood, Lisa made reference to the theme of 'saving' Afghan women, stating that 'so much of the rhetoric when people first came to Afghanistan, was about women and you know the burka and the veiling and blah blah blah and needing to save Afghan women'. She went on to explain that both the military and the civilian sides of the international project used the idea of protecting women in their work and justifications: 'I mean when you just say protection and women and Afghanistan, obviously what instantly comes to mind is a lot of the rhetoric surrounding programming, and like the NGOs and I suppose military' (Lisa, American NGO worker).

Other respondents, both Afghan and international, linked the idea of protection to that of honour, articulating that a mode of protection promoted by social norms and patriarchal constructs in Afghanistan was about keeping women out of the public sphere for the wider purpose of family honour and reputation management. A military respondent spoke about his perspective of this dynamic:

> [Some] people here they really believe that killing people, killing women, treating women as bad as possible, is really the only way possible because God say that and that's what God told them . . .
>
> Women are the object of the honour of these men but they are not – yeah it is an abstract way of thinking about honour. So, if you look at a woman, if another man look at your woman, it is not an honourable thing, if the woman not behave according to the strict traditions – Islamic law – it is not good. But it is really more abstract than that, they do it because they're used to doing it.

This respondent clearly echoes an understanding of Afghan women as bound to universalising cultural expectations that produce victimised subjectivities. His words are deeply racialised and falsely universalising. Yet he is also not fully totalising; he suggests that 'the younger generation are changing' indicating an understanding of multifaceted experiences.

Another international respondent, a civilian research consultant, discussed the discourse of victimhood with me and worried that it was still prevalent in 2014:

> In terms of the way that women are represented, I think that the women who are really outspoken and who are trying to change that discourse that you are talking about, I think that they're gaining voice but they are not necessarily the women that people at high government levels are listening to, and so I think that there is a lot of that idea of the victim Afghan woman, that actually persists even now, so yeah I don't know how much it has changed, I'm not sure. (Kate, Australian research consultant)

Again, there is clear recognition that this discourse of victimhood is a social product and not the lived reality, but equally a concern that practices of power invest in the idea of the 'victim Afghan woman'.

Moreover, some internationals reflected on the complicity of the international project in perpetuating certain understandings of and practices around the idea of Afghan femininity. Lisa articulated an affective link between the security measures of liberal peace actors and the reification of protection as a gendered cultural norm. She told me a story about how her Afghan partner felt a social pressure to protect his sisters, and while this was partly framed as an Afghan social dynamic, she also linked it to wider affective norms of protection and security in the military–peace paradigm:

> [T]he illusion of protecting women because of the need to protect women in this place, because of the sustained insecurity and I think that all of these security measures just perpetuate that – if you didn't have police everywhere, an armed guard at your door etc., this illusion of needing to protect everything, home, self, car, everything, then I don't think there would be as much of a need to display the protection of women. (Lisa, American NGO worker)

Mike suggested that the presence of foreign military personnel, who were predominantly male, had increased the seclusion of women and exacerbated the desire for their removal from public spaces:

> I remember going down into a village once and saying, 'Where are all the women, you know?' And the guys said, 'Yeah you know, you always tell us this, that we don't let our women out a lot you know'. And he said, 'Do you know why we don't let our women out? We don't let our women out because you're here. Like if you weren't here, and in years before you were here, our women were out all the time, you would see them going from house to house and to the market within this village or this cluster of villages. And we know that you're here to help us and do all this good and do this stuff, but we're not going to let them go out'. (Mike, civilian liaison to the US military)

Another respondent contested the de-historicisation process of abstracting an 'average' Afghan woman by highlighting the role that narratives of the past had to play in shaping gendered praxis in the present:

> Of course there has been a gradual sort of public participation of women, during the last communist regime, for example, some changes happened, but because of the fear of what King Amanullah suffered because his wife came

out and she went to Europe and this is what even our current president – he says it in public meeting that 'Oh you remember how the King made his wife naked-face to the outside world and how much he lost?' So, the politicians, the men in power in this country are afraid of that sort of distain for themselves. That's why nobody has seen President Karzai's wife so far in public but of course she has a different role somewhere else. (Asal, Afghan activist)

Moreover, respondents highlighted that patriarchal social structures in Afghanistan were invested in maintaining a social category similar to the 'average third world woman' removed from the public sphere and silenced, despite the very active resistance of Afghan women and their allies. Controlling women in the name of national or religious identity or culture has long been recognised as a political move that entrenches patriarchal power and is designed to galvanise particular political feelings. Afghanistan exemplifies this at times and it would seem that conservative and militant forces have often found it useful to marginalise and repress women where possible and mobilise gendered discourses.

I consider the multiplicities circulating around the idea of the Afghan woman as part of an 'average third world woman' trope because they elucidate that, though this notion was often contested and rarely simplistically promoted by my respondents, it nonetheless held cognitive and discursive power to the point that it must be seen as somehow definitional in wider narratives around Afghanistan. I suggest that this deep trope was so ensconced within the idea of intervention and resistance to it, so intertextually woven into the discursive and visual imaginary of Afghanistan in the eyes of the international, that it continued to structure the possibilities for thought and knowledge around Afghan women's lives. Yet, equally, the complexity of my respondents' encounters with the idea of a 'victim Afghan woman' trope highlights not only its power but the labour involved in maintaining it as an ideational and justificatory category.

To conclude this section, what I have wanted to articulate here is threefold: first, that the idea of the 'average third world' Afghan woman was established partially in the visual imaginary of the country and circulated for specific political reasons; second, that this abstracted framework played a role in international self-definition, emphasising that the gendered 'international' itself functioned as a social category only possible because of particular ideas of the gendered 'local' against which it was to be defined (this will be covered in more detail in the following section); third and finally, that the trope of the 'average third world'

Afghan woman in practice was constantly destabilised, contradicted, criticised and partial yet still functioned to structure meaning, and that feminist lenses elucidate the importance of noticing this.

The Third Gender[2]

The idea of the third sex or gender has a diverse and complex history (Herdt 1996; Knafo 2001; Mirande 2015).[3] Heteronormative and binary understandings of gender can be understood as mainstream within recent Western history, and the politics and normative categories that accompany this reductionist frame of reference have been widely imposed and brutally policed, not least through imperial and racist forms of violence and governmentality. Yet, binary categories of male and female do not adequately reflect human experience.

The third sex or gender as a category transcends gender dimorphism, indicating neither simplistically 'man' nor 'woman'; it is an idea that has been referred to in multiple contexts in different temporal moments, with both biological and social meaning (sometimes incorporating sex organs, sometimes gendered social performance and/or ontology) – referencing intersex people, gay people, men who cross-dress, transgender people and others throughout history (Herdt 1996; Knafo 2001; Leng 2014; Mirande 2015; True and Nederman 2016). Put simply, however, the term 'third sex' or 'third gender' in the context of my research refers to those who identify as international women in Afghanistan – military or civilian actors. It is used primarily by these women to describe themselves purely in a social, perception-based and performative sense, without any implication of shifts in biological sex (hormones, sex organs and so on) or ontology (understanding of the gendered self). Importantly, the term is understood to depict the Afghan perception of international women, especially the Afghan male perception, though the framing of this term came from international women themselves.[4]

It is worth drawing attention here to the historical association between the third sex or gender, citizenship, race and the queer body. As Cynthia Weber points out, the depiction of a savage, racialised Other as sexualised, deviant and 'homosexual' actually 'played a role in licensing Victorian sovereign states to subject entire colonialised populations to imperial rule' (Weber 2016: 21). Manchanda (2014) argues that elements of this trope are also at work in depictions and framings of the Afghan context in the West. As previously stated, the third sex has been used as a term to refer to a queer or subversive body, one that does not neatly adhere to socially normative gender dimorphism and can thus at times be understood as dangerous or deviant (Herdt 1996; Weber 2016). There is an affective link then between, on the one hand, the history of the third sex as a term of reference, marking particular gendered bodies which fall outside the parameters of binary gender norms (in both socially sanctioned and socially deviant ways), and, on the other hand, the framing of subversive non-binary sexuality/gender identity as a mechanism through which racialised politics/violence is played out. So here, drawing, perhaps unconsciously, on a trajectory of meaning which situates them in a wider history of both subversive sexuality and imperial violence, actors in a liberal peace/statebuilding mode call to action a term which indicates non-binary liberation from gendered heteronormativity.

The understanding of the 'third sex/gender' which I analyse and which my interview respondents refer to is heavy with the history of interaction between Afghanistan and the 'West', between the liberal and the perceived 'illiberal' in the global order. As such, 'we must acknowledge that how a certain body (marked through signs of gender, sexuality, race, etc.) feels about another (differently marked) body is not simply a matter of individual impressions but that this "contact is shaped by past histories of contact"' (Ahmed 2015: 7, cited in Laliberté and Schurr 2016: 74).

One of the core ideas that informs the analysis of the third sex/gender construct in this chapter is the notion that certain women ('liberal' citizens of the international) in spaces of exception and violence occupy a liminal position and are generative of unease. This idea of liminality has been traced by feminist scholars in relation to female soldiers in particular. For instance, Katharine Millar (2015) uses Judith Butler's concept of grievability and the anthropological notion of liminality to argue that female soldiers pose a challenge to public mourning processes. Millar has analysed female soldiers' obituaries and argues that there is a dual narrative within them whereby women are framed both as true soldiers (brave, competent) and specifically as feminine (through the mentioning of children or maternal roles, for example), articulating the discomfort inherent in the representation of military women by pointing to the incoherence in their remembrance (Millar 2015: 6). This incoherence signals the tension implicit in women's links with militaries and militarised praxis more generally and the debates around their engagement with militarism (Eichler 2014: 87). As I explain, within the military–peace complex this tension and liminality applies to both civilian and military women, marked by their international bodies and 'liberal' citizenship (by which I mean relationship to the international project and association with the West).

As such, part of the function of the 'third sex/gender' as described by my respondents and in wider research was as a mechanism of negotiated performance, a means to navigate their own liminal embodied meaning as liberal emblems. One NGO worker explained that her gendered performance in Afghanistan was a complex one: '[m]y perception of what it means to be a woman, I don't necessarily act that out in Afghanistan, it's a compromise between what I perceive as my gender and what I know is perceived of me because I'm a woman' (Lisa, American NGO worker). Her words speak to a process of navigation between what she saw as two gendered worlds. She and others seek to reconcile their understandings of themselves with the way that they think people react to them, the ways that they believe they are expected to perform gender in Afghanistan and their experiences of these expectations. Yet, on top of this, it is also clear that their 'liberal' citizenship creates a sense of confusion and unease around the notion of 'woman'. 'Liberal' citizenship bestows expectations around how women are allowed to behave, their capacity to enter the public sphere, hold power and positions of authority in different situations, and possess at least a nominal sense of equality and freedom. What comes up continually within the notion of the 'third gender' is the disruption but not dispersal of these expectations, the uneasy in-betweenness that comes with bringing ideas about 'liberal' and perceived 'illiberal' womanhood into confluence.

Anna suggests this sense of in-betweenness as pervasive:

Women there, foreign women, are kind of this third gender for Afghans, especially Afghan men. From an Afghan male perspective, again I'm generalising, but in general there are men and foreign men, and then there are Afghan women and then there are foreign women. For them foreign women are just sort of this like strange amalgamation of woman and man. (Anna, American education worker)

Within the notion of the 'third sex/gender' in Afghanistan, therefore, was the idea that foreign women were not entirely women but not men either (Dyvik 2013: 418). Thus it contained a complex uncertainty that was both gendered and racialised (Partis-Jennings 2017). The interaction between some concept of the 'foreign' and some concept of the 'female' played out as a site of friction in which 'porous boundaries' (Schia and Karlsrud 2013: 246) between different notions of 'woman' were marked by distinctions between foreign and local bodies in terms of differential freedom and access. Kate exemplified this well in the following comments: '[p]eople talk a lot about foreign women being like the third sex. I don't really like the analogy but there is certainly things that you can do that Afghan women can't do' (Kate, Australian research consultant).

This comment elucidates, as I have argued above, that there would be no 'third sex/gender' in this context without the idea of a 'second sex/gender' (Beauvoir 1997), that is the 'average third world woman', lacking agency and freedom. Luise illustrated that the very ownership of a gender identity became context-dependent:

> [B]ecause my socialisation is German, or European, I would certainly identify, if I would identify, I would identify as a woman, like I would never say I identify as third gender. I identify as third gender in the Afghan context if that makes sense. (Luise, German UN worker)

Her words point to this category as contextually bound, and again illustrate that it is rendered intelligible in relation to specific perceptions of the Afghan gendered social order.

The 'third sex/gender' also applied to military women. Sarah, a female military respondent, commented that 'that female/male thing doesn't seem to exist with female soldiers' and that 'on the whole I think that the Afghans were . . . dealing with females and I sort of feel that a girl in uniform is like a third sex to them, it is not a woman, it is not a man' (Sarah, Major, British Army). Eva, speaking of military women, said, 'female soldiers don't really count as a gender because they are soldiers' (Eva, international personnel). This trope reflects a liminality that privileges the space of male soldiering and reifies the connection between soldiering and masculinity by emphasising the exceptionalism of women in soldiering roles. One FET member notes that

> since female Marines have power and responsibility, they are viewed by Afghan men as being on the same level as a male. Yet, FETs are still viewed as females, allowing the teams to have access and ability to engage Afghan females. (NATO 2011, cited in Dyvik 2013: 417)

Dyvik points out that this is a common characterisation: 'FETs are often characterized as representing a kind of "third gender" in relation to Afghan civilians' (Dyvik 2013: 412). Feminist scholarship has elucidated ways in which 'the presence of servicewomen is identified as a problem; women are essentialised and characterised as instigators of sexual tensions . . . that have the potential to undermine military goals' (Basham 2013: 57; see also Millar 2015; Pin-Fat and Stern 2005). The idea of the 'third sex/gender' here is indicative again of complex performative process whereby women are, or perceive themselves as, recoded to allow space for their gender identities. Thus, the threat of their disruptive womanhood is managed. Indeed, this gendered liminality is highlighted as a military asset by a female British soldier writing for a website on military thought: 'The "Third Sex" became a term applied to female soldiers, perceptually located between male and female, which allowed local men to engage beyond their socio-cultural constraints, thereby enabling greater military access to, understanding, and inclusion of the whole community' (Stone 2019).

She goes on to explain:

> The 'Third Sex' or 'Third Gender' was used as a coping mechanism to enable direct collaboration with men who had constraints on conversing with women who are not related (non-mahram), but it also enabled access to women who are forbidden from interacting in any way with a man outside their family network (Stone 2019).

Thus, in this view, transcending gender dimorphism can offer strategic advantage to the militaries, drawing upon the space between expectations of maleness and expectations of femaleness in a given context, in addition to the privilege of an international body in order to pursue intelligence gathering and biometric data collection from civilian populations.

Luise expressed a similar idea about the value of liminal gendered performances in relation to her work for the UN: 'Because I feel like every human being should be able to do what they want to do, and by falling in-between being a man and being an Afghan woman, you can, actually'. She suggested increased possibilities in her work as a result: 'ultimately, when it comes to the work, I actually think as that third gender you actually have access . . . you are a lot better equipped to talk to both parts of society' (Luise, German UN worker).

It is important to note here that the character of work being discussed is substantively different in nature and, in the military case, is motivated explicitly by war-based objectives rooted, at their heart, in violence, whereas UN programming in most cases is not, and certainly not to the same extent. Yet, unquestionably there is some common ground here in terms of the complex liminality that sticks to international female bodies,[5] delineating them in gendered terms as expressly not Afghan female bodies, embodying borders between 'liberal' and perceived 'illiberal' lifeworlds and mobilising that liminality within the overarching strategic goals of the military–peace complex. In both cases, there is an attempt to fit to the perceived gender order of Afghanistan, to be culturally respectful and to achieve the aims of statebuilding, while at the same time both masculinity and liberal femininity are reified as always already disaggregated from a passive, culturally subjugated Afghan femininity.

Gendered Negotiations

In this final section of this chapter, I want to further explore the issue of gendered negotiations, the processes that require women in particular to negotiate and curate their gendered performances in particular ways within and alongside the military–peace complex.

One form these negotiations took was between the social categories of the 'international' and the 'local'. Safia, an Afghan-Canadian, described the negotiated nature of her everyday life: 'I'm trying to fit in, I don't fit in, but then sometimes I don't really want to fit in' (Safia, Afghan-Canadian IO worker). She talked about the manner in which some colleagues would assign her 'local' status, yet she felt her identity was in fact a complicated and hybridised one: 'I think that the way they see it is I'm just a local, I can go hang out with the locals, but I work here as an international'. Safia suggested that some Afghan men she encountered through her work saw her identity as problematic and would try to redefine her in gendered ways: 'they are really trying to push back and put this Afghan label on me, and I think by doing that they want to set parameters or maybe restrict what I should be doing and what I should not be doing' (Safia, Afghan-Canadian IO worker). Similarly, Masha, another Afghan-Canadian, discussed a sense of 'ownership' that came with her Afghan heritage and that she needed to negotiate carefully (Masha, Afghan-Canadian NGO founder/director).

In our interview Safia spoke of the complexity at work within her performance as an 'international' whose body (in the eyes of others) tied her to different expectations from those placed on foreign bodies. She gave the example of how foreign-educated Afghan men reacted to her:

> because they are men, and they are foreign educated but they are still Afghan, I don't know, I feel I am sensing more of an issue with that, the way that I am not actually an Afghan woman, but I look like it. (Safia, Afghan-Canadian IO worker)

Her implication is that her Afghan-ness sticks to her in an affective as well as a bodily sense; she somehow ought to perform Afghan femininity in line with her bodily image, but she is equally tied affectively to a sense of her own foreignness which sticks (see Ahmed 2015) just as strongly to her gendered identity and performative expectations of her work and lifestyle.

Equally, Afghan women, particularly those in positions of authority such as prominent activists and community leaders and those who headed up civil society organisations or worked with the government, needed to navigate the idea of Western influence/interference carefully. As such, 'in their quest for a "voice," women have to express themselves in terms of actions and performances, which have local cultural resonance' (Billaud 2015: 12).

For Asal, an Afghan activist, engagement with feminism in Afghanistan had entailed a process of adaptation and learning, whereby she felt that she had learned to adapt her work to the communities she was working with. Esin, an Afghan NGO director, explained that this could sometimes be a question of language and framing:

> We had a campaign called Healthy Family Fortune Society and the interesting part was when I first shared the name of the campaign and the whole initiative in the staff meeting everybody started laughing because it was such a basic childish name, Healthy Family Fortune Society, but the idea beyond this was actually the elimination of domestic violence and I could not go with that name because it was perceived as a blueprint from the Western countries, so I had to choose a name that was more acceptable for communities where it was coming in there. (Esin, Afghan NGO director)

In her words her capacity for negotiation and careful attempts to pursue a feminist agenda that is culturally respectful and framed accordingly are clear.

This negotiation was also expressed through the politics of clothing. Esin spoke of the complex interplay between Western-centric expectations of the performance of liberation, marked by clothing, particularly in the Afghan case, and her own agency as an activist and campaigner:

> I've had to change from everything that I was doing, my get-up, from the way that I was clothing, so I wouldn't go with the clothes I have on now, with my jeans and pants on and all that. I mean wearing a black, long hijab didn't cost me anything, it didn't affect my personality or activism . . . Rather than, you know, getting this very typical idea that I have to go and make them accept my very Western type of clothing and all that. (Esin, Afghan NGO director)

Rebecca highlighted the centrality of appearance to modes of acceptance in her experience, and the differing regional politics of clothing in rural areas:

> [Names organisation] had a gender team coming over once and they were all like Kabuli and fancy girls in jeans and yeah, it had the opposite effect in the communities because they were just like 'Well, who are these slutty women from the city, what are they doing here?' And it was not accepted at all. (Rebecca, NGO worker)

Despite the symbolism of the burka often acting as a shorthand for repression in the narratives around the Afghan context, it too was an item of negotiation. Paying attention to different narratives highlights complex experiences and perceptions of the burka. Researcher Kate pointed out that there was a link between women who wore the burka and their capacity or desire to send their children to school. Her research had shown that some women who wore the burka felt safer walking with their children. Since they were more willing to accompany them to school, they were more willing to send them (Kate, Australian research consultant). An Afghan woman I spoke to informally during a lunch meeting had been a teacher in a covert girls' school under the Taliban. She told me that the burka helped her to go unnoticed, and to escape punishment when the Taliban inspected her classroom (see also Joya 2009).

In the international domain, processes of gendered navigation often centred on security practices, sexuality and unease around the female body and its presence in the context of violence. For instance, Sarah explained how she needed to navigate a sense of unease produced by her status as a female soldier (a theme that was also echoed by other respondents). She highlighted how this unease often centred on the concept of protection and questions of her vulnerability to violence as a woman, as well as the increased politics of her status as a soldier.

She suggested that the British military was overprotective of female soldiers in part because of the public perception of their wellbeing, and the media issues that might occur in the event of their death:

> I found that being a female, my boss was really scared, my British Lieutenant-Colonel boss was so worried and he wanted a male to go out instead of me, but it wasn't his job, it was definitely my job. So, he was scared, and I said, 'What are you worried about?', and he said, 'Well I'm just worried that something bad will happen to you and I'm also worried that it will look worse in

the press'. And I know what he means, because if a female soldier dies there is so much more, it is front page news, whereas it is tragic but if a male soldier dies now it is, sort of you know, page three or four. (Sarah, Major, British Army)

Sarah went on to claim, 'it is almost like the West is so overprotective that we're tripping over ourselves', and then repeated a little later, 'it is almost like we're overprotective when it comes to this, sort of the cultural take on a gender dynamic' (Sarah, Major, British Army).

James (former British Army) described his dread when his company was assigned a female medic. He told me that he was worried she would cause his men to disobey his orders under fire. He explained that if one of the company was badly injured when on patrol, the other soldiers needed to leave that person where they were until the situation was secure and they could then provide assistance. James was concerned that the protective feelings his men would feel towards a woman would mean that if she were hurt they would not be able to refrain from helping her. He said that this had thankfully never been put to the test. He also praised the medic and said that she would have had to have been extraordinarily good at her job in order to get to that position as a woman. He suggested that the medic had become a 'sister' to the men and commended that she did not 'use her sexuality' in interactions with her colleagues (James, former British Army).[6]

Sarah's experience and James's concerns evoke Gentry and Sjoberg's unpacking of the female soldier as an ideal-type figure 'capable as a male soldier, but as vulnerable as a civilian woman' (Gentry and Sjoberg 2007: 86). To some extent and to varying degrees the modes of unease Sarah experienced around her femaleness map onto what Enloe (2007), and Bulmer (2013) following Enloe, have described as 'patriarchal confusion':

> [W]hen we pay close attention to women in the military, there are many times when promoters of patriarchy find it difficult to sustain the naturalness of the dichotomy between 'masculinity' and 'femininity' and the propriety (positive value) of a certain mode of feminine behaviour. (Enloe 2007: 81)

The link between masculinised protection and war is in fact central to the construction, justification and maintenance of state-sanctioned violence whereby '[i]t is men's masculine duty to protect women; this duty fuels men's desire and ability to fight in wars' (Sjoberg 2006: 897), and so disruption of this relationship might fuel unease. The concern expressed by an officer around how Sarah's death might be viewed in the media speaks of a wider public response to the death of women in war, which might be markedly different from the public response to the death of men in war (Millar 2015). Relatedly, it points to questions about how women function as a political symbol in warfare in different ways.

The relationship between the symbol of the dead female soldier and wider perceptions of warfare is crafted through an inherent discomfort and a sense of inappropriateness illustrating the 'difficulty, if not impossibility, of expressing a form of subjectivity independent of broader social norms of mourning and grievability' (Millar 2015: 16). In the UK, the US, and in many other places as well, there is a natural link forged historically, and through media and popular representations, between the male body and sacrifice in war (Baggiarini 2015: 38). However, the female body is incongruous in this domain and representations of dead female soldiers in mainstream media are thus defined by attempts to re-inscribe their femininity and navigate their liminal position between 'soldier' and 'woman/mother/daughter/sister/wife' (Baggiarini 2015). These attempts at marking the femininity of the individuals at the moment of discursive 'closure' required by death is deeply significant and illustrative of wider questions of gender identity: 'what is said (or unsaid) about a person following death reflects society's understanding of her identity' (Millar 2015: 3).

Part of the inherent discomfort with dead female soldiers can also be traced back to that deep connection between male bodies, sacrifice and the state. Male citizenship (as superior citizenship) has historically been linked to the potential sacrifice of male bodies in defence of the nation (Baggiarini 2015). Notions of sacrifice as relating to the state garner meaning through gendered framings: 'sacrificial discourses are written upon disciplined, sexed bodies and therefore contain a deeply gendered logic of transcendence over the impure feminine: that is over the female/feminised body' (Eichler 2015a: 41). So part of the problematic motivating a visceral and discursive unease with the sacrifice of the female body in the context of war is arguably that it destabilises the long-standing nexus between state-sanctioned violence and true citizenship (Enloe 2007: 63–5).

Complex gendered negotiations and security performances around protection and the female body were also experienced in the civilian domain, for instance between security contractors and female civilian staff. Higate, researching the relationship between protector and protected in a private security context, suggests that the 'cultivation of fear and anxiety . . . was fostered as a disciplinary strategy' which 'cemented the masculinized protector role rooted in control and authority' (Higate 2012b: 14).

In one account that echoes aspects of this analysis a respondent explained that there was a certain kind of gendered governmentality in her everyday life. She described 'international men being really worried about my personal life, which I do think is related to my gender', particularly a situation where

> one of the security officers [was] at a party and he is the guy that is responsible for tracking where we are most of the time. He said . . . "I know you stayed over at the US embassy, do you have a boyfriend there?"' (Luise, German UN worker)

She told me that many women faced inappropriate, searching questions such as this, somehow framed as tied to their security (where men did not) and a lack of any faith in their ability to look after themselves, despite, as in Luise's case, greater knowledge of Kabul than the security personnel themselves. She commented that because of this gendered treatment, 'I feel like I am really in prison' (Luise, German UN worker).

Eva, another respondent, while not discussing security, explained sexist perceptions attached to gender performance within the international sector in Afghanistan. She talked about the way that international men could view their female counterparts as sexually available and also subordinate: 'the perception changes to "oh these women in Afghanistan, who are working here and who are here just for the fun and the wild parties and we don't have to take them really equal"'. She suggested a distinct lack of equality in her experience:

> as a female, all of the kind of bad stuff we had before emancipation kind of kicks in. You are kind of, not so much an equal as you are in the UK or Germany or any kind of normal environment, it is really different. (Eva, international personnel)

Thus, it is clear that different kinds of negotiation, confusion, performance, hybridity and uncertainty in relation to gender, protection and (in)security cut through the military–peace complex and its effects in different ways. Gendered ideas repeatedly facilitated identities, work and daily routines while gendered expectations and negotiations helped to guide various actors through the complexities of their work and everyday life in Afghanistan.

Conclusions

This chapter has had five core areas of focus, addressing different tropes and gendered ideas, relationships and performances. These have been separately discussed but are also clearly related and interconnected, and the interconnections and overlap have been highlighted. I have articulated the gendered nature of the military–peace complex and engaged with the instrumentalisation of gender and especially the women's rights and freedoms within multiple dimensions of the international project. I have discussed an idea of Afghan womanhood, which, drawing on insights from postcolonial feminism, I consider a deep trope, so fundamental that it holds meaning even without direct, individual engagement. In terms of the 'third sex/gender', the label's span across the military and civilian category of female peacebuilder illustrates a distinct parallel between the performances of gender and foreign identity, collapsing the military and civilian together within an interlocking practice of exceptional bodily performance and distinction from the Afghan context. Both the military and the peacebuilding sides of this paradigm demonstrate a specific kind of unease with the female body and the constant comparison between two distinct imaginaries; that of the 'liberal' gender order of the 'international'/West, and the 'illiberal' gender order of Afghanistan.

A feminist lens sits at the heart of the military–peace complex as a paradigm and a way of looking at intervention, not just because of the importance of gendered constructs and intersectional considerations, but because feminist thinking promotes a holistic understanding. Drawing on a feminist lens in this chapter and looking for the operation of gender within the military–peace complex allows me to draw out the processes of negotiation, the ideational slippages and structures, and the contradictions and contentions that constitute it. A feminist lens allows for a rejection of single narratives (Mehta and Wibben 2018); it troubles 'the very meaning of security and what it means *to be secure*' (Mehta and Wibben 2018: 50, original emphasis) and opens up space to see how gendered ideas produce modes of violence while also fuelling resistance to hegemonic power. A feminist lens allows for the innate disjuncture in intervention praxis to come starkly into view without denying agency to those who fight for a little more space and access within its context. Finally, recognising the everyday and ideological constructions of gender that circulated around the international project in Afghanistan elucidate in new ways the entanglements between military and peace work within the military–peace complex.

Notes

1. This was a term used by Cynthia Enloe during a talk at King's College London entitled '#Metoo Shines a Bright Light on Genuine Security' on 25 September 2019.
2. This section and discussions of the 'third gender' concept draw from a published piece in *Peacebuilding* (Partis-Jennings 2019).
3. I use both 'third sex' and 'third gender' here because my respondents used both 'sex' and 'gender' in conversation. Gender is often understood to refer more directly to socially constructed behaviour and social norms, where sex can sometimes be understood as biological in nature. This conception of sex has been strongly contested in some feminist work, and it can be suggested that sex too is performed and constructed rather than fixed (see Nicholson 1994). However, it falls outside the scope of this discussion to explore this distinction further. It is worth noting here that I use both 'third sex' and 'third gender' to indicate a discursive interchangeability that I encountered and 'third sex' to reflect the more common usage among participants.
4. Interestingly, though it falls outside the scope of this discussion, there are parallels with the phenomenon of the bacha posh in Afghanistan: female children who are dressed and raised as male in order for them and their family to gain access to additional freedoms and social privileges associated with masculinity (Nordberg 2014).
5. For an exploration of the idea of 'stickiness' and its complex implications in relation to bodies, emotions and hierarchies, see the work of Sara Ahmed (2015, 2010, 2007).
6. The recording of the second part of my interview with James in which he discusses the female medic and other aspects linked to gender culture in the military was corrupted and inaudible, so I have paraphrased some of his comments where I refer to them.

A Final Conclusion

I will keep this conclusion brief and discuss just a few final points. First, I want to articulate again what engaging with the international project in Afghanistan through the framework of the military–peace complex does. Then I move to consider tensions that I suggest are drawn out by this book and how those tensions might make for productive lines of thinking or imagining.

So, why the military–peace complex? One element that characterises much of the critical scholarship on Afghanistan, and on intervention and war more broadly, is its alertness to connections. When we see a foreign intervention as building on previous foreign interventions; when we know the role the US played in supporting actors who committed violence against civilians in Afghanistan; when we recognise that private companies who, for instance, are at work guarding detainees in refugee detention centres in the UK are also involved in running prisons, and in deconstructing military sites at the behest of Western governments during the troop drawdown in Afghanistan in 2014; when we see an instrumental deployment of gender politics that echoes through history, well, then, we see the world a little differently. What I have tried to do in this book is craft connections in different ways, drawing in the idea of 'everyday international relations' and thinking about the performative practices that generate webs of being and knowing in different political contexts. Few who look at the international project in Afghanistan see a 'success', if that term is even appropriate. NATO framed ideas of 'hope' and success around the notion that the Taliban had been banished by international military action (Wright 2019) yet today, the Taliban are once again primed for power. However, many of the modes of addressing and articulating this absence of 'success' have focused on military strategy, the Afghan context itself or the misuse of resources. Instead, articulating a military–peace complex is about addressing the innate dissonance that manifested in this project, the ways it was always bound to certain kinds of gendered, racialising, disaggregating and material logics, both martial and liberal, and that these self-sustain and produce modes of violence, exclusion and short-termism, even where they can also foster change.

It is important to highlight the fact that my critique is harsh on international actors at times. This often gave me pause as I know that many people within the international domain are doing important work, sometimes risking their lives and pursuing what they understand as positive goals. Thinking about this I draw upon the insights of Olivia Rutazibwa (2019) who points to the good intentions of humanitarian actors in many cases, yet argues that as the global order shifts away from liberal humanitarianism we must go beyond idealisation and vilification and search for something more complex. She writes: '[t]hinking about the role of humanitarianism today requires that we don't reproduce or unwittingly celebrate Western-led order by mourning the end of a history that never actually existed. Given past and present non-Western experiences of liberal order, we might ask: what's there to mourn?' She goes on to argue that '[w]ith humanitarianism itself being redefined, decolonial perspectives can contribute to an understanding of the relevance of the good intentions of humanitarians to the aspirations of their intended "beneficiaries"'. Rutazibwa's insights highlight the importance of questioning more than intentions and considering the complex and messy worlds of intervention and statebuilding from new perspectives.

Thus, what I have outlined in this book are the ways that flaws, negotiations, disjunctures and contradictions in the military–peace complex manifest 'despite the best intentions of the humanitarian aid workers and donors as . . . unequal relationships are established through the practices of aid' (Goetze 2016: 134). Moreover, I have suggested that, practices, lifestyles and routines are woven into the physical structures of the built environment and other elements of materiality, which in turn exercise affective power over the conditions of possibility in which statebuilding work can occur: '[t]hese practices are manifest in the built environment and material objects of humanitarianism, and their effects are so powerful that they belie all discourses about partnerships and participatory approaches' (Goetze 2016: 134). Similarly, I recognise that soldiers might have good or mixed intentions, that many risk their lives daily, that COIN offers some attempt to minimise civilian casualties and that the inclusion of women soldiers in its strategic goals could be framed as important for gender equity within the military.[1] Yet these elements run alongside actions that are short-sighted and misguided as well as being utilitarian and always in service of the logic of war, which complicates the picture.

This is also not to sideline intentionality altogether, as it must be remembered that these approaches stem from ideological and power-bound commitments, some of which have been historically rendered via modes of imperialism and racialised and gendered biopolitics, some of which are intelligible only in relation to the specifics of the contemporary moment marked by war on terror framings and globalised Islamophobia. At the heart of this ideology is what Jörg Meyer articulates: that so often, deep within the ontological presuppositions of the international order, 'the (non-Western) other is represented as unwilling to maintain or incapable of maintaining peace, so that producing peace becomes an obligation – indeed a prerogative – of the (Western) self as the sole agent of order' (Meyer 2008: 555). While the various aspects of the liberal peace and related paradigms can involve friction, hybridisation and change, it arguably maintains a core discourse and ideology: '[l]iberal governmentality ... produces subjects and spaces governed differently within an overall rationality of rule' (Laffey and Nadarajah 2012: 407). Using the idea of the military–peace complex as a framework, which centres on entanglements drawn out though particular logics, performances, gendered, spatial and material factors, allows the complex interplay of intention, failure, ideology and power in the international project to come into view in new ways.

Another point that I wish to note here is that this book has been an exercise in immanent critique. I have argued repeatedly that gendered ideas, material and spatial practices, bodies and performances facilitate the workings of humanitarian and military praxis in different ways, but also expose their contradictions. The concept of immanent critique is central to the Frankfurt School of Critical Theory but also to the writings of Hegel and Marx (Antonio 1981). In essence, immanent critique looks for the inconsistencies and contradictions within a given social order, and exploits these to generate a critique of that social order which is immanent to the order itself. Richard Devetak suggests that immanent critique requires us to 'excavate the principles and values that structure our political society, exposing the contradictions or inconsistencies in the way our society is organised to pursue its espoused values' (Devetak 2013: 169).

In arguing, for instance, that gender facilitates the workings of statebuilding praxis but also exposes its contradictions, I am suggesting that the same social structuring – the relational nexus between masculinities and femininities in this case – both allows the military–peace paradigm to function and provides the tools with which to critique its inherent inconsistencies. I have dedicated this book to highlighting and unpacking some of these inconsistencies and disjunctures from multiple perspectives, yet throughout my research, resistance, hybridity and hopefulness have emerged from that critique too, most especially from my respondents.

And so this brings me to another point, the question of alternatives. It has not been my intention in this book to imagine what could have been done differently in Afghanistan by international actors and those linked to the international project. Rather, I have focused on paying attention to the disjunctures and problematics inherent in the ways that things happened, yet I see great hope in this disjuncture and in the fact that so many within or proximal to the international project were so attentive to its flaws.

Within my research materials there were endless examples of individuals resisting, hybridising or subverting hierarchies and inequalities in important ways. Among the military, there were examples of individual soldiers striving to overcome the disjuncture in the COIN paradigm and make it a genuinely better strategy for Afghans or other soldiers. Jack spoke about using his extensive military experience to guide younger soldiers towards respecting female colleagues and keeping civilians safe from collateral damage (Jack, former US Special Forces). Carlo spoke of empathising with Afghan partners and seeking to understand their emotional experiences (Carlo, defence attaché). Christopher spoke of accountability and avoiding a mentality of revenge as well as the value of education in fostering military coping strategies (Christopher, former German military). On the civilian side, Lisa refused the distancing mechanisms of larger statebuilding organisations and instead chose to work for a small Afghan NGO for a much smaller salary than she could have earned and lived without heightened security measures (Lisa, American NGO worker). Esin rejected the conflation of dress with liberal modernity, arguing that traditional Afghan attire did not affect her activism (Esin, Afghan activist). Kate made a point of hiring and giving opportunities to Afghan women, and actively worked to subvert their designation as victims in wider narratives (Kate, Australian research consultant). Esin and Luise spoke of leveraging aspects of their gender identity in service of others and their work. Esin, Asal, Damsa and others spoke of their constant, almost lifelong fight for Afghan women's safety and rights. These examples and many, many more matter a great deal in and of themselves, but they also contribute to a wider affective mode which pushes back against the distancing, Othering and negatively gendered components of the military–peace complex that I have mentioned in this research.

Feminist scholar Fiona Robinson highlights the possibilities of viewing the world in new ways by centring an ethic of care. This ethical paradigm, when applied to state- or peacebuilding, emphasises acceptance of vulnerability, relationality and the productive potential of difference. It is also focused on the long term (over short-term projects) and highlights contextualisation, relationship-building and emotional investment (Robinson 2011: 103–4). Thus:

> [t]he ethics of care provides the basis for an approach to peacebuilding that rejects the idea of state liberalization as a fast track to peace; rather care ethics displays a commitment to a slow process of listening to needs, building trust, and rebuilding relations and institutions for the long-term well-being of societies. (Robinson 2011: 104)

Paying attention to the moments of resistance that I have outlined as well as many more not mentioned elucidates that this ethics of care is already a part of the military–peace complex, yet in addition to structural change (such as to the neoliberal economic framework (Duncanson 2016)) within statebuilding this ethic needs to be centred and re-imagined as something more than personal choice. Afghan society is one marked by solidarity and the power of resistance. People in Afghanistan have lost their homes, their loved ones and sometimes their lives as part of the succession of violent manoeuvrings and as a society they continue to demand peace. The past cannot be undone or changed, but going forward it is clear that Afghans know what is best for the future of their nation, and that peace activism and peace movements within the country must be supported, while at the same time, serious consideration must be given to the deep and devastating inadequacies of intervention praxis, especially when it produces such significant entanglements between peace and war work.

Some forms of peace work are too deeply bound to the legacies of imperial inequality and violence to be salvageable. But thinking about the consequences of gendered, racialised, spatial and material logics, of modes of distancing and disaggregation, while also embracing the complexity and template-defying nature of human life and the possibilities of an empathetic and critical ethic, might facilitate a reorientation away from modes of peace work that are built on threat, risk management and military entanglement and towards hope, remembering that 'practicing hope', as Shepherd points out, is a 'profoundly political activity' most especially when one is supposed to be practising fear (2014: 99).

Perhaps practising hope means that security logics are constantly questioned, that militaries are not conflated with development actors, that security actors are always held accountable for their actions and that, if security must be made corporate, clear boundaries are maintained to keep peace work separate from private militarism and indeed wider entanglements with military logics and work. It means '[r]ecognising the social – and therefore relational – aspect of . . . peacebuilding' and statebuilding so that 'we think beyond technocratic "solutions" to the "problem" of peace and instead ask what we might learn from studies of human society' (Shepherd 2014: 102). It means disaggregating corporate and people-focused economic strategies and consistently applying ethical standards to practices of partnership and collaboration, even in times of violence and upheaval.

More than anything it means a constant process of re-evaluation. It means a feminist refusal. A refusal to be turned away from common-sense constructs, no matter how naturalised or difficult to question, how convoluted or everyday. A refusal not to hope that everyday bordering practices can be dismantled, that guns can be silenced and a refusal to forget that they – both the everyday borders and the guns – are only a product of our own making.

I hope that the military–peace complex as a framework can be of use in this endeavour, that it can help to unpack different elements of global political actions and demonstrate the significance of entanglements between military and peace work in everyday and geopolitical ways across contexts beyond Afghanistan, highlighting the centrality of the undernoticed, the material and the gendered to seeing another section of the whole picture.

Note

1. The activism and writing of former Marine Anuradha Bhagwati is important to consider in relation to these arguments; see Miller (2019).

BIBLIOGRAPHY

Abbas, Hassan (2014), *The Taliban Revival: Violence and Extremism on the Pakistan-Afghanistan Frontier*. New Haven, CT: Yale University Press.

Abirafeh, Lina (2009), *Gender and International Aid in Afghanistan: The Politics and Effects of Intervention*. Jefferson, NC: McFarland & Company Inc.

Abrahamsen, Rita and Anna Leander (eds) (2016), *Routledge Handbook of Private Security Studies*. Abingdon: Routledge.

Abu-Lughod, Lila (2002), 'Do Muslim Women Really Need Saving? Anthropological Reflections on Cultural Relativism and Its Others', *American Anthropologist* 104(3): 783–90.

Ackerly, Brooke A., Elisabeth Jay Friedman, Meenakshi Gopinath and Marysia Zalewski (2019), 'Resisting Global Anti-Genderism with Global Feminist Research', *International Feminist Journal of Politics* 21(2): 165–7, https://doi.org/10.1080/14616742.2019.1596386

Agathangelou, Anna M. (2019), 'A Conversation with Emma Hutchison and Frantz Fanon on Questions of Reading and Global Raciality', *Millennium – Journal of International Studies* 47(2): 249–62, https://doi.org/10.1177/0305829818808387

Agius, Christine (2017), 'Ordering without Bordering: Drones, the Unbordering of Late Modern Warfare and Ontological Insecurity', *Postcolonial Studies* 20(3): 370–86, https://doi.org/10.1080/13688790.2017.1378084

Åhäll, Linda (2019), 'Feeling Everyday IR: Embodied, Affective, Militarising Movement as Choreography of War', *Cooperation and Conflict* 54(2): 149–66, https://doi.org/10.1177/0010836718807501

Ahmed-Ghosh, Huma (2003), 'A History of Women in Afghanistan: Lessons Learnt for the Future', *Journal of International Women's Studies* 4(3): 1–14.

Ahmed, Azam and Matthew Rossenburg (2014), 'Deadly Attack at Kabul Restaurant Hints at Changing Climate', *The New York Times*, 18 January. Available at: https://www.nytimes.com/2014/01/19/world/asia/afghanistan-restaurant-attack.html

Ahmed, Leila (1992), *Women and Gender in Islam: Historical Roots of a Modern Debate*. New Haven, CT: Yale University Press.

Ahmed, Sara (2007), 'A Phenomenology of Whiteness', *Feminist Theory* 8(2): 149–68, https://doi.org/10.1177/1464700107078139

Ahmed, Sara (2008), 'Open Forum Imaginary Prohibitions: Some Preliminary Remarks on the Founding Gestures of the "New Materialism"', *European Journal of Women's Studies* 15(1): 23–39, https://doi.org/10.1177/1350506807084854

Ahmed, Sara (2010), 'Happy Objects', in Melissa Gregg and Gregory J. Seigworth (eds), *The Affect Theory Reader*. Durham, NC: Duke University Press, pp. 29–51.

Ahmed, Sara (2015), *The Cultural Politics of Emotion* (2nd edn). London: Routledge.

Aikins, Matthieu (2014), 'Last Tango in Kabul', *Rolling Stone*, August. Available at: http://www.rollingstone.com/politics/news/last-tango-in-kabul-20140818?page=2

Alimia, Sanaa (2019), 'Performing the Afghanistan–Pakistan Border Through Refugee ID Cards', *Geopolitics* 24(2): 391–425, https://doi.org/10.1080/14650045.2018.1465046

Allin, Dana (2011), 'US Policy and Afghanistan', in Nicholas Redman and Toby Dodge (eds), *Afghanistan to 2015 and Beyond*. Abingdon: Routledge, pp. 47–68.

Alvi, Hayat (2012), 'Women in Afghanistan: A Human Rights Tragedy a Decade After September 11', *Middle East Journal of International Affairs* 16(3). Available at: http://www.gloria-center.org/2012/11/women-in-afghanistan-a-human-rights-tragedy-a-decade-after-september-11/

Amini, Mariam (2018), 'Privatizing War in Afghanistan Endangers Civilians'. *Human Rights Watch*, 2 October. Available at: https://www.hrw.org/news/2018/10/03/privatizing-war-afghanistan-endangers-civilians

Amnesty International (2018), 'Afghanistan 2017/2018'. Available at: https://www.amnesty.ie/wp-content/uploads/2018/02/AIR201718_English_2018_EMBARGOED-22-FEB.pdf

Anderson, Craig, Arlin. J. Benjamin and Bruce. D. Bartholow (1998), 'Does the Gun Pull the Trigger? Automatic Priming Effects of Weapon Pictures and Weapon Names', *Psychological Science* 9(4): 308–14, https://doi.org/10.1111/1467-9280.00061

Anonymous (2016), 'Secret Aid Worker: "The Field" Is Not a Lab Where You Can Experiment without Consequence', *The Guardian*, 12 July. Available at: https://www.theguardian.com/global-development-professionals-network/2016/jul/12/secret-aid-worker-field-fieldwork-neocolonial-vocabulary

Antonenko, Oksana (2011), 'The Central Asian States and Russia', in Nicholas Redman and Toby Dodge (eds), *Afghanistan to 2015 and Beyond*. Abingdon: Routledge, pp. 199–218.

Antonio, Robert J. (1981), 'Immanent Critique as the Core of Critical Theory: Its Origins and Developments in Hegel, Marx and Contemporary Thought', *The British Journal of Sociology* 32(3): 330–45.

Aradau, Claudia (2010), 'Security That Matters: Critical Infrastructure and Objects of Protection', *Security Dialogue* 41(5): 491–514, https://doi.org/10.1177/0967010610382687

Aradau, Claudia and Jef Huysmans (2013), 'Critical Methods in International

Relations: The Politics of Techniques, Devices and Acts', *European Journal of International Relations* 20(3): 596–619, https://doi.org/10.1177/1354066116124 74479

Arendt, Hannah (1970), *On Violence*. New York: Harcourt.

Atkinson, Rowland and John Flint (2007), 'Fortress UK?: Gated Communities, the Spatial Revolt of the Elites and Time–Space Trajectories of Segregation', *Housing Studies* 19(6): 875–92, https://doi.org/10.1080/0267303042000293982

Auchter, Jessica (2012), 'Reimagining the Burqa', *International Feminist Journal of Politics* 14(3): 370–88, https://doi.org/10.1080/14616742.2012.659854

Autesserre, Severine (2014), *Peaceland*. Kindle edn. Cambridge: Cambridge University Press.

Azarbaijani-Moghaddam, Sippi (2012), 'Manly Honor and the Gendered Male in Afghanistan'. Available at: https://www.mei.edu/publications/manly-honor-and-gendered-male-afghanistan

Azarbaijani-Moghaddam, Sippi (2014), 'Seeking out Their Afghan Sisters: Female Engagement Teams in Afghanistan'. CMI Working Paper. Available at: https://www.cmi.no/publications/file/5096-seeking-out-their-afghan-sisters.pdf

Azarbaijani-Moghaddam, Sippi, Mirwais Wardak, Idrees Zaman and Annabel Taylor (2008), 'Afghan Hearts, Afghan Minds: Exploring Afghan Perceptions of Civil-Military Relations'. Available at: https://reliefweb.int/sites/reliefweb.int/files/resources/48BF3AFE30E5D1F5492575C200193A3B-Full_Report.pdf

Baggiarini, Bianca (2015), 'Military Privatization and the Gendered Politics of Sacrifice', in Maya Eichler (ed.), *Gender and Private Security in Global Politics*. Oxford: Oxford University Press, pp. 38–54.

Bakhtin, Mikhail (2002), 'Forms of Time and of the Chronotope in the Novel: Notes toward a Historical Poetics', in Brian Richardson (ed.), *Narrative Dynamics: Essays on Time, Plot, Closure and Frames*. Columbus, OH: The Ohio State University Press, pp. 15–24.

Barad, Karen (2003), 'Posthumanist Performativity: Toward an Understanding of How Matter Comes to Matter', *Signs: Journal of Women in Culture and Society* 28(3): 801–31, https://doi.org/10.1086/345321

Barad, Karen (2007), *Meeting the Universe Halfway: Quantum Physics and the Entanglement of Matter and Meaning*. Durham, NC: Duke University Press.

Barfield, Thomas (2010), *Afghanistan: A Cultural and Political History*. Princeton, NJ: Princeton University Press.

Barkawi, Tarak (2017), *Soldiers of Empire: Indian and British Armies in World War Two*. Cambridge: Cambridge University Press.

Basham, Victoria M. (2009), 'Effecting Discrimination: Operational Effectiveness and Harassment in the British Armed Forces', *Armed Forces & Society* 35(4): 728–44.

Basham, Victoria M. (2013), *War, Identity and the Liberal State: Everyday Experiences of the Geopolitical in the Armed Forces*. London: Routledge.

Basham, Victoria M. (2016), 'Gender, Race, Militarism and Remembrance: The Everyday Geopolitics of the Poppy', *Gender, Place & Culture* 23(6): 883–96, https://doi.org/10.1080/0966369X.2015.1090406

Basham, Victoria M. and Sarah Bulmer (2017), 'Critical Military Studies as Method: An Approach to Studying Gender and the Military', in Rachel Woodward and Claire Duncanson (eds), *The Palgrave International Handbook of Gender and the Military*. London: Palgrave Macmillan, pp. 59–71.

Basham, Victoria M. and Nick Vaughan-Williams (2013), 'Gender, Race and Border Security Practices: A Profane Reading of "Muscular Liberalism"', *The British Journal of Politics and International Relations* 15: 509–27, https://doi.org/10.1111/j.1467-856X.2012.00517.x

BBC News (2020), 'Afghan Conflict: US and Taliban Sign Deal to End 18-Year War', 29 February. Available at: https://www.bbc.co.uk/news/world-asia-51689443

Beauvoir, Simone de (1997), *The Second Sex*. London: Vintage.

Bennett, Jane (2010), *Vibrant Matter: A Political Ecology of Things*. Durham, NC: Duke University Press.

Bezhan, Faridullah (2014), 'Exile, Gender and Identity: The Short Stories of Afghanistani Author Maryam Mahboob', *Social Identities* 20(2–3): 239–56, https://doi.org/10.1080/13504630.2014.936374

Bhabha, Homi K. (1994), *The Location of Culture*. London: Routledge

Bialasiewicz, Luiza, David Campbell, Stuart Elden, Stephen Graham, Alex Jeffrey and Alison J. Williams (2007), 'Performing Security: The Imaginative Geographies of Current US Strategy', *Political Geography* 26(4): 405–22, https://doi.org/10.1016/j.polgeo.2006.12.002

Billaud, Julie (2012), 'The Making of Modern Afghanistan: Reconstruction, Transnational Governance and Gender Politics in the New Islamic Republic', *Anthropology of the Middle East* 7(1): 18–37, https://doi.org/10.3167/ame.2012.070103

Billaud, Julie (2015), *Kabul Carnival: Gender Politics in Postwar Afghanistan*. Philadelphia, PA: University of Pennsylvania Press.

Bird, Tim and Alex Marshall (2011), *Afghanistan: How the West Lost Its Way*. New Haven, CT: Yale University Press.

Björkdahl, Annika and Susanne Buckley-Zistel (eds) (2016), *Spatializing Peace and Conflict: Mapping the Production of Places, Sites and Scales of Violence*. Basingstoke: Palgrave Macmillan.

Bleiker, Roland and Emma Hutchison (2008), 'Fear No More: Emotions and World Politics', *Review of International Studies* 34(S1): 115–35, https://doi.org/10.1017/S0260210508007821

Blomqvist, Olof (2016), 'The Millions Left Behind in Afghanistan'. Amnesty International. Available at: https://www.amnesty.org/en/latest/news/2016/06/afghanistan-the-millions-left-behind/

Blunt, Alison and Cheryl McEwan (eds) (2002), *Postcolonial Geographies*. London: Continuum.

Bourdieu, Pierre (1972), *Esquisse d'une théorie de la pratique. Précédé de trois études d'ethnologie kabyle*. Paris: Droz.

Bourdieu, Pierre (1979), *La Distinction: critique sociale du jugement*. Paris: Éditions de Minuit.

Braudel, Fernand (1977), *Afterthoughts on Material Civilisation and Capitalism*. Baltimore, MD: Johns Hopkins University Press.

Brian, Danielle (2009), 'POGO Letter to Secretary of State Hillary Clinton Regarding U.S. Embassy in Kabul', Project on Government Oversight. Available at: https://www.pogo.org/letter/2009/09/pogo-letter-to-secretary-of-state-hillary-clinton-regarding-us-embassy-in-kabul/

Bucher, Jessica, Lena Engel, Stephanie Harfensteller and Hylke Dijkstra (2013), 'Domestic Politics, News Media and Humanitarian Intervention: Why France and Germany Diverged over Libya', *European Security* 22(4): 524–39, https://doi.org/10.1080/09662839.2013.766597

Bulmer, Sarah (2013), 'Patriarchal Confusion?', *International Feminist Journal of Politics* 15(2): 137–56, https://doi.org/10.1080/14616742.2012.746565

Bulmer, Sarah and Maya Eichler (2017), 'Unmaking Militarized Masculinity: Veterans and the Project of Military-to-Civilian Transition', *Critical Military Studies* 3(2): 161–81, https://doi.org/10.1080/23337486.2017.1320055

Bulmer, Sarah and David Jackson (2016), '"You Do Not Live in My Skin": Embodiment, Voice and the Veteran', *Critical Military Studies* 2(1–2): 25–40, https://doi.org/10.1080/23337486.2015.1118799

Burki, Shireen Khan (2011), 'The Politics of Zan from Amanullah to Karzi: Lessons for Improving Afghan Women's Status', in Jennifer Heath and Ashraf Zatiedi (eds), *Land of the Unconquerable: The Lives of Contemporary Afghan Women*. Berkeley, CA: University of California Press, pp. 45–59.

Bush, Laura (2001), 'Radio Address by Mrs. Bush'. The American Presidency Project. Available at: http://www.presidency.ucsb.edu/ws/?pid=24992

Butler, Judith (1999), *Gender Trouble: Feminism and the Subversion of Identity*. Abingdon: Routledge, https://doi.org/10.1016/j.jconhyd.2010.08.009

Campbell, Susanna, David Chandler and Meera Sabaratnam (eds) (2011), *A Liberal Peace? The Problems and Practices of Peacebuilding*. London: Zed Books.

Chandler, David (2012), 'Resilience and Human Security: The Post-Interventionist Paradigm', *Security Dialogue* 43(3): 213–29, https://doi.org/10.1177/0967010612444151

Charlesworth, Hilary and Christine Chinkin (2002), 'Sex, Gender and September 11', *The American Journal of International Law* 96(3): 600–5.

Chisholm, Amanda (2014), 'The Silenced and Indispensible', *International Feminist Journal of Politics* 16(1): 26–47, https://doi.org/10.1080/14616742.2013.781441

Chisholm, Amanda (2015), 'From Warriors of Empire to Martial Contractors: Reimagining Gurkas in Private Security', in Maya Eichler (ed.), *Gender and Private Security in Global Politics*. Oxford: Oxford University Press, pp. 95–113.

Chisholm, Amanda and Hanna Ketola (2020), 'The Cruel Optimism of Militarism: Feminist Curiosity, Affect, and Global Security', *International Political Sociology*, https://doi.org/10.1093/ips/olaa005

Chishti, Maliha (2010), 'Gender and the Development Battlefield in Afghanistan: Nation Builders versus Nation Betrayers', *Comparative Studies of South Asia, Africa and the Middle East* 30(2): 250–61, https://doi.org/10.1215/1089201X-2010-011

Cloud, Dana L. (2004), '"To Veil the Threat of Terror": Afghan Women and the "Clash of Civilizations" in the Imagery of the U.S. War on Terrorism', *Quarterly Journal of Speech* 90(3): 285–306, https://doi.org/10.1080/0033563042000270726

Coburn, Noah (2015), 'Afghanistan: The 2014 Vote and the Troubled Future of Elections'. Chatham House. Available at: https://www.chathamhouse.org/publi cation/afghanistan-2014-vote-and-troubled-future-elections

Cockburn, Cynthia (2012), 'Gender Relations as Causal in Militarization and War: A Feminist Standpoint', in Annica Kronsell and Erica Svedberg (eds), *Making Gender, Making War: Violence, Military and Peacekeeping Practices*. London: Routledge, pp. 19–34.

Cockburn, Cynthia (2014), 'A Continuum of Violence: Gender, War and Peace', in Ruth Jamieson (ed.), *The Criminology of War*. London: Routledge, pp. 357–75.

Cohn, Carol (1987), 'Sex and Death in the Rational World of Defense Intellectuals', *Signs: Journal of Women in Culture and Society* 12(4): 687–718, https://doi. org/10.1086/494362

Cohn, Carol (1999), 'Missions, Men and Masculinities', *International Feminist Journal of Politics* 1(3): 460–75, https://doi.org/10.1080/146167499359835

Cohn, Carol (2011), '"Feminist Security Studies": Toward a Reflexive Practice', *Politics & Gender* 7(4): 581–6, https://doi.org/10.1017/S1743923X11000389

Cohn, Carol (ed.) (2013), *Women and Wars*. Kindle edn. Cambridge: Polity Press.

Connell, R.W. (2005), *Masculinities* (2nd edn). Cambridge: Polity Press.

Connell, R. W. and James W. Messerschmidt (2005), 'Hegemonic Masculinity: Rethinking the Concept', *Gender & Society* 19(6): 829–59, https://doi.org/10.11 77/0891243205278639

Connolly, William E. (2013), 'The "New Materialism" and the Fragility of Things', *Millennium – Journal of International Studies* 41(3): 399–412, https://doi. org/10.1177/0305829813486849

Coomaraswamy, Radhika (2015), 'Preventing Conflict, Transforming Justice, Securing the Peace: A Global Study on the Implementation of United Nations Security Council Resolution 1325'. Available at: https://www.peacewomen.org/ sites/default/files/UNW-GLOBAL-STUDY-1325-2015 (1).pdf

Council on Foreign Relations (2019), 'Women and the Afghan Peace Process: A Conversation with Wazhma Frogh', May 2019. Available at: https://www.cfr.org/ blog/women-and-afghan-peace-process-conversation-wazhma-frogh

Cox, Robert W. (1981), 'Social Forces, States and World Orders: Beyond International Relations Theory', *Millennium – Journal of International Studies* 10(2): 126–55, https://doi.org/10.1177/03058298810100020501

Crenshaw, Kimberlé (1989), 'Demarginalizing the Intersection of Race and Sex: A Black Feminist Critique of Antidiscrimination Doctrine, Feminist Theory and Antiracist Politics', *University of Chicago Legal Forum* 1989(1): 139–67. Available at: https://chicagounbound.uchicago.edu/uclf/vol1989/iss1/8

Crenshaw, Kimberlé (1991), 'Mapping the Margins: Intersectionality, Identity Politics, and Violence Against Women of Color', *Stanford Law Review* 43(6): 1241–99, https://doi.org/10.2307/1229039

Cronin, Stephanie (2011), 'Building and Rebuilding Afghanistan's Army: An Historical Perspective', *The Journal of Military History* 75: 45–92.

Daggett, Cara (2015), 'Drone Disorientations', *International Feminist Journal of Politics* 17(3): 361–79, https://doi.org/10.1080/14616742.2015.1075317

Dalrymple, William (2013), 'The Afghanistan Massacre on the Roof of the World', *The Telegraph*, 18 January. Available at: https://www.telegraph.co.uk/news/world news/asia/afghanistan/9811223/The-Afghanistan-massacre-on-the-roof-of-the-world.html

Davidson, Jason W. (2013), 'France, Britain and the Intervention in Libya: An Integrated Analysis', *Cambridge Review of International Affairs* 26(2): 310–29, https://doi.org/10.1080/09557571.2013.784573

Davies, Tracy C. (2008), 'Introduction: The Pirouette, Detour, Revolution, Deflection, Deviation and Yaw of the Performative Turn', in Tracy C. Davies (ed.), *The Cambridge Companion to Performance Studies*. Cambridge: Cambridge University Press, pp. 1–8.

Davis, Angela (2016), *Freedom Is a Constant Struggle: Ferguson, Palestine, and the Foundations of a Movement*. Chicago, IL: Haymarket Books.

Davis, Noela (2009), 'New Materialism and Feminism's Anti-Biologism: A Response to Sara Ahmed', *European Journal of Women's Studies* 16(1): 67–80, https://doi.org/10.1177/1350506808098535

Detraz, Nicole (2012), *International Security and Gender*. Cambridge: Polity Press.

Devetak, Richard (2013), 'Critical Theory', in Scott Burchill, Andrew Linklater, Richard Devetak, Jack Donnelly, Terry Nardin, Matthew Paterson, Christian Reus-Smit and Jacqui True (eds), *Theories of International Relations* (5th edn). Basingstoke: Palgrave Macmillan, pp. 162–86.

Dietler, Michael (2006), 'Alcohol: Anthropological/Archaeological Perspectives', *Annual Review of Anthropology* 35: 229–49, https://doi.org/10.1146/annurev.anthro.35.081705.123120

Dodge, Toby (2011), 'Domestic Politics and State-Building', in Nicholas Redman and Toby Dodge (eds), *Afghanistan to 2015 and Beyond*. Abingdon: Routledge, pp. 69–95.

Dodge, Toby (2013), 'Intervention and Dreams of Exogenous Statebuilding: The Application of Liberal Peacebuilding in Afghanistan and Iraq', *Review of International Studies* 39(5): 1189–212, https://doi.org/10.1017/S0260210513000272

Dodge, Toby and Nicholas Redman (eds) (2011), *Afghanistan to 2015 and Beyond*. Abingdon: Routledge.

Dogra, Nandita (2011), 'The Mixed Metaphor of "Third World Woman": Gendered Representations by International Development NGOs', *Third World Quarterly* 32(2): 333–48, https://doi.org/10.1080/01436597.2011.560472

Duffield, Mark (2001), *Global Governance and the New Wars*. London: Zed Books.

Duffield, Mark (2010), 'Risk-Management and the Fortified Aid Compound: Everyday Life in Post-Interventionary Society', *Journal of Intervention and Statebuilding* 4(4): 453–74, https://doi.org/10.1080/17502971003700993

Duffield, Mark (2012), 'Risk Management and the Bunkering of the Aid Industry', *Development Dialogue* 58: 21–36, https://doi.org/10.1177/0967010612457975

Duncanson, Claire (2008), 'Forces for Good? British Military Masculinities on Peace Support Operations'. Edinburgh Research Archive. Available at: http://hdl.handle.net/1842/2752

Duncanson, Claire (2013), *Forces For Good? Military Masculinities and Peacebuilding in Afghanistan*. Basingstoke: Palgrave Macmillan.

Duncanson, Claire (2016), *Gender and Peacebuilding*. Cambridge: Polity Press.

Duriesmith, David and Noor Huda Ismail (2019), 'Militarized Masculinities beyond Methodological Nationalism: Charting the Multiple Masculinities of an Indonesian Jihadi', *International Theory* 11 (May): 139–59, https://doi.org/10.1017/S1752971919000034

Durkheim, Emile (2012), *The Elementary Forms of the Religious Life*, ed. and trans. Joseph Ward Swain. New Orleans, LA: Quid Pro Books.

Dyvik, Synne Laastad (2013), 'Women as "Practitioners" and "Targets"', *International Feminist Journal of Politics* 16(3): 410–29, https://doi.org/10.1080/14616742.2013.779139

Edney, Matthew H. (1997), *Mapping an Empire: The Geographical Construction of British India 1765–1843*. Chicago, IL: The University of Chicago Press.

Edwards, Holly (2006), 'Unruly Images: Photography in and of Afghanistan', *Artibus Asiae* 66(2): 111–36, https://doi.org/10.2307/25261858

Egnell, Robert (2010), 'Winning "Hearts and Minds"? A Critical Analysis of Counter-Insurgency Operations in Afghanistan', *Civil Wars* 12(3): 282–303, https://doi.org/10.1080/13698249.2010.509562

Egnell, Robert (2011), 'Lessons from Helmand, Afghanistan: What Now for British Counterinsurgency?', *International Affairs* 87(2): 297–315, https://doi.org/10.1111/j.1468-2346.2011.00974.x

Eichler, Maya (2013), 'Gender and the Privatization of Security: Neoliberal Transformation of the Militarized Gender Order', *Critical Studies on Security* 1(3): 311–25, https://doi.org/10.1080/21624887.2013.848107

Eichler, Maya (2014), 'Militarized Masculinities in International Relations', *The Brown Journal of World Affairs* xxi(1): 81–94.

Eichler, Maya (ed.) (2015a), *Gender and Private Security in Global Politics*. Oxford: Oxford University Press.

Eichler, Maya (2015b), 'Gender and the Privatization of Military Security: An Introduction', in Maya Eichler (ed.), *Gender and Private Security in Global Politics*. Oxford: Oxford University Press, pp. 1–15.

Eley, Tom (2010), 'Wikileaks Private Security Contractors Killed Iraqis with Impunity'. World Socialist Web Site. Available at: http://www.wsws.org/articles/2010/oct2010/iraq-o27.shtml

Elshtain, J. B. (1987), *Women and War*. Chicago, IL: The University of Chicago Press.

Elshtain, J. B. (1991), 'Sovereignty, Identity, Sacrifice', *Millennium – Journal of International Studies* 20(3): 395–406, https://doi.org/10.1177/03058298910200031301

Enloe, Cynthia (2000), *Maneuvers: The International Politics of Women's Lives*. Berkeley, CA: University of California Press.

Enloe, Cynthia (2004), *The Curious Feminist: Searching for Women in a New Age of Empire*. Berkeley, CA: University of California Press.

Enloe, Cynthia (2007), *Globalisation and Militarism: Feminists Make the Link*. Lanham, MD: Rowman & Littlefield.

Enloe, Cynthia (2010), *Nimo's War, Emma's War: Making Feminist Sense of the Iraq War*. Berkeley, CA: University of California Press.

Eroukhmanoff, Clara (2015), 'The Remote Securitisation of Islam in the US Post-9/11: Euphemisation, Metaphors and the "Logic of Expected Consequences" in Counter- Radicalisation Discourse', *Critical Studies on Terrorism* 8(2): 246–65, https://doi.org/10.1080/17539153.2015.1053747

Eroukhmanoff, Clara (2019), 'Responding to Terrorism with Peace, Love and Solidarity: "Je Suis Charlie", "Peace" and "I Heart MCR"', *Journal of International Political Theory* 15(2): 167–87, https://doi.org/10.1177/1755088219829884

Fanon, Frantz (1986), *Black Skin, White Masks*. London: Pluto Press.

Farrell, Theo and Stuart Gordon (2009), 'COIN Machine: The British Military in Afghanistan', *Orbis* 53(4): 665–83, https://doi.org/10.1016/j.orbis.2009.07.002

Fenster, Tovi, 'Belly Dancing in Israel: Body, Embodiment, Religion and Nationality', in Adam Pine and Olaf Kuhlke (eds), *Geographies of Dance: Body, Movement and Corporeal Negotiations*. Plymouth: Lexington Books, pp. 191–206.

Ferguson, Lucy (2014), '"This Is Our Gender Person": The Messy Business of Working as a Gender Expert in International Development', *International Feminist Journal of Politics* 17(3): 1–18, https://doi.org/10.1080/14616742.2014.918787

Ferguson, Michaele L. (2005), '"W" Stands for Women: Feminism and Security Rhetoric in the Post-9/11 Bush Administration', *Politics & Gender* 1(1): 9–38, https://doi.org/10.1017/S1743923X05050014

Fierke, Karin (2010), 'Besting the West: Russia's Machiavella Strategy', *International Feminist Journal of Politics* 1(3):403–34, https://doi.org/10.1080/146167499359817

Finnemore, Martha and Kathryn Sikkink (1998), 'International Norm Dynamics and Political Change', *International Organization* 52(4): 887–917.

Fluri, Jennifer (2009a), '"Foreign Passports Only": Geographies of (Post)Conflict Work in Kabul, Afghanistan', *Annals of the Association of American Geographers* 99(5): 986–94, https://doi.org/10.1080/00045600903253353

Fluri, Jennifer (2009b), 'The Beautiful "Other": A Critical Examination of "Western" Representations of Afghan Feminine Corporeal Modernity', *Gender, Place & Culture: A Journal of Feminist Geography* 16(3): 241–57, https://doi.org/10.1080/09663690902836292

Fluri, Jennifer (2011a), 'Armored Peacocks and Proxy Bodies : Gender Geopolitics in Aid/Development Spaces of Afghanistan', *Gender, Place & Culture: A Journal of Feminist Geography* 18(4): 519–36, https://doi.org/10.1080/0966369X.2011.583343

Fluri, Jennifer L. (2011b), 'Bodies, Bombs and Barricades: Geographies of Conflict and Civilian (In)security', *Transactions of the Institute of British Geographers* 36(2): 280–96, https://doi.org/10.1111/j.1475-5661.2010.00422.x

Foucault, Michel (1972), *The Archaeology of Knowledge and the Discourse on Language*. New York: Pantheon.

Fox, Jeremy (2016), 'What's the Origin of the Term "Field Work"?', *Dynamic Ecology*. Available at: https://dynamicecology.wordpress.com/2016/09/13/whats-the-ori gin-of-the-term-field-work/

Fraser, Nancy (2009), 'Feminism, Capitalism and the Cunning of History', *New Left Review* 56 (March/April): 97–117. Available at: https://newleftreview.org/issues/ II56/articles/nancy-fraser-feminism-capitalism-and-the-cunning-of-history

Frerks, Georg, Annelou Ypeij and Reinhilde Sotiria Konig (eds) (2014), *Gender and Conflict: Embodiments, Discourses and Symbolic Practices*. Surrey: Ashgate.

Friedman, Rebekka (2016), 'Culturally Mediated Grieving and Recovery: Reflections on Women's Experiences in Northern Sri Lanka', in Roslyn Warren and Mayesha Alam (eds), *Occasional Paper Series: Women and Transitional Justice*. Washington, DC: Georgetown Institute for Women, Peace and Security, pp. 20–34.

Friis, Karsten (2012), 'Which Afghanistan? Military, Humanitarian, and State-Building Identities in the Afghan Theater', *Security Studies* 21(2): 266–300, https:// doi.org/10.1080/09636412.2012.679206

Galtung, Johan (1969), 'Violence, Peace and Peace Research', *Journal of Peace Research* 6(3): 167–91.

'Gandamack Lodge' (2014). Tripadvisor. Available at: https://www.tripadvisor.co.uk/ Hotel_Review-g660089-d1173113-Reviews-Gandamack_Lodge-Kabul_Kabul_ Province.html

Gani, Jasmine K. (2019), 'Escaping the Nation in the Middle East: A Doomed Project? Fanonian Decolonisation and the Muslim Brotherhood', *Interventions* 21(5): 652–70, https://doi.org/10.1080/1369801X.2019.1585916

Gentry, Caron E. (2014), 'The Neo-Orientalist Narratives of Women's Involvement in Al-Qaeda', in Laura Sjoberg and Caron E. Gentry (eds), *Women, Gender, and Terrorism*. Athens, GA: University of Georgia Press, pp. 176–93.

Gentry, Caron E. (2015), 'Anxiety and the Creation of the Scapegoated Other', *Critical Studies on Security* 3(2): 133–46, https://doi.org/10.1080/21624887.201 5.1027600

Gentry, Caron E. and Laura Sjoberg (2007), *Mothers, Monsters, Whores*. London: Zed Books.

Gentry, Caron E. and Laura Sjoberg (2015), *Beyond Mothers Monsters Whores: Thinking About Women's Violence in Global Politics*. London: Zed Books.

Geranpayeh, Sarvy (2019), 'Meet Afghanistan's First Female Graffiti Artist, Who Is Risking It All for Her Murals', *The National*, 14 April. Available at: https://www. thenational.ae/arts-culture/art/meet-afghanistan-s-first-female-graffiti-artist-who-is-risking-it-all-for-her-murals-1.848877

Gilmore, Jonathan (2011), 'A Kinder, Gentler Counter-Terrorism: Counterinsurgency, Human Security and the War on Terror', *Security Dialogue* 42(1): 21–37, https:// doi.org/10.1177/0967010610393390

Goetze, Catherine (2016), 'Review: Spaces of Aid: How Cars, Compounds and Hotels Shape Humanitarianism', *Journal of Intervention and Statebuilding* 10(1): 133–5, https://doi.org/10.1080/17502977.2015.1094268

Goffman, Erving (1959), *The Presentation of Self in Everyday Life*. New York: Doubleday.

Goldstein, Joseph (2001), *War and Gender: How Gender Shapes the War System and Vice Versa*. Cambridge: Cambridge University Press.

Goldstein, Joseph (2015), 'U.S Soldiers Told to Ignore Sexual Abuse of Boys by Afghan Allies', *The New York Times*, 20 September. Available at: http://www. nytimes.com/2015/09/21/world/asia/us-soldiers-told-to-ignore-afghan-allies-abuse-of-boys.html?_r=0

Goodhand, Jonathan (2002), 'Aiding Violence or Building Peace? The Role of International Aid in Afghanistan', *Third World Quarterly* 23(5): 837–59, https://doi.org/10.1080/014365902200002862

Goodhand, Jonathan (2008), 'Corrupting or Consolidating the Peace? The Drugs Economy and Post Conflict Peacebuilding in Afghanistan', *International Peacekeeping* 15(3): 405–23, https://doi.org/10.1080/13533310802058984

Goodhand, Jonathan (2010), 'Stabilising a Victor's Peace? Humanitarian Action and Reconstruction in Eastern Sri Lanka', *Disasters* 34(S3): 342–67, https://doi.org/10.1111/j.0361

Goodhand, Jonathan (2013), 'Contested Boundaries: NGOs and Civil–Military Relations in Afghanistan', *Central Asian Survey* 32(3): 287–305, https://doi.org/10.1080/02634937.2013.835211

Goodhand, Jonathan and Mark Sedra (2013), 'Rethinking Liberal Peacebuilding, Statebuilding and Transition in Afghanistan: An Introduction', *Central Asian Survey* 32(3): 239–54, https://doi.org/10.1080/02634937.2013.850769

Gordon, Avery F. (2008), *Ghostly Matters: Haunting and the Sociological Imagination*. Minneapolis, MN: University of Minnesota Press.

Gregory, Derek (2016), 'The Natures of War', *Antipode* 48(1): 3–56, https://doi.org/10.1111/anti.12173

Gregory, Thomas (2019), 'Dangerous Feelings: Checkpoints and the Perception of Hostile Intent', *Security Dialogue* 50(2): 131–47, https://doi.org/10.1177/0967010618820450

Gregory, Thomas (2020), 'The Costs of War: Condolence Payments and the Politics of Killing Civilians', *Review of International Studies* 46(1): 156–76, https://doi.org/10.1017/S026021051900038X

Grobl, Karl (2009), 'The Gandamack Lodge, Kabul'. Available at: http://karlgrobl.blogspot.com/2009/12/gandamack-lodge.html

Grove, Jairus (2016), 'An Insurgency of Things: Foray into the World of Improvised Explosive Devices', *International Political Sociology* 10: 332–51, https://doi.org/10.1093/ips/olw018

Grove, Nicole Sunday (2015), 'The Cartographic Ambiguities of HarassMap: Crowdmapping Security and Sexual Violence in Egypt', *Security Dialogue* 46(4): 345–64, https://doi.org/10.1177/0967010615583039

Haastrup, Toni (2017), 'The Undoing of a Unique Relationship? Peace and Security in the EU – South Africa Strategic Partnership', *South African Journal of International Affairs* 24(2): 197–213, https://doi.org/10.1080/10220461.2017.1338615

Habashi, Janette (2013), 'Palestinian Children: Authors of Collective Memory', *Children & Society* 27: 421–33, https://doi.org/10.1111/j.1099-0860.2011.00417.x

Hadley, Stephen (2015), 'Lessons Learned Interview', 16 September. Office of the Special Inspector General for Afghanistan Reconstruction. Available at: https://www.washingtonpost.com/graphics/2019/investigations/afghanistan-papers/documents-database/?document=hadley_stephen_ll_01_d12_09162015

Hakimi, Aziz A. (2013), 'Getting Savages to Fight Barbarians: Counterinsurgency and the Remaking of Afghanistan', *Central Asian Survey* 32(3): 388–402, https://doi.org/10.1080/02634937.2013.843300

Hamdouni Alami, Mohammed (2011), *Art and Architecture in the Islamic Tradition*. London: I. B. Tauris & Co.

Hanifi, Shah Mahmoud (2018), 'A Genealogy or Orientalism in Afghanistan: The Colonial Image Lineage', in Tugrul Keskin (ed.), *Middle East Studies after September 11: Neo-Orientalism, American Hegemony and Academia*. Leiden: Brill, pp. 50–80.

Harsch, Michael F. (2015), *The Power of Dependence: NATO-UN Cooperation in Crisis Management*. Oxford: Oxford University Press.

Hastings, Michael (2010), 'The Runaway General', *Rolling Stone*, June. Available at: https://www.rollingstone.com/politics/politics-news/the-runaway-general-the-profile-that-brought-down-mcchrystal-192609/

Heath, Jennifer and Ashraf Zahedi (eds) (2011), *Land of the Unconquerable: The Lives of Contemporary Afghan Women*. Berkeley, CA: University of California Press.

Heck, Axel and Gabi Schlag (2013), 'Securitizing Images: The Female Body and the War in Afghanistan', *European Journal of International Relations* 19(4): 891–913, https://doi.org/10.1177/1354066111433896

Hehir, Aidan (2007), 'The Myth of the Failed State and the War on Terror: A Challenge to the Conventional Wisdom', *Journal of Intervention and Statebuilding* 1(3): 307–32, https://doi.org/10.1080/17502970701592256

Henderson, Errol A. (2013), 'Hidden in Plain Sight: Racism in International Relations Theory', *Cambridge Review of International Affairs* 26(1): 71–92, https://doi.org/10.1080/09557571.2012.710585

Henry, Marsha G. (2018), 'Why Critical Military Studies Needs to Smash Imperial White Supremacist Capitalist Heteropatriarchy: A Rejoinder', *Critical Military Studies* 6(1): 107–10, https://doi.org/10.1080/23337486.2018.1429049

Henry, Marsha, Paul Higate and Gurchathen Sanghera (2009), 'Positionality and Power: The Politics of Peacekeeping Research', *International Peacekeeping* 16(4): 467–82, https://doi.org/10.1080/13533310903184499

Herdt, Gilbert (ed.) (1996), *Third Sex, Third Gender: Beyond Sexual Dimorphism in Culture and History*. Cambridge, MA: The MIT Press.

Higate, Paul (2003), *Military Masculinities, Identity and the State*. Westport, CN: Praeger.

Higate, Paul (2012a), '"Cat Food and Clients": Gendering the Politics of Protection in the Private Militarised Security Company'. Available at: http://www.bristol. ac.uk/media-library/sites/spais/migrated/documents/higate-08-11.pdf

Higate, Paul (2012b), 'Drinking Vodka from the "Butt-Crack": Men, Masculinities and Fratriarchy in the Private Militarized Security Company', *International Feminist Journal of Politics* 14(4): 450–69. Available at: https://doi.org/10.1080/14616742 .2012.726092

Higate, Paul (2012c), 'The Private Militarized and Security Contractor as Geocorporeal Actor', *International Political Sociology* 6(4): 355–72, https://doi. org/10.1111/ips.12004

Higate, Paul and Marsha Henry (2009), *Insecure Spaces: Peacekeeping, Power and Performance in Haiti, Kosovo and Liberia*. London: Zed Books.

Hirschmann, Nancy J. (1989), 'Freedom, Recognition, and Obligation: A Feminist Approach to Political Theory', *American Political Science Association* 83(4): 1227–44, https://doi.org/10.2307/1961666

Hodges, Adam (2011), *The 'War on Terror' Narrative: Discourse and Intertextuality in the Construction and Contestation of Sociopolitcal Reality*. New York: Oxford University Press.

Hokayem, Emile (2011a), 'Iran', in Nicholas Redman and Toby Dodge (eds), *Afghanistan to 2015 and Beyond*. Abingdon: Routledge, pp. 187–98.

Hokayem, Emile (2011b), 'Saudi Arabia', in Nicholas Redman and Toby Dodge (eds), *Afghanistan to 2015 and Beyond*. Abingdon: Routledge, pp. 247–52.

Holland, Jack and Mike Aaronson (2014), 'Dominance through Coercion: Strategic Rhetorical Balancing and the Tactics of Justification in Afghanistan and Libya', *Journal of Intervention and Statebuilding* 8(1): 1–20, https://doi.org/10.1080/1750 2977.2013.856126

Holland, Jack and Ty Solomon (2014), 'Affect Is What States Make of It: Articulating Everyday Experiences of 9/11', *Critical Studies on Security* 2(3): 262–77.

hooks, bell (2000), *Feminism Is for Everybody: Passionate Politics*. Cambridge, MA: South End Press, https://doi.org/10.4324/9781315743189

Howell, Alison (2018), 'Forget "Militarization": Race, Disability and the "Martial Politics" of the Police and of the University', *International Feminist Journal of Politics* 20(2): 117–36, https://doi.org/10.1080/14616742.2018.1447310

Howell, Alison and Melanie Richter-Montpetit (2019), 'Is Securitization Theory Racist? Civilizationism, Methodological Whiteness, and Antiblack Thought in the Copenhagen School', *Security Dialogue* 51(1): 3–22, https://doi. org/10.1177/0967010619862921

Huber, Marie S. (2014), 'Of Habermas and Hypocrisy: Discounting Nonviolence in Afghanistan's Elections', *E-International Relations*, 13 September. Available at: https://www.e-ir.info/2014/09/13/of-habermas-and-hypocrisy-discounting-non violence-in-afghanistans-elections/

Hudson, Heidi (2012), 'A Double-Edged Sword of Peace? Reflections on the Tension between Representation and Protection in Gendering Liberal Peacebuilding', *International Peacekeeping* 19(4): 443–60, https://doi.org/10.1080/13533312.20 12.709753

Hudson, Heidi (2014), 'Gendercidal Violence and the Technologies of Othering in Libya and Rwanda', *Africa Insight* 44(1): 103–20.

Hudson, Heidi (2018), 'Larger Than Life? Decolonising Human Security Studies Through Feminist Posthumanism', *Strategic Review for Southern Africa* 40(1): 46–62.

Hutchings, K. (2008), 'Making Sense of Masculinity and War', *Men and Masculinities* 10(4): 389–404, https://doi.org/10.1177/1097184X07306740

Hyndman, Jennifer and Malathi De Alwis (2003), 'Beyond Gender: Towards a Feminist Analysis of Humanitarianism and Development in Sri Lanka', *Women's Studies Quarterly* 31(1): 212–26.

Hyndman, Jennifer and Malathi De Alwis (2004), 'Bodies, Shrines, and Roads: Violence, (Im)mobility and Displacement in Sri Lanka', *Gender, Place and Culture: A Journal of Feminist Geography* 11(4): 535–57, https://doi.org/10.1080/0966369042000307960

ISAF (2011), 'International Security Assistance Force (ISAF), CIVCAS (2008 to 2010) as of January 2011'. Available at: http://science.sciencemag.org/highwire/filestream/592180/field_highwire_adjunct_files/1/CIVCASJan2011.%0Axls

Jabri, Vivienne (2013), 'Peacebuilding, the Local and the International: A Colonial or a Postcolonial Rationality?" *Peacebuilding* 1(1): 3–16, https://doi.org/10.1080/21647259.2013.756253

Jachens, Liza, Jonathan Houdmont and Roslyn Thomas (2016), 'Effort–Reward Imbalance and Heavy Alcohol Consumption Among Humanitarian Aid Workers', *Journal of Studies on Alcohol and Drugs* 77(6): 904–13, https://doi.org/10.15288/jsad.2016.77.904

Jalalzai, Zubeda and David Jeffress (2011), 'Globalizing Afghanistan', in Zubeda Jalalzai and David Jeffress (eds), *Globalizing Afghanistan: Terrorism, War and the Rhetoric of Nation Building*. Durham, NC: Duke University Press, pp. 223–34.

Jilani, Seema (2010), 'Getting Drunk in Kabul Bars? Pass the Sick Bag', *The Guardian*, 31 August. Available at: https://www.theguardian.com/commentisfree/2010/aug/31/kabul-expat-bars-war-afghanistan

Jiwani, Yasmin and Aliaa Dakroury (2009), 'Veiling Differences – Mediating Race, Gender, and Nation', *Global Media Journal – Canadian Edition* 2(2): 1–6.

Johnson, Thomas H. and Matthew C. DuPee (2012), 'Analysing the New Taliban Code of Conduct (Layeha): An Assessment of Changing Perspectives and Strategies of the Afghan Taliban', *Central Asian Survey* 31(1): 77–91, https://doi.org/10.1080/02634937.2012.647844

Joshi, Madhav, Sung Yong Lee and Roger Mac Ginty (2014), 'Just How Liberal Is the Liberal Peace?' *International Peacekeeping* 21(3): 364–89, https://doi.org/10.1080/13533312.2014.932065

Joya, Malalai (2009), *A Woman Among Warlords*. New York: Scribner.

Kakar, Mohammad Hassan (2003), 'Afghan Nation-State. Myth or Reality'. Available at: http://www.kakarfoundation.com/pubs/uploads/publications/articles/Afghannation-statemythorreality.pdf

Kakar, Mohammad Hassan (2011), 'Taliban'. Available at: http://www.kakarfoundation.com/pubs/uploads/publications/articles/Taliban.pdf

Kearns, Matthew (2017), 'Gender, Visuality and Violence: Visual Securitization and the 2001 War in Afghanistan', *International Feminist Journal of Politics* 19(4): 491–505, https://doi.org/10.1080/14616742.2017.1371623

Kelsall, Helen Louise, Millawage Supun, Dilara Wijesinghe, Mark Christopher Creamer, Dean Philip Mckenzie, Andrew Benjamin Forbes, Matthew James Page and Malcolm Ross Sim (2015), 'Alcohol Use and Substance Use Disorders in Gulf War, Afghanistan, and Iraq War Veterans Compared With Nondeployed Military Personnel', *Epidemiologic Reviews* 37 (January): 38–54, https://doi.org/10.1093/epirev/mxu014

Khalid, Maryam (2011), 'Gender, Orientalism and Representations of the "Other" in the War on Terror', *Global Change, Peace and Security* 23(1): 15–29, https://doi.org/10.1080/14781158.2011.540092

Khalili, Laleh (2011), 'Gendered Practices of Counterinsurgency', *Review of International Studies* 37(4): 1471–91, https://doi.org/10.1017/S026021051000121X

Kirby, Paul and Marsha Henry (2012), 'Rethinking Masculinity and Practices of Violence in Conflict Settings', *International Feminist Journal of Politics* 14(4): 445–9, https://doi.org/10.1080/14616742.2012.726091

Klinesmith, Jennifer, Tim Kasser and Francis T. McAndrew (2006), 'Guns, Testosterone, and Aggression: An Experimental Test of a Mediational Hypothesis', *Psychological Science* 17(7): 568–71, https://doi.org/10.1111/j.1467-9280.2006.01745.x

Knafo, Danielle (2001), 'Claude Cahun: The Third Sex', *Studies in Gender and Sexuality* 2(1): 29–61, https://doi.org/10.1080/15240650209349169

Kothari, Uma (2006a), 'An Agenda for Thinking about "Race" in Development', *Progress in Development Studies* 6(1): 9–23, https://doi.org/10.1191%2F1464993406ps124oa

Kothari, Uma (2006b), 'From Colonialism to Development: Reflections of Former Colonial Officers', *Commonwealth & Comparative Politics* 44(1): 118–36, https://doi.org/10.1080/14662040600624502

Kothari, Uma (2006c), 'Spatial Practices and Imaginaries: Experiences of Colonial Officers and Development Professionals', *Singapore Journal of Tropical Geography* 27(3): 235–53, https://doi.org/10.1111/j.1467-9493.2006.00260.x

Laffey, M. and S. Nadarajah (2012), 'The Hybridity of Liberal Peace: States, Diasporas and Insecurity', *Security Dialogue* 43(5): 403–20, https://doi.org/10.1177/0967010612457974

Laliberté, Nicole and Carolin Schurr (2016), 'Introduction', *Gender, Place & Culture* 23(1): 72–8, https://doi.org/10.1080/0966369X.2014.992117

Lampton, William (1818), 'An Abstract of the Results Deduced from the Measurement of an Arc on the Meridian Extending from Latitude 8 Degrees 9' 38",4, to Latitude 18 Degrees 3' 23",6, N. Being an Amplitude of 9 Degrees 53' 45", 2', *Philosophical Transactions of the Royal Society of London* 108: 486–517.

Lee, Jonathan L. (2018), *Afghanistan: A History from 1260 to the Present*. London: Reaktion Books.

Le Miere, Christian, Gary Li and Nigel Inkster (2011), 'China', in Nicholas Redman and Toby Dodge (eds), *Afghanistan to 2015 and Beyond*. Abingdon: Routledge, pp. 219–30.

Lemke, Thomas (2015), 'New Materialisms: Foucault and the "Government of Things"', *Theory, Culture & Society* 32(4): 3–25, https://doi.org/10.1177/0263276413519340

Leng, Kirsten (2014), 'Permutations of the Third Sex: Sexology, Subjectivity, and Antimaternalist Feminism at the Turn of the Twentieth Century', *Signs: Journal of Women in Culture and Society* 40(1): 227–54, https://doi.org/10.1086/676899

Lorimer, Hayden (2008), 'Cultural Geography: Non-Representational Conditions and Concerns', *Progress in Human Geography* 32(4): 551–9, https://doi.org/10.1177/0309132507086882

Lundborg, Tom and Nick Vaughan-Williams (2015), 'New Materialisms, Discourse Analysis, and International Relations: A Radical Intertextual Approach', *Review of International Studies* 41(1): 3–25, https://doi.org/10.1017/S0260210514000163

McBride, Keally and Annick T. R. Wibben (2012), 'The Gendering of Counterinsurgency in Afghanistan', *Humanity: An International Journal of Human Rights, Humanitarianism, and Development* 3(2): 199–215, https://doi.org/10.1353/hum.2012.0012

McChrystal, Stanley (2013), *My Share of the Task*. New York: Portfolio/Penguin.

Macfarlane, Julie (2018), 'Why Palestinians Throw Stones: A Reporter's Notebook', *ABC News*, 16 May. Available at: https://abcnews.go.com/International/palestinians-throw-stones-reporters-notebook/story?id=55200067

Mac Ginty, Roger (2010a), 'Hybrid Peace: The Interaction Between Top-Down and Bottom-Up Peace', *Security Dialogue* 41(4): 391–412, https://doi.org/10.1177/0967010610374312

Mac Ginty, Roger (2010b), 'Warlords and the Liberal Peace: State-Building in Afghanistan', *Conflict, Security & Development* 10(4): 577–98, https://doi.org/10.1080/14678802.2010.500548

Mac Ginty, Roger (2012), 'Routine Peace: Technocracy and Peacebuilding', *Cooperation and Conflict* 47(3): 287–308, https://doi.org/10.1177/0010836712444825

Mac Ginty, Roger (2017), 'A Material Turn in International Relations: The 4×4, Intervention and Resistance', *Review of International Studies* 43(5): 855–74, https://doi.org/10.1017/S0260210517000146

Mcgirk, Tim (2010), 'Kabul Nightlife: Thriving in Between Bombs', *Time Magazine*, 13 April. Available at: http://content.time.com/time/magazine/article/0,9171,1983874,00.html

MacGregor, Col Douglas (2009), 'Refusing Battle: An Alternative to Persistent Warfare', *Armed Forces Journal*, 1 April. Available at: http://armedforcesjournal.com/refusing-battle/

MacKenzie, Megan H. (2012), *Female Soldiers in Sierre Leone: Sex, Security and Post-Conflict Development*. New York: New York University Press.

McLeod, Laura (2015), 'A Feminist Approach to Hybridity: Understanding Local and International Interactions in Producing Post-Conflict Gender Security', *Journal of Intervention and Statebuilding* 9(1): 48–69, https://doi.org/10.1080/17502977.2014.980112

Mcleod, Laura and Maria O'Reilly (2019), 'Critical Peace and Conflict Studies: Feminist Interventions', *Peacebuilding* 7(2): 127–45, https://doi.org/10.1080/21 647259.2019.1588457

McMullin, Jaremey R. (2013), 'Integration or Separation? The Stigmatisation of Ex-Combatants after War', *Review of International Studies* 39: 385–414, https://doi.org/10.1017/S0260210512000228

Mahmud, Tayyab (2010), 'Colonial Cartographies, Postcolonial Borders, and Enduring Failures of International Law: The Unending Wars Along the Afghanistan-Pakistan Frontier', *Brooklyn Journal of International Law* 36(1): 1–74. Available at: https://ssrn.com/abstract=1596835

Mälksoo, Maria (2012), 'The Challenge of Liminality for International Relations Theory', *Review of International Studies* 38(2): 481–94, https://doi.org/10.1017/S0260210511000829

Manchanda, Nivi (2014), 'Queering the Pashtun: Afghan Sexuality in the Homo-Nationalist Imaginary', *Third World Quarterly* 36(1): 130–46, https://doi.org/10.1080/01436597.2014.974378

Manchanda, Nivi (2017), 'Rendering Afghanistan Legible: Borders, Frontiers and the "State" of Afghanistan', *Politics* 37(4): 386–401, https://doi.org/10.1177/0263395717716013

Manchanda, Nivi (2018), 'The Imperial Sociology of the "Tribe" in Afghanistan', *Millennium – Journal of International Studies* 46(2): 165–89, httEps://doi.org/10.1177/0305829817741267

Manchanda, Nivi (2019), 'The Graveyard of Empires: Haunting, Amnesia and Afghanistan's Construction as a Burial Site', *Middle East Critique* 28(3): 307–20, https://doi.org/10.1080/19436149.2019.1633745

Mann, Bonnie (2014), *Sovereign Masculinity: Gender Lessons from the War on Terror.* Oxford: Oxford University Press.

Medie, Peace A. (2015), 'Women and Postconflict Security: A Study of Police Response to Domestic Violence in Liberia', *Politics & Gender* 11: 478–98, https://doi.org/10.1017/S1743923X15000240

Mehta, Akanksha (2015), 'The Aesthetics of "Everyday" Violence: Narratives of Violence and Hindu Right-Wing Women', *Critical Studies on Terrorism* 8(3): 416–38, https://doi.org/10.1080/17539153.2015.1091656

Mehta, Akanksha and Annick T. R. Wibben (2018), 'Feminist Narrative Approaches to Security', in Caron E. Gentry, Laura J. Shepherd and Laura Sjoberg (eds), *Routledge Handbook of Gender and Security.* London: Routledge.

Mehta, Rimple (2014), 'So Many Ways to Love You/Self', *International Feminist Journal of Politics* 16(2): 181–98, https://doi.org/10.1080/14616742.2014.9129 15

Mel, Neloufer de (2007), *Militarizing Sri Lanka: Popular Culture, Memory and Narrative in the Armed Conflict.* Thousand Oaks, CA: Sage Publications.

Meyer, Jörg (2008), 'The Concealed Violence of Modern Peace(-Making)', *Millennium – Journal of International Studies* 36(3): 555–74, https://doi.org/10.1177/030582 98080360030901

Millar, Katharine M. (2015), 'Death Does Not Become Her: An Examination of the Public Construction of Female American Soldiers as Liminal Figures', *Review of International Studies* 41(4): 757–79, https://doi.org/10.1017/S0260210514000424

Miller, Stuart (2019), 'Former Marine Anuradha Bhagwati Waged a Battle against Military Misogyny', *Los Angeles Times*, 12 April. Available at: https://www.latimes.com/books/la-ca-jc-fob-unbecoming-anuraha-bhagwati-20190412-story.html

Mirande, Alfredo (2015), 'Hombres Mujeres: An Indigenous Third Gender', *Men and Masculinities* 19(4): 384–409, https://doi.org/10.1177/1097184X15602746

Moghadam, Valentine M. (2004), 'Patriarchy in Transition: Women and the Changing Family in the Middle East', *Journal of Comparative Family Studies* 35(2): 137–62.

Mohanty, Chandra Talpade (1984), 'Under Western Eyes: Feminist Scholarship and Colonial Discourses', *Boundary 2* 12(3): 333–58, https://doi.org/10.2307/1395054

Mohanty, Chandra Talpade (2003), 'Under Western Eyes: Feminist Scholarship and Colonial Discourse', in Chandra Talpade Mohanty, *Feminism without Borders: Decolonizing Theory, Practicing Solidarity.* Durham, NC: Duke University Press.

Moses, Jonathon W. and Torbjorn L. Knutsen (2007), *Ways of Knowing: Competing Methodologies in Social and Political Research.* Basingstoke: Palgrave Macmillan.

Murer, Jeffrey Stevenson (2009), 'Overcoming Mixed Feelings about Mixed Methodologies: Complex Strategies for Research among Hidden Populations', *eSharp Special Volume: Critical Issues in Researching Hidden Communities* 14: 99–130.

Murer, Jeffrey Stevenson (2010), 'The Myth of Autonomy: Subjectivity, Heteronomy and the Violence of Liberal Individualism', *Polish Political Science* XXXIX: 126–48. Available at: https://czasopisma.marszalek.com.pl/images/pliki/ppsy/39/ppsy2010007.pdf

Myrttinen, Henri (2019), 'Packing for Kabul', in Althea-Maria Rivas and Brendan Ciaran Brown (eds), *Experiences in Researching Conflict and Violence: Fieldwork Interrupted.* Bristol: Policy Press.

Nadarajah, Suthaharan (2013), '"Conflict-Sensitive" Aid & Making Liberal Peace', in Mark Duffield and Vernon Hewitt (eds), *Empire, Development and Colonialism: The Past in the Present.* Martlesham: James Currey, pp. 59–73

Nadarajah, Suthaharan and David Rampton (2015), 'The Limits of Hybridity and the Crisis of Liberal Peace', *Review of International Studies* 41(1): 49–72, https://doi.org/10.1017/S0260210514000060

Nash, Catherine (2004), 'Post-Colonial Geographies', in Paul Cloke, Philip Crang and Mark Goodwin (eds), *Envisioning Human Geographies.* London: Hodder Arnold, pp. 104–27.

Nasimi, Rabia (2016), 'Ethnicity and Politics in Afghanistan: An Analysis of the 2014 Presidential Election', *LSE Blog*, 5 October. Available at: https://blogs.lse.ac.uk/southasia/2016/10/05/ethnicity-and-politics-in-afghanistan-an-analysis-of-the-2014-presidential-election/

NATO (2011), 'Engaging Women on the Frontline'. Available at: http://www.nato.int/cps/en/natolive/news_76542.htm

Nayak, Meghana (2006), 'Orientalism and "Saving" US State Identity after 9/11', *International Feminist Journal of Politics* 8(1): 42–61, https://doi.org/10.1080/14616740500415458

Ndlovu-Gatsheni, Sabelo J. (2009), *The Ndebele Nation: Reflections on Hegemony, Memory and Historiography*. Pretoria: UNISA Press.

Nicholson, Linda (1994), 'Interpreting Gender', *Signs: Journal of Women in Culture and Society* 20(1): 79–105.

Nicoll, Alexander (2011), 'The Road to Lisbon', in Nicholas Redman and Toby Dodge (eds), *Afghanistan to 2015 and Beyond*. Abingdon: Routledge, pp. 21–46.

Nordberg, Jenny (2014), 'The Afghan Girls Raised as Boys', *The Guardian*, 22 September. Available at: https://www.theguardian.com/lifeandstyle/2014/sep/22/girls-boys-afghanistan-daughters-raised-as-sons-puberty-bacha-posh

Nordland, Rod (2014), 'To Protect Foreigners, Afghanistan Shuts Down Their Hangouts', *The New York Times*, 2 April. Available at: https://www.nytimes.com/2014/04/02/world/asia/to-protect-foreigners-afghanistan-shuts-down-their-hangouts.html

Norfolk, Simon (n.d.), 'Afghanistan. Chronotopia'. Available at: https://www.simonnorfolk.com/afghanistan-chronotopia

Omidi, Maryam (2014), 'Anti-Homeless Spikes Are Just the Latest in "Defensive Urban Architecture"', *The Guardian*, 12 June. Available at: http://www.guardian.com/cities/2014/jun/12/anti-homeless-sprikes-latest-defensive-urban-architecture

Omrani, Bijan (2014), 'The Iron Amir', *History Today* 64(6): 48–53. Available at: https://www.historytoday.com/archive/iron-amir-britain-afghanistan-1880

O'Reilly, Maria (2012), 'Muscular Interventionism', *International Feminist Journal of Politics* 14(4): 529–48, https://doi.org/10.1080/14616742.2012.726096

Orford, Anne (1999), 'Muscular Humanitarianism: Reading the Narratives of the New Interventionism', *European Journal of International Law* 10(4): 679–711, https://doi.org/10.1093/ejil/10.4.679

Oxfam (2011), 'How Not to Run an Aid Programme: Afghanistan'. Available at: https://oxfamblogs.org/fp2p/how-not-to-run-an-aid-programme-afghanistan/

Paffenholz, Thania (2015), 'Unpacking the Local Turn in Peacebuilding: A Critical Assessment towards an Agenda for Future Research', *Third World Quarterly* 36(5): 857–74, https://doi.org/10.1080/01436597.2015.1029908

Parashar, Swati (2009), 'Feminist International Relations and Women Militants: Case Studies from Sri Lanka and Kashmir', *Cambridge Review of International Affairs* 22(2): 235–56, https://doi.org/10.1080/09557570902877968

Parashar, Swati (2012), 'Women in Militant Movements: (Un)Comfortable Silences and Discursive Strategies', in Annica Kronsell and Erika Svedberg (eds), *Making Gender, Making War: Violence, Military and Peacekeeping Practices*. London: Routledge, pp. 166–81.

Parashar, Swati (2013), 'What Wars and "War Bodies" Know about International

Relations', *Cambridge Review of International Affairs* 26(4): 615–30, https://doi.org /10.1080/09557571.2013.837429

Paris, Roland (2001), 'Echoes of the *Mission Civilisatrice*: Peacekeeping in the Post-Cold War Era', in Edward Newman and Oliver Richmond (eds), *The United Nations and Human Security*. London: Palgrave Macmillan, pp. 100–20.

Paris, Roland (2010), 'Saving Liberal Peacebuilding', *Review of International Studies* 36(2): 337–65, https://doi.org/10.1017/S0260210510000057

Paris, Roland (2013), 'Afghanistan: What Went Wrong?', *Perspectives on Politics* 11(2): 538–48, https://doi.org/10.1017/S1537592713000911

Partis-Jennings, Hannah and Marie S. Huber (2014), 'Women, Peace and Security in Afghanistan: Looking Back to Move Forward'. Available at: http://reliefweb. int/sites/reliefweb.int/files/resources/Women Peace and Security in Afghanistan. pdf

Partis-Jennings, Hannah (2017), 'The (In)security of Gender in Afghanistan's Peacebuilding Project: Hybridity and Affect', *International Feminist Journal of Politics* 19(4): 411–25, https://doi.org/10.1080/14616742.2017.1279418

Partis-Jennings, Hannah (2019), 'The "Third Gender" in Afghanistan: A Feminist Account of Hybridity as a Gendered Experience', *Peacebuilding* 7(2): 178–93, https://doi.org/10.1080/21647259.2019.1588455

Pateman, Carole (1989), 'Feminist Critiques of the Public/Private Dichotomy', in Carole Pateman, *The Disorder of Women: Democracy, Feminism and Political Theory*. Cambridge: Polity Press.

Piccolino, Giulia (2019), 'Local Peacebuilding in a Victor's Peace. Why Local Peace Fails Without National Reconciliation', *International Peacekeeping* 26(3): 354–79, https://doi.org/10.1080/13533312.2019.1583559

Pin-Fat, Véronique and Maria Stern (2005), 'The Scripting of Private Jessica Lynch: Biopolitics, Gender, and the "Feminization" of the U.S. Military', *Alternatives* 30: 25–53, https://doi.org/10.1177/030437540503000102

Pratt, Nicola and Sophie Richter-Devroe (2011), 'Critically Examining UNSCR 1325 on Women, Peace and Security', *International Feminist Journal of Politics* 13(4): 489–503, https://doi.org/10.1080/14616742.2011.611658

Prugl, Elisabeth (2001), 'Gender and War: Causes, Constructions, and Critique', *Symposium* 1(2): 335–42, https://doi.org/10.1017/S1537592703000252

Pugh, Michael C. (2004), 'Peacekeeping and Critical Theory', *International Peacekeeping* 11(1): 39–58, https://doi.org/10.1080/1353331042000228445

Rashid, Ahmed (2006), 'The View from Swimming Pool Hill', *The New York Times*, 26 June. Available at: https://www.nytimes.com/2006/06/26/opinion/26iht-edrashid.2057067.html

Rasmussen, Sune Engel (2016a), 'Kabul's Expat Bubble Used to Be like Boogie Nights – Now It's More like Panic Room', *The Guardian*, 18 July. Available at: https://www.theguardian.com/world/2016/jul/18/kabul-expat-bubble-boogie-nights-panic-room-afghanistan-war

Rasmussen, Sune Engel (2016b), 'Isis Claims Responsibility for Kabul Bomb Attack on Hazara Protesters', *The Guardian*, 24 July. Available at: https://www.theguard

ian.com/world/2016/jul/23/hazara-minority-targeted-by-suicide-bombs-at-kab
ul-protest

Razack, Sherene H. (2004), *Dark Threats and White Knights: The Somalia Affair, Peacekeeping and the New Imperialism*. Toronto: University of Toronto Press.

Razack, Sherene H. (2008), *Casting Out: The Eviction of Muslims from Western Law and Politics*. Toronto: University of Toronto Press.

Read, Róisín (2018), 'Embodying Difference: Reading Gender in Women's Memoirs of Humanitarianism', *Journal of Intervention and Statebuilding* 12(3): 300–18, https://doi.org/10.1080/17502977.2018.1482079

Reardon, Betty A. (1996), *Sexism and the War System*. New York: Syracuse University Press.

Richmond, Oliver P., Stefanie Kappler and Annika Björkdahl (2015), 'The "Field" in the Age of Intervention: Power, Legitimacy, and Authority Versus the "Local"', *Millennium – Journal of International Studies*, 23–44, https://doi.org/10.1177/0305829815594871

Richmond, Oliver P. (2009a), 'A Post-Liberal Peace: Eirenism and the Everyday', *Review of International Studies* 35: 557–80, https://doi.org/10.1017/S0260210509008651

Richmond, Oliver P. (2009b), 'Becoming Liberal, Unbecoming Liberalism: Liberal-Local Hybridity via the Everyday as a Response to the Paradoxes of Liberal Peacebuilding', *Journal of Intervention and Statebuilding* 3(3): 324–44, https://doi.org/10.1080/17502970903086719

Robinson, Fiona (2011), *The Ethics of Care: A Feminist Approach to Human Security*. Philadelphia, PA: Temple University Press.

Romaniuk, Scott Nicholas and Steward Tristan Webb (2016), *Insurgency and Counterinsurgency in Modern War*. Boca Raton, FL: CRC Press.

Rostami-Povey, Elaheh (2007), *Afghan Women: Identity and Invasion*. London: Zed Books.

Roy, Olivier (2015), 'Introduction', in Micheline Centlivres-Demont, *Afghanistan: Identity, Society and Politics*. London: I. B. Tauris & Co., pp. xv–xxiii.

Roy-Chaudhury, Rahul (2011), 'India', in Nicholas Redman and Toby Dodge (eds), *Afghanistan to 2015 and Beyond*. Abingdon: Routledge, pp. 231–46.

Rubin, Barnett R. (2013), *Afghanistan from the Cold War through to the War on Terror*. New York: Oxford University Press.

Rutazibwa, Olivia Umurerwa (2019), 'What's There to Mourn? Decolonial Reflections on (the End of) Liberal Humanitarianism', *Journal of Humanitarian Affairs* 1(1): 65–7.

Sabaratnam, Meera (2013), 'Avatars of Eurocentrism in the Critique of the Liberal Peace', *Security Dialogue* 44(3): 259–78, https://doi.org/10.1177/0967010613485870

Sabaratnam, Meera (2017), *Decolonising Intervention: International Statebuilding in Mozambique*. London: Rowman & Littlefield.

Said, Edward W. (1979), *Orientalism*. New York: Vintage Books.

Saikal, Amin (2010), 'Afghanistan and Pakistan: The Question of Pashtun

Nationalism?', *Journal of Muslim Minority Affairs* 30(1): 5–17, https://doi.org/10.1080/13602001003650572

Sasson-Levy, Orna (2003), 'Feminism and Military Gender Practices: Israeli Women Soldiers in "Masculine" Roles', *Sociological Inquiry* 73(3): 440–65, https://doi.org/10.1111/1475-682X.00064

Schia, Niels Nagelhus and John Karlsrud (2013), '"Where the Rubber Meets the Road": Friction Sites and Local-Level Peacebuilding in Haiti, Liberia and South Sudan', *International Peacekeeping* 20(2): 233–48, https://doi.org/10.1080/13533312.2013.791581

Shameem, Shaista (2010), 'Report of the Working Group on the Use of Mercenaries as a Means of Violating Human Rights and Impeding the Exercise of the Right of Peoples to Self-Determination'. United Nations General Assembly. Available at: https://undocs.org/A/HRC/15/25/Add.2

Shannon, Róisín (2009), 'Playing with Principles in an Era of Securitized Aid: Negotiating Humanitarian Space in Post-9/11 Afghanistan', *Progress in Development Studies* 9(1): 15–36, https://doi.org/10.1177/146499340800900103

Shepherd, Laura J. (2006), 'Veiled References: Constructions of Gender in the Bush Administration Discourse on the Attacks on Afghanistan Post-9/11', *International Feminist Journal of Politics* 8(1): 19–41, https://doi.org/10.1080/14616740500415425

Shepherd, Laura J. (2008), 'Visualising Violence: Legitimacy and Authority in the "War on Terror"', *Critical Studies on Terrorism* 1(2): 213–26, https://doi.org/10.1080/17539150802184611

Shepherd, Laura J. (2009), 'Gender, Violence and Global Politics: Contemporary Debates in Feminist Security Studies', *Political Studies Review* 7(2): 208–19.

Shepherd, Laura J. (2012), 'Introduction: Rethinking Gender, Agency and Political Violence', in Linda Ahall and Laura J. Shepherd (eds), *Gender, Agency and Political Violence*. Basingstoke: Palgrave Macmillan, pp. 1–18.

Shepherd, Laura J. (2014), 'The Road to (and from) "Recovery": A Multidisciplinary Feminist Approach to Peacekeeping and Peacebuilding', in Gina Heathcote and Dianne Otto (eds), *Rethinking Peacekeeping, Gender Equality and Collective Security*. Basingstoke: Palgrave Macmillan, pp. 99–117.

Shepherd, Laura J. (2017), *Gender, UN Peacebuilding, and the Politics of Space: Locating Legitimacy*. New York: Oxford University Press.

Shilliam, Robert (2008), 'What the Haitian Revolution Might Tell Us about Development, Security, and the Politics of Race', *Comparative Studies in Society and History* 50(3): 778–808, https://doi.org/10.1017/S0010417508000339

Shouse, Eric (2005), 'Feeling, Emotion, Affect', *Journal of Media and Culture* 8(6). Available at: http://journal.media-culture.org.au/0512/03-shouse.php

Siddiqui, Azhar Javed (2014), 'Afghanistan-Soviet Relations during the Cold War. A Threat for South Asian Peace', *South Asian Studies* 29(2): 617–31.

Silva, Jennifer M. (2008), 'A New Generation of Women? How Female ROTC Cadets Negotiate the Tension between Masculine Military Culture and Traditional Femininity', *Social Forces* 87(2): 937–60.

Simon, Eszter (2015), 'Cognitivism, Prospect Theory, and Foreign Policy Change: A Comparative Analysis of the Politics of Counterinsurgency in Malaya and Afghanistan', *Small Wars & Insurgencies* 26(6): 886–911, https://doi.org/10.1080/09592318.2015.1095842

Singer, Peter Warren (2003), *Corporate Warriors: The Rise of the Privatized Military Industry*. Ithica, NY: Cornell University Press.

Sjoberg, Laura (2006), 'Gendered Realities of the Immunity Principle: Why Gender Analysis Needs Feminism', *International Studies Quarterly* 50(4): 889–910.

Sjoberg, Laura (2013), *Gendering Global Conflict: Towards a Feminist Theory of War*. New York: Columbia University Press.

Smirl, Lisa (2008), 'Building the Other, Constructing Ourselves: Spatial Dimensions of International Humanitarian Response', *International Political Sociology* 2(3): 236–53, https://doi.org/10.1111/j.1749-5687.2008.00047.x

Smirl, Lisa (2009), 'Spaces of Aid: The Spatial Turn and Humanitarian Intervention'. Available at: https://spacesofaid.wordpress.com/category/writing-teaching/papers/

Smirl, Lisa (2012), 'The State We Are(n't) in: Liminal Subjectivity in Aid Worker Autobiographies', in Berit Bliesemann de Guevara (ed.), *Statebuilding and State-Formation: The Political Sociology of Intervention*. London: Routledge, pp. 230–45.

Smirl, Lisa (2015), *Spaces of Aid: How Cars, Compounds and Hotels Shape Humanitarianism*. London: Zed Books.

Smith, Shane A. (2014), 'Afghanistan After the Occupation: Examining the Post-Soviet Withdrawal and the Najibullah Regime It Left Behind 1989–1992', *The Historian* 76(2): 308–42, https://doi.org/https://doi.org/10.1111/hisn.12035

Solomon, Ty (2012), '"I Wasn't Angry, Because I Couldn't Believe It Was Happening": Affect and Discourse in Responses to 9/11', *Review of International Studies* 38(4): 907–28, https://doi.org/10.1017/S0260210511000519

Spearin, Christopher (2008), 'Private, Armed and Humanitarian? States, NGOs, International Private Security Companies and Shifting Humanitarianism', *Security Dialogue* 39(4): 363–82, https://doi.org/10.1177/0967010608094034

Spivak, G. C. (1988), 'Can the Subaltern Speak?', in Cary Nelson and Lawrence Grossberg (eds), *Marxism and the Interpretation of Culture*. Urbana, IL: University of Illinois Press, pp. 271–313.

Stachowitsch, Saskia (2015), 'Military Privatization as a Gendered Process: A Case for Integrating Feminist International Relations and Feminist State Theories', in Maya Eichler (ed.), *Gender and Private Security*. Oxford: Oxford University Press, pp. 19–36.

Stepputat, Finn (2012), 'Knowledge Production in the Security–Development Nexus: An Ethnographic Reflection', *Security Dialogue* 43(5): 436–55, https://doi.org/10.1177/0967010612457973

Stern, Maria and Joakim Öjendal (2010), 'Mapping the Security–Development Nexus: Conflict, Complexity, Cacophony, Convergence?', *Security Dialogue* 41(1): 5–30, https://doi.org/10.1177/0967010609357041

Steward, Rodney J. (2011), 'Afghanistan in a Globalized World – A Longer View', in Zubeda Jalalzai and David Jefferess (eds), *Globalizing Afghanistan:Terrorism,*

War, And the Rhetoric of Nation Building. Durham, NC: Duke University Press, l. 1022–514.

Stiehm, Judith (1982), 'The Protected, the Protector, the Defender', *Women's Studies International Forum* 5(3/4): 367–76.

Stone, Rosie (2019), 'The 3rd Sex: Gender and Contemporary Conflict', *Wavell Room: Contemporary British Military Thought*, 29 January. Available at: https://wavellroom.com/2019/01/29/the-3rd-sex-gender-and-contemporary-conflict/

Suhrke, Astri (2011), *When More Is Less. The International Project in Afghanistan*. New York: Columbia University Press/Hurst.

Suhrke, Astri (2013), 'Statebuilding in Afghanistan: A Contradictory Engagement', *Central Asian Survey* 32(3): 271–86, https://doi.org/10.1080/02634937.2013.834715

Sylvester, C. (2012), 'War Experiences/War Practices/War Theory', *Millennium – Journal of International Studies* 40(3): 483–503, https://doi.org/10.1177/0305829812442211

Taplin, Shahnaz (2014), 'Muslim Women: Movers and Shakers Fight for Women's Rights', *Huffpost*, 7 March. Available at: https://www.huffpost.com/entry/muslim-women-movers-and-s_b_4546673

Terrill, Chris (2014), *Marine 'A': Criminal or Casualty of War?* BBC. Available at: http://www.bbc.co.uk/programmes/b040mzfc

The Guardian (2016), 'Secret Aid Worker: We Were There to Win Hearts and Minds, but Every War Gets Its Own Comedy', 31 May. Available at: https://www.theguardian.com/global-development-professionals-network/2016/may/31/secret-aid-worker-we-were-there-to-win-hearts-and-minds-but-every-war-gets-its-own-comedy-whiskey-tango-foxtrot

The New Humanitarian (2010), 'Afghanistan: Security Firm Ban Will Not Hurt Us – NGOs', 25 October. Available at: https://reliefweb.int/report/afghanistan/afghanistan-security-firm-ban-will-not-hurt-us-ngos

Thobani, Sunera (2007), 'White Wars: Western Feminisms and the "War on Terror"', *Feminist Theory* 8(2): 169–85, https://doi.org/10.1177/1464700107078140

Tickner, J. Ann (2005), 'What Is Your Research Program? Some Feminist Answers to International Relations Methodological Questions', *International Studies Quarterly* 49(1): 1–21.

Trnka, Susanna (1995), 'Living a Life of Sex and Danger: Women, Warfare, and Sex in Military Folk Rhymes', *Western Folklore* 54(3): 232–41, https://doi.org/10.2307/1500350

True, Jacqui and Cary J. Nederman (2016), 'The Third Sex: The Idea of the Hermaphrodite in Twelfth-Century Europe Author', *Journal of the History of Sexuality* 6(4): 497–517.

Tuastad, Dag (2003), 'Neo-Orientalism and the New Barbarism Thesis: Aspects of Symbolic Violence in the Middle East Conflict(s)', *Third World Quarterly* 24(4): 591–9.

Tuin, Iris van der (2011), 'New Feminist Materialisms', *Women's Studies International Forum* 34(4): 271–7, https://doi.org/10.1016/j.wsif.2011.04.002

Vaittinen, Tiina, Amanda Donahoe, Rahel Kunz and Silja Bára Ómarsdóttir (2015), 'Care as Everyday Peacebuilding', *Peacebuilding* 7(2): 194–209, https://doi.org/10.1080/21647259.2019.1588453

Vannini, P. (2015), 'Non-Representational Ethnography: New Ways of Animating Lifeworlds', *Cultural Geographies* 22(2): 317–27, https://doi.org/10.1177/1474474014555657

Wahab, Shaista and Barry Youngerman (2007), *A Brief History of Afghanistan*. New York: Infobase Publishing.

Waldman, Matt (2015), 'Opportunity in Crisis: Navigating Afghanistan's Uncertain Future'. Available at: https://www.chathamhouse.org/sites/default/files/field/field_document/20150731NavigatingAfghanistanUncertainFutureWaldmanFinal.pdf

Walter, Ben (2016), 'The Securitization of Development and Humans' Insecurity in Nangarhar Province, Afghanistan', *Global Change, Peace and Security* 28(3): 271–87, https://doi.org/10.1080/14781158.2016.1197896

Ward, Adam, Nicholas Redman and Toby Dodge (2011), 'Conclusion', in Nicholas Redman and Toby Dodge (eds), *Afghanistan to 2015 and Beyond*. Abingdon: Routledge, pp. 253–70.

Weber, Cynthia (2016), 'Queer Intellectual Curiosity as International Relations Method: Developing Queer International Relations Theoretical and Methodological Frameworks', *International Studies Quarterly* 60(1): 11–23, https://doi.org/10.1111/isqu.12212

Weizman, Eyal (2010), 'Forensic Architecture: Only the Criminal Can Solve the Crime', *Radical Philosophy* 4 (164): 9–24.

Weizman, Eyal (2011), *The Least of All Possible Evils: Humanitarian Violence from Arendt to Gaza*. London: Verso.

Wekker, Gloria (2016), *White Innocence: Paradoxes of Colonialism and Race*. Durham, NC: Duke University Press.

Welland, Julia (2013), 'Militarised Violences, Basic Training, and the Myths of Asexuality and Discipline', *Review of International Studies* 39(4): 881–902, https://doi.org/10.1017/S0260210512000605

Welland, Julia (2015), 'Liberal Warriors and the Violent Colonial Logics of "Partnering and Advising"', *International Feminist Journal of Politics* 17(2): 289–307, https://doi.org/10.1080/14616742.2014.890775

Whitlock, Craig, Leslie Shapiro and Armand Emamdjomeh (2019), 'A Secret History of the War', *The Washington Post*, 9 December. Available at: https://www.washingtonpost.com/graphics/2019/investigations/afghanistan-papers/documents-database/

Whitworth, Sandra (2004), *Men, Militarism and UN Peacekeeping: A Gendered Analysis*. Boulder, CO: Lynne Rienner Publishers.

Wibben, Annick T. R. (2011), *Feminist Security Studies: A Narrative Approach*. Abingdon: Routledge.

Wilcox, Lauren (2013), 'Explosive Bodies and Bounded States', *International Feminist Journal of Politics* 16(1): 66–85, https://doi.org/10.1080/14616742.2012.750947

Williams, Michael. J. (2011), *The Good War: NATO and the Liberal Conscience in Afghanistan*. Basingstoke: Palgrave Macmillan.

Wright, Katharine A. M. (2019), 'Telling NATO's Story of Afghanistan: Gender and the Alliance's Digital Diplomacy', *Media, War & Conflict* 12(1): 40–2, https://doi.org/10.1177/1750635217730588

Young, Iris Marion (2003a), 'Political Responsibility and Structural Injustice', Lindley Lecture, Philosophy Department, University of Kansas, 5 May. Available at: http://www.bc.edu/content/dam/files/schools/cas_sites/sociology/pdf/Political Responsibility.pdf

Young, Iris Marion (2003b), 'The Logic of Masculinist Protection: Reflections on the Current Security State', *Signs: Journal of Women in Culture and Society* 29: 1–25, https://doi.org/ 10.1086/375708

Young, Iris Marion (2006), 'Responsibility and Global Justice: A Social Connection Model', *Social Philosophy and Policy* 23(1): 102–30, https://doi.org/10.1017/S0265052506060043

Yousaf, Farooq (2019), 'Pakistan's Colonial Legacy', *Interventions* 21(2): 172–87, https://doi.org/10.1080/1369801X.2018.1487322

Yuhas, Alan (2015), 'Mere Sight of a Gun Makes Police – and Public – More Aggressive, Experts Say', *The Guardian*, 5 August. Available at: http://www.theguardian.com/us-news/2015/aug/05/gun-police-public-more-aggressive-psychology-weapons-effect

Zalewski, Marysia (1995), '"Well, What Is the Feminist Perspective on Bosnia?"', *International Affairs* 71(2): 339–56, https://doi.org/ 10.2307/2623438

Zaman, Wesal (2006), 'U.S. Troops Fire on Crowd in Kabul After Crash, Riots', *Los Angeles Times*, 29 May. Available at: https://www.latimes.com/archives/la-xpm-2006-may-29-fg-afghcrash29-story.html

Zanotti, Laura (2006), 'Taming Chaos: A Foucauldian View of UN Peacekeeping, Democracy and Normalization', *International Peacekeeping* 13(2): 150–67, https://doi.org/10.1080/13533310500436524

Zehfuss, Maja (2012), 'Culturally Sensitive War? The Human Terrain System and the Seduction of Ethics', *Security Dialogue* 43(2): 175–90, https://doi.org/10.1177/0967010612438431

Zulfacar, Maliha (2006), 'The Pendulum of Gender Politics in Afghanistan', *Central Asian Survey* 25(1–2): 27–59, https://doi.org/10.1080/02634930600903007

INDEX

EU representative:
Easy Access System Europe
Mustamäe tee 50, 10621 Tallinn, Estonia
Gpsr.requests@easproject.com

www.ingramcontent.com/pod-product-compliance
Lightning Source LLC
Chambersburg PA
CBHW070844300326
41935CB00039B/1438